The University
in Medieval Life,
1179–1499

The University in Medieval Life, 1179–1499

Hunt Janin

McFarland & Company, Inc., Publishers

Jefferson, North Carolina, and London

Library of Congress Cataloguing-in-Publication Data

Janin, Hunt, 1940–
    The university in medieval life, 1179–1499 / Hunt Janin.
        p.   cm.
    Includes bibliographical references and index.

    ISBN 978-0-7864-3462-6
    softcover : 50# alkaline paper ∞

    1. Universities and colleges — Europe — History.   2. Education,
Medieval.   3. Middle Ages.   I. Title.
LA177.J36 2008
378.009'02 — dc22   2008029600

British Library cataloguing data are available

©2008 Hunt Janin. All rights reserved

Cover photograph of Exeter College, 1860 ©2008 Photos.com

Manufactured in the United States of America

McFarland & Company, Inc., Publishers
    Box 611, Jefferson, North Carolina 28640
    www.mcfarlandpub.com

With thanks and appreciation to
Dr. Paul Brand,
Senior Research Fellow and Academic Secretary,
All Souls College, Oxford.

"And gladly wold he lern and gladly teeche."
(Chaucer, *Canterbury Tales*)

Acknowledgments

I am very conscious of my heavy debt to scholars and friends for their patience in reading my rough drafts, for their insightful comments, and for answering my endless questions. The highest praise is due to Dr. Ursula Carlson, who read the entire manuscript with a critical eye and forced me to clarify a number of substantive and procedural points. If this book reads well, it is largely due to her efforts.

Let me also extend my sincere thanks, in alphabetical order, to Francine de Booy, Dr. Robert Black, Dr. Paul Brand, Dr. Helen Castor, Dr. W. J. Courtenay, Ken Croswell, Dr. Jeremy Cato, Grant Dean, Heidi van Eck, Ria van Eil, Saadia Eisenberg, Dr. Paul Grendler, Dr. Noga Hartmann, the Historical Association for Joan of Arc Studies, Corinne Janin, Henk 't Jong, Dr. Sharon Kaye, Martine Kommer, Dr. Andrew E. Larsen, Ginger Lester, Dr. John Longeway, Gotthard von Manteuffel, Bernard Monjauze, Fr. Louis Pascoe, James M. Robinson, Dr. Erika Rummel, Dr. Elizabeth Teviotdale, Virginia Tobiassen, Ginny Wagner, Dr. Nicholas Watson, Dr. Olga Weijers, Dr. Thomas Williams, and Dr. Anders Winroth.

Needless to say, I alone am responsible for any mistakes or misjudgments in this book.

Contents

Acknowledgments   vii

Prologue   xi

Preface   1

Setting the Stage: Medieval Life   7

I. MEDIEVAL UNIVERSITIES: AN OVERVIEW   25

II. THE UNIVERSITY OF BOLOGNA   55

III. LEGAL SCHOLARS AT BOLOGNA   63

IV. THE UNIVERSITY OF PARIS   71

V. THREE SCHOLARS AND A HERETIC (OR A SAINT)   97

VI. THE UNIVERSITY OF OXFORD   107

VII. LUMINARIES AT OXFORD   115

VIII. TEN OTHER UNIVERSITIES   127

IX. MEDIEVAL UNIVERSITIES AND HUMANISM   140

X. THE IMPACTS OF THE UNIVERSITIES
ON MEDIEVAL LIFE   165

Appendix 1. A University Student's Possessions   177

Appendix 2. Three Excerpts from Peter Abelard's *Historia Calamitatum* (*The Story of My Misfortunes*) 179

Appendix 3. John of Garland on "How Students Should Behave" 182

Appendix 4. The *Pecia* System 183

Appendix 5. Two Letters of 21 November 1430 from the University of Paris 185

Appendix 6. Medieval Requirements for Becoming a Physician 187

Chronology 189

Glossary 197

Chapter Notes 199

Bibliography 209

Index 217

Prologue

Following is part of Geoffrey Chaucer's description of an Oxford University student, taken from *The Canterbury Tales*— an epic poem that Chaucer began in 1386–1387 but never finished (Penguin edition, 1996):

> A Clerk there was of Oxenford also
> That unto logic hadde long y-go.
> As leene was his horse as is a rake,
> And he was not right fat, I undertake,
> But looked hollwe, and thereto sobrely.
> Full thredbare was his overest courtepy —
> For he had geten him yet no benefice,
> Ne was so worldly for to have office;
> For him was lever have at his beddes heed
> Twenty bookes, clad in black or red,
> Of Aristotle and his philosophye,
> Than robes riche, or fithel, or gay sautrye.
> But all be that he was a philosophre
> Yet hadde he but litel gold in coffre;
> But all that he might of his freendes hente,
> Of bookes and on lerning he it spente,
> And bisily gan for the soules praye
> Of hem that yaf him wherewith to scholeye.
> Of study took he most cure and most heede.
> Not oo word spak he more than was need....

Paraphrased in modern English and with a few explanations added, it reads as follows:

> One of Chaucer's pilgrims on the road to Canterbury was a graduate student

or a postdoctoral fellow at Oxford University. He had long since finished all
his introductory courses and was now doing advanced work, i.e., studying
logic. He looked undernourished and, in addition, grave. He was very poor:
his short outer coat was threadbare because he did not yet have any income
from a church position [a benefice] or any employment outside the church.
Rather than possessing fine robes or lovely stringed instruments, he would have
preferred to have had at his bedside 20 copies of Aristotle's works, handsomely
bound in black or red. [He could not afford these books: they would have
cost as much as a small house in the city of Oxford.] And although he was
a philosopher [a pun: the word also meant an alchemist, someone who tried
to turn base metals into gold], he had but little cash. He spent on books and
learning all that he could get from his friends, and prayed for the souls of
those who helped him finance his studies. He attached the greatest importance
to study and never said one word more than was absolutely necessary.

Preface

The medieval universities of Western Europe rested on two mutually reinforcing foundations: *people* and *ideas*. Both were equally important and both will be discussed here. This book is an introductory survey written for the general reader — that is to say, for someone with no detailed knowledge of the medieval period. It begins by describing briefly some key aspects of medieval life and then traces at greater length the growth of selected universities from their beginnings to the end of the Middle Ages, which we will date as finishing by 1500. Personalities, ideas and events will be presented to the reader not as links in an unbroken chain of causes and events but as convenient stepping stones across the river of medieval university life.

This book deliberately steers clear of the learned controversies usually studding academic treatises on this subject. Its goals are clarity, simplicity and human interest, not scholarly hairsplitting. Such an approach makes for a more readable text but it does have one drawback: it does not permit the painstaking, carefully hedged qualifications that are hallmarks of a formal academic study. The reader who wants such qualifications can find them in the specialized works listed in the bibliography.

While this book touches on earlier periods, it really begins in 1179, when Pope Alexander III ordered that every cathedral should have a *magister* (master) who would, free of charge, teach Latin grammar — the cornerstone of academic knowledge in the Middle Ages — to bright but impoverished students. One chapter of this book will extend into the Renaissance and Reformation to discuss scholasticism and humanism.

These movements overlapped chronologically. The Renaissance, a transitional movement in European culture between medieval and modern times, began in Italy in the fourteenth century. It extended into the seventeenth century and is known for its flowering of the arts and literature and for the beginnings of modern science. The Reformation, for its part, was a sixteenth-century religious movement which ultimately led to the rejection or modification of some Roman Catholic beliefs and to the establishment of Protestant churches.

Our basic account of medieval universities themselves will end in the closing days of the Middle Ages, specifically in 1499, when the French king Louis XII rescinded the right of the University of Paris to go on strike. His edict deprived the great university of its most powerful weapon and thus most of its independence from royal control.

I believe that, for two reasons, this introductory survey will help to fill a gap in the literature. The first reason is that in recent years very little has been published on this subject for the general reader. The best beginners-level introduction to medieval universities is still Charles Homer Haskins' classic study, *The Rise of the Universities*, which appeared in 1923. A later editor of that book did not overstate its excellence when he described it as "a work which has remained unsurpassed in the conciseness and vividness of its account."[1] It has only one drawback: it is too short, with only 93 pages of text.

Another useful work, published in 1980, is the Swedish Latinist Anders Piltz's *The World of Medieval Learning*. This is an excellent account of the Latin terms and concepts used in medieval universities. The downside of the book is that it is rather narrowly focused.

A wider ranging and, indeed, truly outstanding reference book is *Universities in the Middle Ages* (1992), the first volume of a projected four-volume series entitled *A History of the University in Europe* (Walter Rüegg general editor). The only shortcomings of this first volume, which is edited by Hilda de Ridder-Symoens, are that it is too complicated (with contributions by 17 authors) and too long (506 pages) for easy use by the general reader.

A. B. Cobban's *English University Life in the Middle Ages* (1999) is very good but as its title suggests it focuses chiefly on the English university experience.

There are other recent books as well. The best of them, in my opinion, is an excellent primer in French: *Des nains sur des épaules de géants: Maîtres et élèves au Moyen Age* (*Dwarfs on the shoulders of giants: Masters and students of the Middle Ages*), published by the French medievalists Pierre Riché and Jacques Verger in 2006. It contains many extremely interesting contemporary quotations that are published in modern French: the best of them have been edited, used and translated here. Fine as it is, this work is of no use to those who do not read French.

Taken collectively, these considerations suggest that it is now time for a new introductory survey that will introduce readers of English, clearly and concisely, to the era of medieval universities. This is the goal of my book.

The second reason why this book may help to fill a gap in the literature is that many earlier works on this subject have focused on medieval universities chiefly as *institutions*, rather than as exciting arenas of people and ideas. This is because — quite remarkably — no personal diaries or memoirs written by the students themselves have survived from the years before 1500. When masters wrote about their own profession, they did so only in academic commentaries, scholarly tracts and official texts. These provide, at best, only partial and idealized glimpses of their work.[2] They tell us nothing about the personal lives of the masters. Walter Rüegg, general editor of the multivolume *History of the University in Europe*, was therefore driven to conclude that

> biographical accounts of teachers and students, their social and familial origins, their patterns of association in the course of their studies, and their subsequent careers are markedly lacking. Such prosopographical investigations [i.e., studies that identify and relate groups of persons or characters within a particular historical context] ... are indispensable for a genuinely social history of universities.[3]

A few contemporary medieval sources, such as the financial record (*computus*) of a tax levied on members of the University of Paris during the academic year 1329–1330, can enlighten us on certain aspects of university life.[4] These sources, however, do not reveal very much: as the French medievalists Pierre Riché and Jacques Verger tell us, "elles sont loin de satisfaire toutes nos curiosités" ("they fall far short of satisfying our curiosity").[5] Medieval sources on the universities — or, more accurately, *the lack of such sources* — remain a serious problem for historians today. Indeed, when discussing a book by a well-known British medievalist, an independent American scholar told me:

> If you've read his book, you know that it's deadly boring because the sources he relies on are so dry. If you want to appeal to a wider audience than a handful of academic medievalists, you're going to need much richer sources — which are usually scarce. The definitive statement on any period of the Middle Ages all too often seems to be "the sources don't allow us to make any definitive conclusions."[6]

Part of the "deadly boring" problem is the fact that most of the sources that have survived are official university statutes and regulations. These were written to define what medieval university life *should be*, not what it actually was in practice. This lacuna in firsthand sources has forced many later writers to concentrate chiefly on the institutional aspects of university life. Such a scholarly approach can be instructive and valuable for experts in this field but it cannot interest the general reader: lacking *a human dimension*, it is insufferably dull.

Compared with older and more formal academic studies of medieval universities, the book you now have in your hands is simple and straightforward, even though the subject matter is quite complex. This book looks not only at medieval ideas but also at some of the men (and a few of the women) who left visible imprints on the medieval university experience. Many of them would be truly outstanding figures in any day and age. To the extent possible at this chronological distance, we shall try to meet most of them on their own ground — as individuals in their own right — and will let them speak for themselves.

Their words will be quoted extensively, sometimes in French or in Latin, followed by English translations. These quotations will give us good insights into a society that was very different from our own. One small caveat is necessary here. In French publications today, medieval texts that were originally written in Latin or, less likely, possibly in Old French or Middle French, are printed in modern French. To give as much of the original flavor of these texts as is feasible, in such cases I have quoted the modern French version, followed by an English translation.

The introductory essay sets the stage for the rest of the book by highlighting, in terms of specific historical figures, some key points about medieval life. It must be remembered that medieval life was anything but monolithic. This book covers more than 300 years of medieval history in Western Europe: no introductory chapter can hope to capture its remarkable diversity and complexity. Nevertheless, I believe it is critically important to offer some basic information for any reader who may be approaching medieval life for the first time. Without some kind of basic introduction, he or she will, figuratively speaking, be lost in mid-ocean without a lifeboat.

Here the lifeboat is a lifeboat of my own devising: a unique *people-oriented* description of medieval life. This approach has both merits and defects. On the one hand, it is hopefully interesting and concise; on the other, it will appall medievalists *by what it does not say*— that is, by how much it leaves out.

To avoid cluttering the text with explanations about the ever-changing political map of Europe, modern names for countries are used here (e.g.,

France, Germany, Italy, Sweden) even if they did not exist then in their present form. Endnotes have been used extensively but only for attribution, not to comment on substantive matters, all of which are covered in the text itself or in the appendices. In the few places where this is necessary, CE (Common Era) and BCE (Before Common Era) are used in place of A.D. and B.C. Bullets and numbered points have been used to highlight important people and ideas and to break up what might otherwise be an overly dense text.

In the usage of the medieval university, the three traditional academic titles — namely, master, doctor, and professor — were synonymous.[7] Of these, *magister* was by far the most common. Only a small number of masters went on to advanced studies in divinity, canon law, civil law or, occasionally, medicine. Once they had earned their doctorates they were known as doctors.

A word is needed about the famous English medievalist Hastings Rashdall (1858–1924), author of a magisterial three-volume analysis entitled *The Universities of Europe in the Middle Ages*. Rashdall is so well known in the field of medieval university studies that hereafter we shall refer to him and to his great work (which was written in 1895, edited in 1936 by the Oxford scholars F. M. Powicke and A. B. Emden, and runs to nearly 1,500 heavily footnoted pages) simply as "Rashdall." His three volumes remain our most accessible source on medieval universities, especially on the 10 "lesser" — that is to say, less prominent — universities briefly described here in Chapter VIII. Rashdall's volumes will therefore be cited frequently here.

Hunt Janin
St. Urcisse
Fall 2008

Setting the Stage:
Medieval Life

The university is indigenous to Western Europe and is probably the greatest and most enduring achievement of the Middle Ages. It did not exist in a vacuum but was part and parcel of medieval life. Our first task must therefore be to come to grips with medieval life itself—and to do so in a way that is historically accurate, interesting and accessible to the general reader. An original and highly selective approach will be used here. With cavalier disregard for the usual scholarly devotion to chronological order, we will move around freely in time and space and will look — non-chronologically — at a potpourri of first-hand medieval accounts.

These accounts cover a wide range of topics at various times and places. They are, in effect, snapshots of different but very representative aspects of medieval life. Their goal is not to "explain" medieval life as a whole or to argue for or against any particular thesis. These accounts usually will not surface again in the body of the text. They are put forward here only to give the reader some of the flavor of medieval life and to demonstrate its diversity. With this background in mind we can then move on to consider the universities themselves.

The first thing to bear in mind is that medieval universities are an excellent latch-key to medieval life. The medievalist Léo Moulin explains why:

"Qui comprend la vie des universités médiévales," écrit Hastings Rashdall, l'historien par excellence de ces institutions, "a fait un grand pas vers une meilleure compréhension de l'Église médiéval et du monde médiéval.... Les universités sont plus grandes — et pourraient se montrer moins périssables — que les cathédrales elles-mêmes." Et de fait, elles sont aujourd'hui moins désertées.[1]

["He who understands the life of medieval universities," wrote Hastings Rashdall, the most outstanding historian of these institutions, "has made a big step towards a better understanding of the medieval church and the medieval world.... The universities were greater — and could prove themselves to be less perishable — than the cathedrals themselves." And, in fact, today the universities are less deserted than the cathedrals.]

Taking Rashdall's big step is important because medieval society was really quite complicated. To use but one of many possible examples from the medieval history of Western Europe, in about 1188 the anonymous author of *Glanville*, the first treatise on English common law, complained: "To put into writing, in their entirety, the laws and customs of the realm would be utterly impossible today ... such a confused mass they are."[2] Before the fourteenth century, a young man traveling from one country to another might find that his legal status had changed radically during the course of a single day's journey. During the day, while crossing country A, he might have been an adult; in the evening, safely ensconced at a tavern in country B, he might again be a minor.[3]

One result of these complexities was that the Middle Ages were very litigious times. Most of the records that have come down to us from this era are in fact legal documents: European and American libraries now hold about 7,000 manuscripts on civil law and some 8,000 manuscripts on canon law.[4] To use an example of legal activity in medieval England, during the two-year period of 1327–1328 a total of 13,031 cases came before the Court of Common Pleas, the busiest branch of the king's court. Each year, more than 15,000 different men and women were involved as litigants in this one court alone.[5]

To impose some order on the variety of medieval life during the more than 300-year era of the medieval universities, we shall now embark on a novel and ambitious experiment: examining three different aspects of medieval culture and some of the individuals associated with them. There are many other different and often contradictory aspects of medieval life but the ones chosen here will give us some good if necessarily limited insights into the times. These three aspects are:

- *The structure of medieval society.* Our personalities here will be the Prince of Wales, a famous warrior known as the Black Prince; the English monk and chronicler Matthew Paris; Guillaume Bélibaste, a French heretic who was burned at the stake; an anonymous bourgeois householder in Paris;

and an unnamed, hypothetical, impoverished law student at the University of Orléans.

- *The natural disasters* that spread suffering and death so widely in the Middle Ages. By contributing to the palpable uncertainty of life in medieval Europe, they also strengthened popular reliance on the doctrines and personnel of the Christian church. The Black Death (bubonic plague) and the calamitous weather will be our prime examples, as chronicled by the Benedictine monk Thomas Walsingham, the Italian chronicler Matteo Villani, and Matthew Paris.

- *The renaissance of the twelfth century*— the great revival of learning and economic life that gave birth to the universities themselves. Our examples will be John of Salisbury, perhaps the most influential scholar of his age, and the French scholastic philosopher and logician Peter Abelard. Because Abelard is one of the most engaging personalities of the Middle Ages, he will get a good deal of attention here.

The Structure of Medieval Society

Beginning in the ninth century, contemporary theories about life revolved around the belief that it should consist of only "three estates," that is, three different but mutually supporting walks of life. In Latin, those who followed them were known, respectively, as *bellatores* (those who fought), e.g., knights; *oratores* (those who prayed), e.g., ecclesiastics; and *laboratores* (those who worked with their hands), e.g., chiefly peasants, who constituted the bulk of the medieval population, but other manual workers as well. An early thirteenth-century poem, *Miserere*, illustrates the theory of this traditional social structure very clearly:

> Labours de clerc est Dieu priër
> Et justice de chavalier.
> Pain lor truevent li loborier.
> Chil paist, chil prie, et chil deffent.
> Au camp, a la ville, au moustier
> S'entreaïdent de lor mestier
> Chil troi par bel ordenement.[6]

[It is the work of a cleric to pray to God and that of a knight to render justice. The laborer earns their bread. This man works, this one prays, and that one defends. In the field, in town, and in church these three groups help one another, thanks to a beautiful arrangement made by God.]

Medieval society, however, was far more complicated than a simple tripartite division suggests. In fact, this model never accurately reflected the changing social landscape and by the twelfth century it was hopelessly out of date. A new "middle class" of city dwellers — lawyers, doctors, merchants, professors, artisans, masters and students — would make itself felt in the burgeoning cities. These newcomers were chiefly motivated by the desire to make money: status meant much less to them than it did to the hereditary nobility. In terms of the social pecking order, the townsmen fell midway between the aristocrats and prelates who still monopolized the top positions at the narrow apex of the social pyramid and the commoners who still formed its broad base.[7]

Medieval towns and cities usually began as military strongholds, as refuges near a castle, or as hamlets with market days and other opportunities for local trade.[8] As these settlements expanded economically during the Middle Ages, they flourished socially as well. The constant drive to build, strengthen and decorate city walls, towers, houses, town halls, churches and cathedrals offered plenty of work for supervisors, architects, artisans, skilled and unskilled workers. Entrepreneurial townsfolk were eager to provide, for a price, the food, clothing, shelter, tools and entertainment these men needed. Cities thus became the magnets of medieval life. Living in a city freed a person from onerous obligations to the lords, ecclesiastics and village elders who dominated rural life. The Germans put it best. "*Stadtluft macht frei*," they said: "City air makes you free." The cities offered freedom, jobs, and physical space for all social groups.

Universities, for their part, were the marketplaces of learning and intellectual debate: students and masters traded in ideas. The universities also made major contributions to the economic vitality of Oxford, Cambridge and other university cities. Such enclaves of students, masters and university employees were entirely dependent on the accommodations, foodstuffs, ale and wine, clothes, shoes and other necessities of life provided by the men and women of the towns.[9] At the same time, officials, law courts and businessmen in the cities increasingly relied on the universities to supply them with the capable men they needed to run their affairs.

The best way to understand the structure of medieval society is to look at medieval people themselves. The fighting man dominated the secular ranks of medieval society; indeed, the medieval era has aptly been called "the heyday of the soldier."[10] Fighting skills were essential because by the beginning of the Middle Ages (which we will set here at about the year 500), Roman rule had ended nearly everywhere west of the Adriatic Sea. This development led to frequent warfare and to the virtual collapse of Roman urban life. In ninth-century France, for example, the decline of the Carolingian monarchy and the ferocious attacks of the Vikings resulted in a state of near-anarchy. Reflecting on these woes, a cleric from Ravenna predicted, correctly, that henceforth "each man will put his trust only in the sword."[11]

To protect their lives, families and properties, medieval men forged reciprocal military, legal and social ties with the nearest leader who had enough armed men at his disposal to guarantee their common defense. Mutual obligations among the warrior nobility of Western Europe involved three key concepts: lords, vassals, and fiefs. Taken collectively, these traits were traditionally said to have constituted "feudalism."

It is important to note here that although this term has now passed into common speech, it has very much fallen out of scholarly favor in recent years. Critics hold that it lumps together unrelated phenomena and that medieval men and women never described themselves or their ways of life as "feudal." The historians Elizabeth Brown and Susan Reynolds, for example, argued that medieval historians have erred in applying later eleventh- and twelfth-century legal texts, which do not use the word "feudal," to a much more diverse earlier ninth- and tenth-century society. In Brown's and Reynolds' view, this misreading of history has created a "feudal world" which did not in fact exist or which, at most, existed only in limited parts of France for short periods of time. Today, however, "feudalism" has not been replaced by any other widely accepted "ism." The closest scholarly approximation is probably "manoralism," which speaks of the relationships between lords and peasants.[12]

One of the most famous examples of the warrior nobility of the Middle Ages is Edward of Woodstock (1330–1376), the Prince of Wales, who is better known as the Black Prince. This sobriquet is said to have come from the black armor he wore or was given. Jean Froissart (c. 1334–c. 1405), the most readable of all medieval chroniclers, tells us that the Black Prince was "courageous and cruel as a lion,"[13] winning his major victory at the Battle of Poitiers in 1356. There he defeated the French forces and captured both John II (the French king) and his son, Louis of Anjou. Despite his ferocity in combat, the Black Prince took elaborate pains to treat John and Louis with the utmost courtesy. He certainly lived up to his motto: *homout; ich dene* ("Courage; I serve"). According to Froissart,

> The same day of the battle at night the prince made a supper in his lodging to the French king and to the most part of the great lords who were prisoners. The prince made the king and his son ... [as well as seven great nobles] to sit all at one board, and the other lords, knights and squires at other tables; and always the prince served before the king as humbly as he could and would not sit at the king's board for any desire that the king could make, but said he was not sufficient to sit at the table with so great a prince as the king was.[14]

Such chivalric treatment of their royal prisoners did not blind the English to how valuable they were. The English drove a hard bargain for the king's release: the 1360 Treaty of Brétigny set his ransom at 3,000,000 gold crowns. John was allowed to return to France to raise this huge sum but he had to leave his son Louis in Calais, which was held by the English, as a replacement hostage. Since Louis was being treated with great respect and was only lightly guarded, he easily escaped. John then surrendered himself to the English. His true motive for so doing remains unclear but when he arrived in England early in 1364 he was greatly admired by both English royalty and ordinary citizens as having behaved with great honor. Held in the Savoy Palace, he died in London a few months later.

For medieval society no concept was more all-embracing or more important than God. In that era, the perceived barrier between "the seen and the unseen"—that is, between natural power and supernatural power—was thinner and more porous than most people think it is today.[15] Medieval men and women referred to God as *dominus* ("Lord") or *Dominus Deus* ("Lord God"). The pope defined himself as *servus servorum Dei* ("servant of the servants of God") and as *vicar Dei* ("representative of God"). Kings were subject to God, too: they reigned only *gracia Dei* ("by the grace of God"). The faithful hailed Jesus Christ as *rex regnum, dominus dominantium* ("king of kings, lord of lords").[16] Understandably, the faithful also valued and supported those who devoted themselves entirely to God—the *oratores*.

Medieval people worried that their own lives here on earth would be brief and, in most cases, unhappy interludes before death ushered them into the world to come. There they hoped for heavenly bliss but were deeply worried that their unconfessed and therefore unforgiven sins might lead God to damn them to the endless torments of hell. Despite the visible shortcomings of some individual clerics, most secular men and women felt that, as a group, *oratores* were fulfilling the highest human calling—a life entirely devoted to God—and the one most likely to earn them a heavenly reward.

There was a world of difference between the lifestyles of the upper echelons of the church and those of the lower level. At the top of the organizational pyramid was the pope, who lived in great splendor. Under him were serried ranks of churchmen, e.g., cardinals, bishops, abbots, priests, monks, and friars. Friars were mendicants, members of one of the religious orders that lived by charity, i.e., by begging. Because one of their main missions was to preach against heresy, friars had to live where there were other people. Thus they settled in the towns and cities instead of living in cloistered monastic communities in the countryside. Some were brilliant and highly educated. At the lower end was the simple country priest of modest means and modest education, who stumbled through the Latin of the Mass and who lived at a level not much above that of one of his poorest parishioners.

One of the most memorable *oratores* is the Benedictine monk and chronicler Matthew Paris (c. 1200–1259). He was an Englishman who may have studied in Paris as a young man but who spent most of his life at St. Albans Abbey in Hertfordshire, England, where he became the abbey's official recorder of events. His *Chronica Majora* (*Major Chronicle*) is an important historical document — indeed, it is one of our best and most candid sources of knowledge about European affairs between 1235 and 1250.

Its usefulness comes from Paris' close personal friendships with contemporary leaders, e.g., King Henry III and Richard, Earl of Cornwall; from the frankness with which he attacked the papacy; and from the appealing illustrations he drew in the pages of his manuscripts. He gives us a more lively "I was there" description of his era than any other English chronicler. In the following excerpt, Paris complains about the extortion of money from the poor:

> Such therefore, are the fruits produced by the rapines and slaughter practised by the magnates on the all-suffering poor with the permission, or rather by the teaching, of the Roman church, in order to fill their purses whenever they set out on pilgrimage to fight for God. It emerges clear as daylight from above how displeasing to God this way of obtaining money is which derives from the oppression and impoverishment of the poor.[17]

As an excellent but unusual example of the *laboratores* we will select a Cathar heretic, Guillaume Bélibaste. The Cathars were a heretical sect that flourished in southern France in the twelfth and thirteenth centuries. They considered themselves to be good Christians but they rejected the church's teachings on many fundamental issues. For example, Cathars believed that Jesus was only an angel, not the son of God. They also condemned the ostentatious wealth, corruption and moral laxity of the church itself. The church's highly visible abuses made it easier for the Cathars to appeal, often successfully, to the "poorest of the poor."

Jacques Fournier, bishop of Palmiers in southern France from 1318 to 1325, was a Cistercian monk who rose from a humble background to become Pope Benedict XII of Avignon in southern France. (During the Avignon Papacy, which extended from 1309 and 1377, seven popes, all of them French, resided in Avignon.) He earned a doctorate at the University of Paris and later conducted a detailed, highly successful inquisitorial campaign against the last remaining Cathar heretics. These were the subsistence farmers and shepherds who lived quietly near Montaillou, a tiny village located in the foothills of the eastern Pyrenees, not far from what is now the Spanish border.

Fourier's court held hundreds of sessions during 370 days between 1318 and 1325. It dealt with 98 cases involving 114 people and conducted 578 interrogations. A wide range of penalties were inflicted on those found guilty of being Cathars. Punishments included imprisonment, of varying degrees of severity; wearing the yellow cross, which was a symbol of ignominy imposed by the Inquisition; pilgrimages; confiscation of personal goods; and burning at the stake.[18] Fourier's remarkable *Inquisition Record* is relevant here because it is one of the very few medieval documents that captures for posterity the words of the men and women who were at the base of the social pyramid.

Most of the *Inquisition Record*, which was taken down verbatim, focuses on the extent to which a suspect was or was not infected by the Cathar heresy. In the process, it includes a great many valuable firsthand observations about life and love in the Montaillou region of southwestern France during the early fourteenth century. Consider, for example, the case of an unmarried young man named Guillaume Bélibaste. He is an excellent and rarely documented example of downward social mobility in the Middle Ages.

This is his story in brief: Guillaume had killed a shepherd in a fight.[19] He was therefore forced to flee from his family's prosperous sheep farm and take to the road. First he became a shepherd himself, then a Cathar leader and prophet. To support himself in this latter calling, he made baskets and wooden combs to card (comb) wool. He also worked with other men as a shepherd, one of whom (Pierre Maury) he cheated out of some sheep. Guillaume also managed to persuade Pierre to marry Raymonde Piquier, Guillaume's long term concubine, who was pregnant. Captured by the Inquisition, Guillaume was eventually burned at the stake as a heretic.

At this point, rather than trying to cast some light on all of the new groups of townsmen in the Middle Ages, we will limit ourselves to only two of these groups: the urban upper-middle class and the university students. These are well represented by two figures. The first was an elderly, prosperous, anonymous Parisian. He is known to posterity only as the *ménagier de Paris* (the householder of Paris) and we will so refer to him here.[20] When he was over 60, he married a much younger woman, who was only 15 years old. We do not know her name. Between 1392 and 1394 the ménagier de Paris wrote out a charming, tender set of instructions to guide her and help her cope with the difficult tasks of supervising his servants and managing his townhouse and his farm.

Here is an example of the householder's clear, simple instructions for his young wife, using familiar incidents drawn from daily life. Throughout the document, he always addresses her as "sister," a term of affection and respect. He advises her as follows:

Wherefore cherish the person of your husband carefully, and, I pray you, keep him in clean linen, for 'tis your business. And because the care of outside affairs lieth with men, so must a husband take heed, and go and come and journey hither and thither, in rain and wind, in snow and hail, now drenched, now dry, now sweating, now shivering, ill-fed, ill-lodged, ill-warmed and ill-bedded; and nothing harms him, because he is upheld by the hope that he has of his wife's care of him on his return.... Certainly, fair sister, such service maketh a man love and desire to return to his home and to see his own wife and to be distant with other women.[21]

Our second illustrative figure comes from the pen of Eustache Deschamps (1346–1406), a medieval French poet who studied law at the University of Orléans before becoming a diplomatic messenger for Charles V of France. He knew all about the financial hardships of student life from his own experience. As we will see shortly, Deschamps introduces us to a hypothetical but very believable impoverished student who is, very probably, studying civil law, i.e., Roman law, at the University of Orléans.

A word about law is first necessary here because of the importance of this convoluted subject in medieval life. As stated earlier, Roman rule had ended west of the Adriatic by about 500 but there was no "decline and fall" of Roman law itself. Roman law, i.e., civil law, never vanished entirely. Indeed, from about the eleventh century onward there was a gradual process of integration, adaptation, and revival of this law throughout Western Europe — with the sole exception of England because it had a common law all its own.[22] (The common law of England was not a code derived from Roman law but was instead a legal labyrinth consisting of the precedents, cases, and decisions of various English royal courts.[23])

We can make an educated guess that civil law was the field of study of Deschamps' mythical student because in *Super specula*, a bull of 1219, Pope Honorius III had prohibited the teaching of civil law at the University of Paris and its environs. (A bull was a formal papal letter, often affixed with a round leaden seal known as a *bulla*.) Honorius justified his action on the grounds that, in France, laymen did not use civil law and that in few ecclesiastical suits was it ever necessary to invoke it.[24] What the pope was actually concerned about, however, was that civil law had become such a popular career track in Paris that it was threatening the traditional primacy of canon law, i.e., ecclesiastical law, and, by extension, it was thus undermining theological studies as well. After the bull was issued, the Paris law facility could teach only canon law: French and other students who wished to study civil law in France had to go to the University of Orléans rather than to Paris.

Like their counterparts at universities today, many medieval students were chronically short of cash. This is reflected in the fact that the only letters from them that come down to us are letters home, pleading, in effect, "Dear Father, please send money." Writing in about 1400, Deschamps gives us in verse the text of an imaginary letter that such an impoverished student might well have sent to his father:

> Lettres des escoliers d'Orliens:
> Treschiers peres, je n'ay denier,
> Ne sanz vous ne puis avoir riens;
> Et si fait a l'estude chier,
> Ne je ne puis estudier
> Et mon Code n'en ma Digeste:
> Caduque sont. Je doy de reste
> De ma prevosté dix escus,
> Et ne treuve homme qui me preste:
> Je vous mande argent et salus!
>
> Trop fault, qui est estudiens;
> Se son fair veult bien advancier,
> It fault que son pere et les siens
> Lui baillent argent sanz dangier,
> Par quoy cause n'ait d'engagier
> Ses livres, ait finance preste,
> Robes, pannes, vesture honneste,
> Ou il sera un malostrus;
> Et qu'om ne me tiengne pour beste,
> Je vous mande argent et salus.
>
> Vins sont chiers, hostelz, autres biens
> Je doy partout; s'ay grant mestier
> D'estre mis hors de tels liens:
> Chiers peres, vueillez moy aidier.
> Je doute l'excommunier,
> Cité suy; cy n'a n'os n'areste:
> S'argent n'ay devant cette feste
> De Pasques, du moustier exclus
> Seray. Ottroiez ma requeste
> Je vous mande argent et salus.
>
> L'Envoy
>
> Treschiers peres, pour m'alegier
> En la taverne, au boulengier,
> Aux docteurs, aux bediaux, conclus,
> Et pour mes coletes payer
> A la burresse et au barbier,
> Je vous mande argent et salus.

In English, this letter reads:

Well beloved father, I have not a penny, nor can I get any save through you, for all things at the University are so dear; nor can I study in my Code or my

Digest [these are legal texts], for their leaves [pages] have the falling sickness. Moreover, I owe ten crowns to the provost, and can find no man to lend them to me. I ask of you greetings and money. The student has need of many things if he will profit here; his father and his kin must supply him freely [so] that he will not be compelled to pawn his books, but [will] have ready money in his purse, with gowns and furs and decent clothing; or he will be damned for a beggar; wherefore, that men may not take me for a beast, I ask of you greetings and money. Wines are expensive, [as are] hostels and other good things; I owe in every street, and am hard put to free myself from such snares. Dear father, deign to help me! I fear being excommunicated; already I have been cited, and there is not even a dry bone in my larder. If I cannot find money before this feast of Easter, the church door will be shut in my face; wherefore grant my supplication. I ask of you greetings and money. [The *Envoi* was a short stanza at the end of a poem, used to address a real or imagined reader. It reads:] Well beloved father, to ease my debts contracted at the tavern, at the baker's, with the professors and the beadles [low-level university officers responsible for ceremonial duties], and to pay my subscriptions to the laundress and the barber, I ask of you greetings and money.[25]

Student pleas for money were founded on real need. A treatise written some time between 1230 and 1240, *De disciplina scholarium*, stressed that it was the responsibility of university masters to make sure that the poverty of students did not prevent their academic progress.[26] Nevertheless, some students were poor as church mice and were even granted licenses by the chancellor that permitted them to beg in the streets. Here we must quote Rashdall, this time to note that

Many a man who would have been ashamed to dig [i.e., to do manual work] was not ashamed to beg; and the begging scholar was invested with something like the sacredness of the begging friar. To support a scholar at the university or to help on a smaller scale by giving him something at the door, in return for a prayer or two, was a recognized work of charity in the medieval world.[27]

Other students had a very modest but apparently sufficient stock of worldly goods. Appendix 1, for example, lists the possessions of a recently deceased student at the College of Saint-Nicholas d'Annecy in Avignon in 1435.

Natural Disasters

Medieval people believed they were living in a world that was entirely dependent on the will of God. They felt themselves at the mercy of disease and of the elements. The Black Death (the plague) was a pandemic that spread from southwestern Asia to Europe, where it is estimated to have killed between one-third and one-half of Europe's population. In Paris alone, it

killed 40,000 to 50,000 people in a single year (1438), according to a contemporary chronicler, "especialement les plus fors et les plus jeunes" ("especially the strongest and the youngest").[28] In 1448 the Black Death struck
Bologna: 14,000 people died in the city itself and 17,000 more in the sur-
rounding areas. At Oxford, university life was interrupted for nearly three
years (1450–1453) by the plague, which returned to Europe virtually every
generation until the 1700s.[29]

Let us see what two earlier chroniclers — one English, the other Italian — have to say about the Black Death.

The Englishman Thomas Walsingham was a Benedictine monk in
charge of the *scriptorium* (writing room) at St. Albans Abbey in Hertfordshire. He was educated at Oxford and wrote the famous *Historia Anglicana*
(*History of England*). It contains this vivid description:

> In the year of grace 1349 ... a great mortal plague spread through the world,
> starting from the southern and the northern areas, and ending with such
> devastating ruins that scarcely a handful of men survived. The towns, once
> densely populated, were emptied of their settlers and so rapidly did the inten-
> sity of the plague grow that the living could scarcely bury the dead.... A disease
> among cattle followed closely on the pestilence; then the crops died; then the
> land remained untilled because of the scarcity of farmers, who were wiped out.
> And such misery followed these disasters that the world never afterwards had
> an opportunity of returning to its former state.[30]

The Italian chronicler Matteo Villani describes the social effects of the
plague in Florence before he himself died of it in 1363. This is how some of
the survivors of the plague conducted themselves:

> Since men were few, and since, by hereditary succession, they abounded in
> earthly goods, they forgot the past as though it had never been, and gave
> themselves up to a more shameful and disordered life that they had led before.
> For, mouldering at ease, they dissolutely abandoned themselves to the sin
> of gluttony, with feasts and taverns and the delight of delicate foods.... And
> the price of labour, and the work of all trades and crafts, rose in disorderly
> fashion beyond the double. Lawsuits and disputes and quarrels and riots
> arose everywhere among citizens of every land, by reason of legacies and
> successions....[31]

The weather could be treacherous and its consequences were as unpre-
dictable and as uncontrollable as disease. Matthew Paris recounts the effects
of torrential rains in and near London in 1236:

> Bridges were hidden, mills and their ponds were destroyed, cultivated lands
> and reed meadows were overrun ... the River Thames overflowed its usual
> bounds, and entered the great palace at Westminster.... In the summer of the
> same year ... it continued dry with an almost intolerable heat for more than

four months in succession. The result was that marshes and ponds were completely empty, the water-mills stood dried up and useless, and cracks opened up in the earth. In many places the ears of corn [wheat] scarcely reached two feet.[32]

The Renaissance of the Twelfth Century

During the twelfth century, far reaching advances were made in Western Europe in education, trade, science, technology, philosophy, literature, architecture and the arts. These changes are captured by the term "the renaissance of the twelfth century," a concept popularized by the great medievalist Charles Homer Haskins (1870–1937), first in a series of lectures he gave at Brown University in 1923 and then, at greater length, in his classic work *The Renaissance of the Twelfth Century*, which was published four years later.

The renaissance of the twelfth century is now seen as gradually extending over a period of some 200 years (from about 1050 to 1250). Regardless of its exact duration, it clearly represents a watershed in European thought. Haskins gives us the reason:

> There came a great influx of new knowledge into western Europe, partly through Italy and Sicily, but chiefly through the Arab scholars of Spain — the works of Aristotle, Euclid, Ptolemy, and the Greek physicians, the new arithmetic, and those texts of the Roman law which had lain hidden through the Dark Ages.... This new knowledge burst the bonds of the cathedral and monastery schools and created the learned professions; it drew over mountains and across narrow seas eager youths who, like Chaucer's Oxford clerk of a later day, "would gladly learn and gladly teach," to form in Paris and Bologna those academic guilds which have given us our first and best definition of a university, a society of masters and scholars.[33]

This influx of knowledge was not easy to master, often because of poor translations into Latin. The Englishman John of Salisbury (c. 1120–1180) had attended cathedral schools in France, studied under Peter Abelard in Paris, become bishop of Chartres and was one of the most influential scholars of his age. He is sometimes considered to have been an early humanist (we will discuss humanism later) but this is stretching the point. Instead, his own brand of humanism held that while church authorities are reliable guides to happiness, their teachings can usefully be buttressed by studying the acts and ideas of worthy pagans.[34]

John found that the excitingly new but very imperfect translations of Aristotle's *Analytica Posteriora* (*Posterior Analytics*) had serious shortcomings. This work, which is part of another work by Aristotle known as the *Organon*, discusses questions of argumentation and knowledge. John says of the translations then available to him:

> The second *Analytics* contains perspicacious scholarship and only a few people understand it. There are evidently several reasons for this as it deals with the science of argumentation which is the most difficult form of exposition. It has fallen into almost total obscurity because so few scholars have concerned themselves with it.... It is without comparison the most impenetrable [of Aristotle's works] as a result of its extraordinary use of terminology and letters of the alphabet to stand for ideas, and the remarkable examples taken from different disciplines. Finally, and for this the author cannot be blamed, it has been so distorted by errors in copying that every new paragraph gives rise to additional obscurity; sometimes the number of obscurities simply exceeds the number of paragraphs. Most people ascribe the difficulty to the translator and maintain that the translation that is available is now inadequate.[35]

The boldest and most interesting of the many historical figures we could use to embody this period is Peter Abelard (1079–1142), a French scholastic philosopher and logician who was one of the greatest intellectuals of the twelfth century. His best known philosophic work was *Sic et Non* (*Yes and No*), a pro-and-con argumentation of 158 philosophical and theological problems on which reputable authorities differed. Arguing that "By doubting we come to inquiry, and by inquiry we perceive truth," Abelard invited scholarly debate on many challenging and controversial propositions, e.g.,

- That faith is to be supported by human reason.
- That to God all things are possible.
- That only Eve, and not Adam, was beguiled by the Devil.
- That Adam was saved.
- That no one can be saved without baptism by water.
- That nothing is yet established concerning the origin of the soul.
- That marriage is lawful for all.
- That works of mercy do not profit those without faith.
- That we sin at times unwillingly.
- That a lie is permissible.
- That it is lawful to kill a man.[36]

Initially a member of the generation of the "wandering scholars" of Europe who traveled, studied and taught before the universities themselves formally appeared in about 1200, Abelard encouraged his students to seek answers to the above problems by using *reason*, specifically, the thesis, antithesis, and synthesis procedure of dialectical reasoning (often referred to as "dialectics"), which had been pioneered by Greek philosophers.[37] This dialectical process has been called "a particularly long lived and fruitful branch of medieval logic."[38] It formed the essence of scholasticism, a word which comes from the Latin *scholasticus* ("that which belongs to the school") and which will be discussed in a later chapter.

Abelard's devotion to reason was unswerving. He tells us about his own intellectual growth, first as pupil and then as master:

> Then it came about that I was brought to the very foundation of our faith by applying the analogies of human reason, and was led to compose for my pupils a theological treatise on the Divine Unity and Trinity. They [the students] were calling for human and philosophical arguments and insisting on something intelligible, rather than mere words, saying that there had been more than enough of talk which the mind could not follow; that it was impossible to believe what was not in the first place understood, and that it was ridiculous for any one to set forth to others what neither he nor they could rationally conceive.[39]

Abelard's intellectual skepticism was to a large degree responsible for the growing fame of Paris as an intellectual center and thus helped to prepare the ground for the later appearance of a university there. In this era, Paris did not yet have a "university" as we use the word today. Rather, the Parisian *universitas* (a word which means "the totality" or "the whole") was initially simply a guild or corporation formed to protect the interests of the students. Later it gradually evolved into a self-regulating, permanent institution of higher learning, i.e., a proper university. By about 1210 it could certainly be termed a *universitas scholarium* (a university of students) or a *universitas magistrorum et scholarium* (a university of masters and students) at a given place.[40] Thus the University of Paris would be known as the *universitas magistrorum et scolarium Parisiensium*.[41]

Abelard's enduring fame, however, rests more on romance than on learning. His crowning literary achievement was *Historia Calamitatum* (*The Story of My Misfortunes*). Written in the form of a letter consoling a friend, this autobiography not only gives us a remarkably candid account of Abelard's own professional and amorous life but also a unique insight into intellectual life in Paris before the gradual formalization of the University of Paris itself in about 1200. Three excerpts from the *Historia Calamitatum* are given in Appendix 2.

A brief account of Abelard's eventful life will be of interest here. A precocious lad, he learned quickly and chose an academic life rather than the military career that would have been more in tune with his family's relatively high social status. He soon mastered the art of dialectical reasoning, which was then based on Aristotelian logic. His academic travels brought him to the great cathedral school of Notre-Dame in Paris. There he was able to defeat a famous philosopher, William of Champeaux, in philosophic arguments.

Abelard was a brilliant teacher. In about 1115, at the age of only 22, he was able to set up his own school. It was not long before he was teaching at Notre-Dame itself, surrounded by crowds of appreciative students drawn from many European countries. His success was so great, he confides to us, that he came to think of himself as the only undefeated philosopher in the world. His pride soon led to his fall.

A 17-year-old girl, Heloise (1100/1101–1163/1164), was living at Notre-Dame under the care of her uncle, the canon (staff clergyman) Fulbert. She is said to have been beautiful, intelligent and accomplished, having mastered Latin, Greek and Hebrew. Abelard, then 40 years old, fell madly in love with her and arranged to become her tutor. They quickly became lovers. Abelard later wrote:

> Under the pretext of study we spent our hours in the happiness of love, and learning held out to us the secret opportunities that our passion craved.... No degree in love's progress was left untried by our passion, and if love itself could imagine any wonder as yet unknown, we discovered it. And our inexperience in such delights made us all the more ardent in our pursuit of them, so that our thirst for one another was still unquenched.[42]

Heloise, for her part, was not just a complaisant young woman. She played an active, passionate role in what the French medievalist Régine Pernoud aptly termed a story of "reason and passion." Heloise said in a letter:

> Quelle reine, quelle princesse n'a point envié et mes joies et mon lit?[43]

> [Which queen, which princess, would not envy my joys and my bed?]

Heloise eventually gave birth to a boy, whom the reason-loving couple named Astrolabe and who was adopted by Abelard's sister. His unusual name refers to a scientific instrument that had recently been introduced from the Islamic world. (Before the invention of the sextant, the astrolabe was used to observe and calculate the position of celestial bodies.) To calm her furious uncle, Abelard and Heloise were married secretly but Fulbert came to believe (incorrectly) that Abelard was planning to abandon his niece. So, together with some accomplices, Fulbert broke into Abelard's room one night and castrated him.

The upshot of this brutal attack was that Heloise entered a convent and Abelard became a monk. He resumed teaching and once again attracted large numbers of students by applying his logical method of inquiry to intractable theological issues. However, his chief enemy, Bernard of Clairvaux, accused him of heresy. Bernard's hostility was based not so much on substance as on the tone, spirit, and method of Abelard's theological teaching. The great medievalist Rashdall uses a nice turn of phrase in his evaluation of Abelard:

He had presumed to endeavour to understand, to explain the mystery of the Trinity: he had dared to bring all things in heaven and earth to the test of reason. For his conservative opponents that was heresy enough: *to accept the doctrines of the Church because they were rational was hardly less offensive than to reject them as irrational.*[44]

En route to Rome to plead his case in person, Abelard fell ill and died at the priory of St. Marcel. His remains and those of Heloise now lie together in the cemetery of Père-Lachaise in eastern Paris. In addition to his other accomplishments, he was also a gifted poet. This is probably the shortest, simplest and most moving of his poems. Drawn from Matthew 2:18, it describes Rachel sorrowing for her children, who had been murdered by King Herod:

> Est in Rama
> Vox audita
> Rachel flentis,
> Super natos
> Interfectos
> Eiulantis.[45]

[The King James Version of the Bible translates Matthew 2:18 thus: In Rama was there a voice heard, lamentation, and weeping, and great mourning, Rachel weeping for her children, and would not be comforted, because they were not.]

Keeping this brief survey of medieval life in mind, let us now turn to the universities themselves.

I

Medieval Universities:
An Overview

The university arose, uniquely, in medieval Europe at a special time and for special reasons — the growing need to expand the scope of higher education to meet the demands of an increasingly literate, prosperous, urbanizing society, and the need of students to organize themselves to prevent exploitation by townsmen. According to the French medievalist Jacques Verger,

> L'université est une des grandes créations du Moyen Âge. Elle se stabilisa dans une institution de type corporatif liée à l'essor urbain et destinée à ce que nous appelons de nos jours l'enseignement supérieur. Elle évolua jusqu'aujourd'hui où elle conserve des traits importants de son origine médiévale.[1]

> [The university is one of the great creations of the Middle Ages. It became stabilized as a corporative institution linked to the expansion of the cities and destined to become what we now call higher education. The university has continued to develop up to the present time and still retains important traits from its medieval past.]

Let us begin at the beginning of the educational process in Western Europe. There the monasteries were the earliest centers of learning, scholarship, and writing in the Middle Ages. They had libraries — very modest ones, to be sure — and skilled, dedicated, low cost workers — namely, their monks. Some of these men were willing and able to spend long years copying texts and illustrating sacred texts, thus multiplying them for a slightly wider readership. Such work was considered highly meritorious in religious terms and very likely to lead to the copyist's salvation.

25

Here are two examples of this widely held belief. During the eleventh century a French monk in Arras recorded that "for every letter, line, and point [that is copied into the text], a sin is forgiven."[2] In the twelfth century an English monk, Orderic Vitalis (1075–1142), wrote one of the great contemporary chronicles of Normandy and England, entitling it the *Historia Ecclesiatica* (*Ecclesiastical History*). In it he recounts the tale, told by the Abbot Thierry, about a sinful monk who was nevertheless a devoted copyist and a fine illustrator of holy texts. When this monk died, so the story runs, God weighed each and every letter of his work against his many sins. In the end, the monk was saved from the clutches of the Devil only because he had copied *one letter more* than the number of his sins. This credit balance of a single letter was enough to offset his transgressions: it saved him from the endless torments of hell.[3]

In 789 King Charles of the Franks, who the next year would become the Emperor Charlemagne, put forward an ambitious program of reforms to improve education. He decreed that all monasteries and cathedrals were to have schools to provide, free of charge, the basic elements of education for any boy who had the ability and self-discipline needed to prepare himself academically for eventual entry into the priesthood. Charlemagne's command on schools read in part:

> Que les prêtres attirent vers eux non seulement les enfants de condition servile, mais aussi les fils d'hommes libres. Nous voulons que des écoles soient créées pour apprendre à lire aux enfants. Dans toutes les monastères et les évêchés, enseignez les Psaumes, les notes, le chant, le comput, la grammaire, et corrigez soigneusement les livres religieux, car, souvent, alors que certains désirent bien prier Dieu, ils y arrivent mal à cause de l'imperfection et des fautes des livres.[4]

> [Let the priests recruit for these schools not only children from servile families but also the sons of free men. We wish that schools be created to teach children how to read. In the monasteries and in the bishoprics, teach the psalms, musical notes, hymns, reckoning the dates of movable feasts in the religious calendar, grammar, and studiously correct the religious books because, often, when students want to pray to God they cannot do so because of imperfections and mistakes in these books.]

Although Charlemagne died before his plan could be fully implemented, some cathedral schools were established and managed to survive the perilous times of the early Middle Ages. These small schools, taught by cathedral clergy, usually had less than 100 pupils and were originally designed to train choirboys and future priests but later they accepted lay students as well — usually boys of noble families who were being prepared for high positions in church, state or business. The most famous and most active cathedral school during the Middle Ages was that of Chartres, although, unlike some of its rivals, it never became a university. Other well-known cathedral schools included those of Liège, Rheims, Laon, Paris and Orléans.

John of Salisbury recounts how Bernard of Chartres, a twelfth-century French philosopher and administrator, ran the school at Chartres:

> Bernard of Chartres, the most abounding spring of letters in Gaul [France] in modern times, followed this method, and in the reading of authors showed what was simple and fell under the ordinary rules; the figures of grammar, the adornments of rhetoric, the quibbles of sophistries; and where the subject of his own lesson had reference to other disciplines, in these matters he brought out clearly, yet in such wise that he did not teach anything about each topic, but in proportion to the capacity of his audience dispensed to them in time the due measure of the subject....
>
> And since the memory is strengthened and the wits are sharpened by exercise, he urged some by warnings and some by floggings and punishments to the constant practice of imitating what they heard. Every one was required on the following day to reproduce some part of what he had heard the day before.... Evening drill, which was called declension, was packed with so much grammar that one who gave a whole year to it would have at his command, unless unusually dull, a method of speaking and writing and could not be ignorant of expressions which are in common use.[5]

By about 1200 the first three universities in the world had come into being. These were Bologna, renowned for civil and canon (ecclesiastical) law; Paris, celebrated for logic, philosophy and speculative theology (i.e., theology concerned with religious ideas rather than with pastoral care); and Oxford, a leader in mathematics and in natural science (the rational study of the universe via the rules or laws of natural order). Because these were by far the most famous universities and were role models for most of the others, they merit and will receive extensive treatment in this book. Ten other "lesser"—i.e., less famous—universities will be discussed in a separate chapter.

The universities appeared on the scene not because of medieval students' *amor sciendi* (love of knowledge for its own sake) but because these young men soon recognized the need to organize and protect themselves from rapacious townsmen and officials who were eager to profit from such a captive market. That said, it must be recognized that *amor sciendi* did in fact have a critically important role to play. The concept of the university as a remote, otherworldly institution selflessly dedicated to the Aristotelian ideal of *bios theoretikos* (intellectual training) has often been reviled but there is much truth in it. It is this truth, in fact, that helped ensure the university's survival in the Middle Ages and its remarkable expansion in later times — up to and including our own day. Indeed, if universities had only been trade schools, they would almost certainly have disappeared during the Renaissance, like so many other medieval institutions.[6]

Only a minority of students ever graduated from universities: most of them were content simply to be there. They dropped out early due to financial problems, poor grades, or perhaps simply because of boredom with academic life. There was no social stigma attached to quitting. Ex-students simply went home and got caught up in the daily round of medieval life. For those that did manage to stay in the universities, the overriding goal for most of them was not intellectual freedom or self-discovery but simply a burning desire to qualify for a limited number of prestigious careers in the church, in the state, or in the universities themselves.

Medieval universities were quite different from today's universities. Classroom instruction was entirely in Latin, which students were strongly encouraged, under the pain of fines, to speak outside the classroom as well. Proficiency in Latin was essential for a student's academic survival. A statute of the University of Paris, for example, required that a student who was seeking a certificate of "scholarity" had to be able to make his case in person to the rector in Latin alone — without any "interposition of French words." If he could not do so, the certificate was refused.[7]

Full fluency in Latin, however, was not very common because Latin was a foreign language for prelates, priests and students alike. In 1318, for example, the Bishop of Durham could neither understand nor pronounce Latin. Once, when ordaining candidates for holy orders, he came across the word *aenigmte* ("through a glass darkly") and swore in English: "By St. Louis, that was no courteous man who wrote this word!"[8]

John of Garland (c. 1195–c. 1272), an English grammarian who taught Latin at the University of Paris and at the University of Toulouse, wrote the *Morale scolarium* (*Morality of Students*) in 1241. To help his students master Latin, he prepared a descriptive vocabulary of the people, professions and objects they would typically see during the course of a stroll through the streets of Paris. Perhaps of more interest to us here is the conservative, sensible advice he offered on "How Students Should Behave." Excerpts can be found in Appendix 3.

One of the reasons why Latin was so important was that students from different countries — and even from different provinces of France itself — could not have understood each other without using Latin. This can be seen by an incident in the life of Pope John XXII (1316–1334). He had grown up in Cahors in southwestern France and, despite having gone to school in Paris and Orléans, he still could not speak the French of the Île-de-France, the Parisian seat of the royal court. Thus when in 1323 he received a letter in this formal French from King Charles IV, he was forced to have it translated into Latin.[9]

Because of the importance of Latin, universities made a serious effort to make sure it was spoken outside the classroom too. The Heidelberg *Manuale Scholarium* (*Scholar's Manual*), a handbook on student life in Germany in about 1480, shows that one of the supervisors of the students was known as *lupus* ("wolf"). His task was to make sure, by imposing increasingly stiff fines, that the students under his charge spoke Latin rather than their native tongues in their free time. The students were furious about this but had no choice but to comply. If they did not abide by university regulations, they risked being locked up in a detention cell or even being "excluded," i.e., losing the all-important legal protection provided by their university privileges.[10]

The *Manuale Scholarium* also gives us a fine account of the ritualized hazing of a newly arrived Heidelberg undergraduate, who was known for reasons that are now lost as a *beanus* or *bejaunus* ("yellow-bill," from the French *bec-jaune*).[11] This young student is considered by his already-initiated fellows as a wild beast who must be civilized before he is fit to be part of university society. The hazing ceremony by which this transformation was accomplished was called the *depositio*.

In the *Manuale Scholarium* the new student is first depicted as meeting with his professor, whom he asks to arrange for his *depositio* and begs that its expenses be held to a minimum. Then, after appearing before the rector for the ceremony of matriculation (formal enrollment in the university), he is visited in his room by two of the other students, named Camillus and Bartoldus, who pretend to be investigating the source of an abominable smell that has assailed their nostrils. They discover to their mock horror that the cause of the odor is a *bejaunus*—a creature they have heard about but never seen. Here is part of their dialogue:

> *Camillus.* What's the stink that's smelling up this place? We can't stand this! There's either been a corpse rotting here, or a goat, filthiest of beasts. Most worthy masters and excellent fellows, how can you sit in the midst of this smell? I can hardly close my nose to keep it out. I must go. If I stay any longer, I'll become so infected that I'll faint, and hit the ground head first. I'm leaving! ...
>
> *Bartoldus.* I will look [at this creature], even though I risk my life. What do you say, Cam? It's actually a *beanus*....
>
> *Camillus.* Never have I laid eyes on any beast that shows such cruelty and savagery as this misshapen animal.[12]

They go on to remark about the wild glare in this creature's eye, the length of his ears, and his long fearsome tusks. They suggest that the tusks and other abnormalities can be removed only by the *depositio*. The young student's face is then smeared with soap; the other students pretend to trim his ears and saw off his tusks. The students explain that since this operation may well prove fatal, the young student must immediately have his confession heard — by a student feigning to be a priest. The young student is then forced to confess, very quietly, to all kinds of imaginary faults; the "priest" then repeats them in a loud voice for the benefit of all the other students. Finally, as his penance for such grievous sins, the young student is ordered to arrange — and pay for — a sumptuous banquet for his new comrades.

Hazing aside, the basic aim of teaching in the medieval university was to transmit to students, uncritically, selected parts of the medieval world's received (inherited) body of learning springing from Greek, Roman, Arabic and early Christian authorities.[13] Masters were almost always supporters, not critics, of the established order and did not encourage original thought. As explained in his autobiographical work, *The Metalogicon* (1159), which was a staunch defense of dialectical reasoning and the importance of the *trivium* (a medieval "foundation course" in arts, which will be discussed later), John of Salisbury traveled to Paris and undertook advanced studies there and in Chartres from 1136 to 1147. He echoes the reverence accorded by medieval society to its time-tested academic knowledge:

> Our own generation enjoys the legacy bequeathed to it by that which preceded it. We frequently know more, not because we have moved ahead by our own natural ability, but because we are supported by the mental strength of others, and possess riches that we have inherited from our forefathers. Bernard of Chartres used to compare us to puny dwarfs perched on the shoulders of giants. He pointed out that we can see more and farther than our predecessors, not because we have keener vision or greater height, but because we are lifted up and borne aloft on their gigantic stature.[14]

At the same time, however, received learning — especially when shielded from new currents of thought, as was usually the case — could easily degenerate into sterility. Thus when John of Salisbury returned to Paris after 12 years away (mostly spent in Chartres) he was quite depressed to find that his former scholarly colleagues on Mont-Sainte-Geneviève, an academic center located on a hilltop overlooking Paris, had made no progress whatsoever during his long absence. He says:

> Je les ai retrouvai comme avant et au même endroit. Ils ne semblaient pas être parvenus au but, en démêlant ces vieux problèmes, et ils n'avaient pas ajouté un iota à leurs propositions; les idéaux qui les avaient inspirés jadis, les inspiraient encore. Ils avaient seulement progressé sur un point: ils avaient oublié la modération, ils ignoraient la modestie, de telle façon que l'on peut craindre pour leur guérison. Et l'expérience m'amena ainsi à une conclusion évidente: si la dialectique sert aux autres études, elle reste inanimée et stérile lorsqu'elle

demeure seule, et ne pousse pas l'esprit à produire les fruits de la philosophie, sinon ceux qui ont été déjà conçus.[15]

[I found them just as they were before and where they were before; nor did they appear to have reached the goal of unraveling the old questions, nor had they added one iota of a proposition. The aims that once inspired them inspired them still: they had progressed in one point only: they had forgotten moderation, they knew not modesty; in such a manner that one must despair of their recovery. And thus experience taught me an evident conclusion, that, whereas dialectic furthers other studies, it remains inert and sterile as long as it stays by itself, and does not uplift the human spirit to produce the fruits of philosophy, except those originating from somewhere else.]

In medieval universities, theology, which was based on exegesis of the Bible, took over the preeminent role which philosophy had played in the Greek world.[16] It was hailed as "Madame la Haute Science" ("My lady the high science") or as "Lady Theology." It was the most prestigious and most difficult course of study. The doctrines of the church were supremely important; heresy was a serious and possibly fatal mistake in medieval times. Doctrinal errors were potentially so threatening to a man's career and livelihood that he was well advised, under the threat of having his teaching license and thus his earning power canceled, to make sure that both his peers and the church approved of what he planned to teach students.[17]

Indeed, during the later Middle Ages university leaders would continue to stress the traditional, primary role accorded to theology. For example, in his 1402 reform program *Contra curiositatem studentium* (*Against the curiosity of students*), which was aimed at the theological faculty of the University of Paris, Jean Gerson, the renowned French theologian and chancellor of the University of Paris who will be discussed later, held that, in comparison with other academic disciplines, theology must be granted the role of *domina* (mistress). The other subjects were thus only *ancillae* (handmaidens) to theology.[18]

All university students were males. In northern Europe, almost all of them were nominally clerics, that is to say, they were members of the *ordo clericalis*. This religious and legal status was reflected by the tonsure, i.e., shaving the dome of the head, leaving a fringe of hair encircling it. In Italy, some university students were clerics but most were laymen. It must be understood that being a *clericus* ("clerk" in Chaucerian English, i.e., a cleric) at a university was very different from being an ordained priest. In the early Middle Ages, the educational monopoly of the church was still intact; for this reason, most *litterati*, i.e., men of learning, were also *clerici* (clerics). Gradually, however, *clericus* came to mean any man who knew how to write. By the end of the fifteenth century, in official documents the German universities were referring to their students as "half-priests."[19]

Under church law, a woman could not become a cleric and, in practice, it was impossible for her to become a university student unless she disguised herself. In one case, a young Polish woman did exactly that, some time between 1400 and 1420. We do not know her name but her story is worth recounting here:

She studied at a grammar school as a girl. When her parents died, she used her inheritance to enter the University of Krakow. She disguised herself as a man and lived in one of the student hostels. She was unmasked only when two men — a soldier in the house of a burgher named Kaltherbrig and his companion — made a bet that she was actually a woman. They tore her clothes off to make sure. When taken before a judge and asked why she had so disguised herself, she replied "For the love of learning." Sent to a convent, she first became a teacher (*Magistra*) there and, later on, the abbess.[20]

Clerical status had two important consequences. First, it placed university students under the legal protection of the church. As a result, they were legally subject not to secular courts but only to ecclesiastical courts, which were not allowed to sentence clerical defendants to any corporal punishment. In practice, this meant that they could disregard minor regulations and laws with little fear of punishment by the secular authorities — a fact which frequently aroused the ire of townsfolk. Second, as clerics they were qualified for benefices (clerical positions that received their revenues from endowments) to help finance their education.

Medieval university students ranged in age from boys of 14 to adults in their 30s. Most of them did not have a good reputation with the townsfolk, who complained that they were always brawling, whoring, dicing, swanking around in inappropriate clothing, singing and dancing, carrying weapons, and insulting not only respectable citizens but also the forces of law and order.[21] But since no detailed, reliable, firsthand accounts by students or masters have come down to us from the years before 1500, we really do not know much about them as individuals or about their daily lives.

What we do know is mainly negative. A handbook dating from 1495 and entitled *Le Manuel du parfait étudiant* (*The manual of the perfect student*) lists a great many things that students must *not* do. These include being outside at night (night began at 8:00 P.M. in winter and at 9:00 P.M. in summer); playing games on Sunday with non-students; swimming on Monday; strolling around the market on Wednesday; failing to attend matins; falling asleep during Mass; missing vespers; beating up children; getting hymn books dirty; stirring up trouble; making stupid remarks; destroying trees; pestering the hangman while he is trying to do his job; and being obnoxious in churches and cemeteries.[22]

Many of the classic sources for the era are long on institutional data and short on human interest. Good examples are the four volumes of the *Chartularium Universitatis Parisiensis* (these are the regulations of the University of Paris between 1200 and 1452 and the papal bulls affecting them), edited in Paris by H. Denifle and E. Chatelain from 1889 to 1897, and the four volumes of M. Fournier's *Les status et privilèges des universités françaises jusq'en 1789* (*The laws and privileges of universities in France up to 1789*), published in Paris between 1890 and 1894.

The result has been that, as mentioned earlier, most later scholars have focused on the institutional side of university life, which to the nonspecialist can be incorrigibly dull. This book will try to redress the balance by looking for more human interest: we will flesh out the story of medieval universities by looking at specific episodes in the lives of some of the people directly or indirectly involved with them.

Medieval accounts can give us valuable insights into the daily lives, if not the personalities, of students. Such sources include the university institutions themselves; their faculties (the main faculties were those of the liberal arts, theology, law, and medicine); the poems and songs of *goliardi* (wandering students who were also known as *vagrantes*); and the student residences known as university colleges. Some of these colleges would later become study and teaching centers in their own right: the colleges of Oxford, Cambridge and the Sorbonne are still world famous today.

It must be remembered that medieval universities and medieval colleges were not at all the same thing. By stretching the point a bit perhaps we can say that, figuratively speaking, the university was a thin canopy-like structure providing bureaucratic shelter for the learned faculties and for the robust colleges. This process began in 1257 when Robert of Sorbon, chaplain and confessor of Louis IX, founded in Paris the college of La Sorbonne. It captured perfectly the essence of the college system: *vivere socialiter et collegiater, et moraliter, et scholariter.* This meant a community, organized like a brotherhood, where students could live together and study at low cost under the supervision of a master.[23] Colleges usually had books. The oldest extant catalogue of the Sorbonne, which served as the chief library for the University of Paris, had 1,722 volumes in 1338.[24] Many of them can still be consulted at the Bibliothèque Nationale in Paris.

Originally the Sorbonne was nothing more than a small college of theologians; in the sixteenth and seventeenth centuries, however, "Sorbonne" would refer to the whole theological faculty of the University of Paris. Indeed, by the reign of the French king François I (r. 1515–1547), all the doctors of theology were calling themselves "doctors of the Sorbonne."[25] Formal university debates, known as disputations (*disputio*), were held in the hall of the Sorbonne beginning in the early fourteenth century. Such disputations became intellectual gladiatorial contests for those seeking the doctorate. In effect, they constituted a rigorous oral examination. Rashdall describes the scene:

> At this disputation, known as the *Sorbonic*, from its taking place in the hall of the Sorbonne, the respondent was required to reply standing, alone, and without the assistance of any moderator or judge except an audience which occasionally signified its approbation or disapprobation by stamping or clapping, to a succession of opponents who relieved each other at intervals from six in the morning until six in the evening, an hour's relaxation only being allowed for refreshment in the middle of the day.[26]

Undergraduates at the Sorbonne had to comply with strict regulations designed to preserve discipline and scholarly decorum. In the fourteenth century, for example, they had to ask for permission to leave the university and were allowed to walk the streets of Paris only in pairs — perhaps to prevent them from being seduced by the city's many prostitutes. Contemporary university records suggest that the students of the Sorbonne were not angels. They were fined for "very inordinately" knocking at the dining room door, trying to gain entrance while dinner was already being served; for being very drunk; for "confabulating" in the university's quadrangle late at night; for refusing to go to their rooms when ordered to do so; and for demanding wine — in the name of a master — at the buttery (a room in an English college stocking provisions for sale to students) and then drinking it themselves.

The Sorbonne's regulations were no respecters of rank. We learn that a Doctor of Divinity was fined for picking a pear off a tree in the garden of the college; for forgetting, yet again, to close the chapel door; and for eating his meals in the kitchen rather than in the dining hall. Finally, the head cook was fined for cooking the meat badly and for not putting enough salt in the soup.[27]

The university college proved itself an exceptionally useful institution for medieval students. From its modest beginnings as an endowed hospice or hall of residence, it flourished to such an extent that by the end of the Middle Ages there were 68 colleges in Paris alone.[28] (The first one at Oxford was appropriately known as University College. It was founded in 1249 by William of Durham, a distinguished master of Paris, to enable masters of arts to complete the long course necessary for the Doctor of Divinity degree.[29])

Over time, some of the Parisian colleges would become *collèges de plein exercice* (colleges providing a full course of study). When this happened, the faculties, which at one point had been the most important influential components of the university, would in practice be limited to conferring formal degrees.[30] In 1445, for example, it was said that in France the entire university was centered in its colleges — a statement that was equally true for Oxford and Cambridge as well.[31]

University authorities were strongly in favor of students living either in the colleges or in the authorized halls of the university itself. They wanted to keep an eye on the students to prevent too many university and civil regulations from being trampled underfoot. Masters tried to reduce the number of students who lived in the town without permission or supervision and who slept by day and raised hell in the brothels and taverns at night. Universities repeatedly passed ordinances to control such unruly students. Vienna did so in 1410 against "outside students" (*extra bursas stantes*); Paris followed its lead in 1452–1457 against what the French, with a playful touch, termed them m*artinets* (swifts, i.e., small plainly colored birds that strongly resemble swallows). Nowhere, however, did such regulatory efforts have any lasting effect.[32]

Many of the *martinets* also seem to have been wandering *goliardi*. These latter were young men who were "students without masters." Their irregular academic status was a clear and vexing violation of university regulations. As early as 1215 the university had ruled that *nullus sit scholaris Parisius que certum magistrum non habeat* ("nobody can be a student at the University of Paris if he does not have a permanent teacher").[33] To become a university student, a young man had to matriculate, that is, he had to be formally enrolled in a register (*matricula*) as an official member of the university. In England, this process was first described at Oxford in a statute of about 1231 and at Cambridge in one dated between 1236 and 1254.

The initial step in matriculation was the student's interview with his prospective master. The student had to pass muster on three counts: being male, being able to pay his own way in his university studies, and knowing enough Latin to be able to follow lectures in that language. If accepted by the master, the student's name would then be inscribed on the *matricula album registrum* (registration roll) and he would be a member of the privileged academic community. Matriculation can best be thought of as a contract: the student agreed to attend the master's formal lectures; in return, the master agreed to protect the student and to be responsible for his behavior.[34]

It is precisely because of their footloose, irregular life that the poems of the *goliardi* give us such a refreshing, intensely human insight into medieval university life. One of their lapidary songs was the well-known *Gaudeamus igitur*, which is still very widely used today, both as a beer-drinking song in European universities and at university graduations. Regarded as the oldest student drinking song, it was originally based on a Latin manuscript of 1287. There are many versions of it now. The one given below will probably be the most familiar. It dates from about 1781; the music we associate with it comes from Johannes Brahms' *Academic Festival Overture* (Opus 80), composed in 1880.

   The text reads as follows:

   Guadeamus igitur
   Juvenes dum sumus.
   Gaudeamus igitur
   Juvenes dum sumus.
   Post jucundam juventutem
   Post molestam senectutem
   Nos habebit humus.

   Via nostra brevis est,
   Brevi finietur,
   Venit mors velociter
   Rapit nos atrociter,
   Nemini parcetur.

   Vivat academia
   Vivant professores
   Vivat membrum quodlibet
   Vivat membra quaelibet
   Simper sint in flore!

   Vivat nostra societas,
   Vivant studiosi
   Cescat una veritas,
   Floreat fraternitas,
   Patriae prosperitas.

   Alma Mater floreat,
   Quae nos educavit;
   Caros et commilitones,
   Dissitas in regiones,
   Sparsos, congregavit.

   [Let us therefore rejoice
   While we are young.
   Let us therefore rejoice
   While we are young.
   After a pleasant youth
   After the troubles of old age
   The earth will have us.

Life is short and all too soon
We emit our final gasp;
Death ere long is on our back;
Terrible is his attack;
None escapes his dread grasp.

Long live our academy,
Teachers we cherish;
Long life to all the graduates;
And the undergraduates;
Ever may they flourish.

Long live our society,
Scholars wise and learned;
May truth and sincerity
Nourish our fraternity
And our land's prosperity.

May our Alma Mater thrive,
A font of education;
Friends and colleagues, where're they are
Whether from near or from afar,
Heed her invitation.][35]

During the Middle Ages there were about 4,000 taverns in Paris, which sold some 700 barrels of wine every day. About 60 of these taverns were special favorites of the Paris students.[36] We shall never know which particular tavern (if there was one) inspired this famous *goliard* poem:

Meum est propositum in taberna mori,
Vinum sit appositum morientis ori
Ut dicant cum venerint angelorum chori:
Deus sit propitius huic potatori![37]

[In the tavern to die
Is my resolution;
Let wine to my lips be nigh
At life's dissolution;
That will make the angels cry
With glad elocution,
"Grant this boozer, God on high,
Grace and absolution!"][38]

The derivation of the name *goliard* remains obscure. Some scholars link it to a mythical "Bishop Golias." Others believe it originates with Pope Innocent II, who in a letter to St. Bernard referred to Peter Abelard as "Goliath," thus creating a link between this Biblical giant and the students clustering around Abelard. Still others hold that *goliard* is a corruption of the French word *gaillard*, meaning a strong, lively fellow. The *goliardi* have now no exact counterparts in modern life: the Western hippies of the late 1960s and early 1970s were the closest approximations.

Regardless of the provenance of their name, *goliardi* were vagabond students from Italian, French, English and German universities who lampooned the abuses of the church through their public performances. They specialized in Latin drinking songs, poems and religious plays. Many of these can now be found in the *Carmina Burana*, a manuscript collection in Munich that contains more than 1,000 satirical works written in the early thirteenth century.

The *goliardi* had a very devil-may-care attitude and happily celebrated all the pleasures of student life. Three examples follow. In the first, a *goliard* is dying. A priest, summoned in haste, tries to comfort the young man and encourages him to make a last confession. We are then treated to a parody of the Credo ("I believe")—the formal statement of religious belief which is often used in the Catholic Mass as a text or in musical form. The italicized Latin words below are from the goliard's Credo. It is too long to quote here in full, but a few excerpts will be instructive.

The *goliard* whispers to his confessor:

> *Credo*—in dice I well believe,
> That got me often bite and sup,
> And many a time hath made me drunk,
> And many a time delivered me
> From every stitch and penny.
> *In Deum* [in God]—never with my will
> Gave Him a thought or ever will....
> Good Sir, I had a father once,
> *Omnipotentem* [all-powerful] in his having,
> Money and horses and fine wearing,
> And by the dice that thieveth all things
> I lost and gamed it all away....
> But when I've drunk a good strong wine
> That leaves me well and warm within,
> Little I care for *peccatorum* [sin]....
> And I would pray to the Lord God
> That He will in no kind of way
> *Resurrectionem* [the resurrection of the dead] make of me,
> So long as I may drench the place
> With good wine where I'll be laid,
> And so pray of all my friends
> That if I can't, themselves will do it,
> And leave me with a full pot of wine
> Which I may to the Judgment bring....[39]

In the second example, we get a good dose, in this mock liturgy, of the cocky attitude adopted by *goliardi*:

Ego sum abbas Cucaniensis
et consilium meum est cum bibulis,
et in secta Decii voluntas mea est,
et qui mane me quesierit in taberna,
post vesperam nudus egredietur,
et sic denudatus veste clamabit:
Wafna, wafna!
quid fecisti sors turpissima?
Nostre vite gaudia abstulisti omnia!

[I am the Abbot of Never-Never Land and all my friends drink gallons of
booze and I worship gambling and if someone finds me in a bar in the morning he will leave completely stripped of everything, whining: "Wafna, wafna!
(an expletive used to express sorrow and anger). Life sucks: what incredibly
lousy luck could have taken away everything good in my life?"][40]

The third example celebrates the joys of yet another round of drinks:

Once for the buyer of the wine,
free men drink out of it;
twice they drink for those in jail,
after that, three times for the living,
four times for all Christians,
five times for those who died in the Faith,
six times for the weak sisters
seven times for the forces on forest duty.

Eight times for errant brothers,
nine times for monks dispersed,
ten times for sailors,
eleven times for quarrelers,
twelve times for penitents,
thirteen times for those going on a journey,
the same for the Pope as for the king,
everyone drinks without license.[41]

More soberly, we can also learn about university life from the specific
courses of study; from the shape of the academic day; and from the general tone and methodology of intellectual life in the universities. As
their primary intellectual tool in the faculties of arts, medieval universities
relied on scholasticism, a rigorous method of learning based on dialectical
reasoning.

Masters taught in two ways: the *lectio* (reading), when they read aloud
and painstakingly explained an authoritative text while the students listened
passively, and the *disputatio* (oral disputation), in which students themselves
played an active role in debate. During the high scholastic period (1250 to
1350), scholasticism expanded beyond theology into many other fields. Its

ultimate aim was to produce a systematic body of knowledge in every important arena of intellectual enquiry.

Scholasticism was, together with the Christian faith, the intellectual powerhouse of medieval universities. The men who devoted themselves professionally to using the scholastic method were known as Schoolmen. They would analyze, logically and meticulously, a question or a proposition found in a text of, say, Aristotle, whose logic was the bedrock of scholastic thought. The opinions of different thinkers on the subject would be researched and considered; pro and con arguments drawn from them were advanced and refuted; and, finally, a carefully structured effort was made to find the best possible rational solution to the question or proposition at issue.[42]

Thus the importance of scholasticism in medieval universities can hardly be exaggerated. The medievalist R. W. Southern may have described it best. He wrote:

> The greatest virtue of the medieval scholastic system was that it stabilized and systematized knowledge of theology and law, which were the subjects of greatest importance for the creation of a fairly orderly and basically hopeful society, and which had been immensely successful in producing works of the highest genius in Christian doctrine, devotion, imagery, and order. The role of the schools was fundamental to their whole effort since they produced the systematic body of doctrine on which a way of life and a body of works of piety and devotion, and of imaginative force, were created which can never lose their power to attract, however much they may lose their power to convince.[43]

We should note here that when Aristotle was at length discovered by the Schoolmen, the first thing they were impressed by was the formidable rationality of his logic. From this observation it was an easy step for them to conclude that the Aristotelian store of wisdom must in its entirety be regarded as the most reliable source of knowledge in the secular sphere, just as the Bible was so regarded in the religious sphere. Indeed, for medieval thinkers Aristotle's position was similar to that accorded to definitive works in scholarship today: his writings were always accepted at face value as long as there was no specific reason to doubt their accuracy.[44]

Medieval scholars were great logicians. With the growth of nominalism (a school of thought, which held that a universal concept such as "father" does not have any independent existence beyond the particular person it names), scholasticism would give greater and greater weight to Aristotelian logic as the Middle Ages advanced. To acquire a baccalaureate degree at the University of Erfurt (Germany) in about 1420, a student had to attend lectures and exercises on the following texts. Most of them dealt chiefly with logic, a subject that was far from easy to master. These texts included[45]:

- The *Ars minor* by Donatus
- The second part of *Doctrinale* by Alexander de Villa Dei
- Works by Thomas Maulevelt, namely *The Supposition of Terms*; *Confusions*; *Alienations*; *Remotions*; *Syncategoremes*; and *Consequences*. An alternative to the last work was John Sutton's *Consequences*
- Richard Billingham's *Proof of Propositions*
- Hollandrinus' *Obligations* and his *Insolubilia*
- Porphyry's *Isagoge*, which will be discussed later
- Aristotle's *Categories*; *Perihermeneias*; first and second *Analytics*; *Elenchi*; *Physics*; and *De Anima*
- John of Hollywood's *Sphaera materialis*

The universities did not have a monopoly over scholastic pedagogy but they were responsible for perfecting it. They were the only medieval institutions of learning that routinely used a system of carefully specialized examinations, i.e., oral disputations, to test what had been taught in the classroom.[46] Over time, however, scholasticism tumbled into the twin pitfalls of logical rigidity and emotional desiccation. Because it was always much more concerned with achieving logical precision and with determining philosophical "truths" than with testing its speculations against empirical evidence, it became intellectually constipated. Under the impact of humanist thought (which will be described later), later reformers would deride the Schoolmen of the past as "obscurantists" who were foolishly opposed to humanistic methods and ideas and who blindly followed sterile, pedantic and frivolous academic procedures.[47]

Some modern scholars of the Middle Ages will defend the scholastics against such denigrations. Unlike the humanists, the Schoolmen were not interested in philology (the study of literature and related disciplines), but they were formidable philosophers and dialecticians in their own right.[48] Today it is easy enough for us to deplore the iron grip of scholasticism on university teaching in the late Middle Ages because of its sterility, formalism, and rigidity. Yet despite these shortcomings it was for many years the hallmark of the educated man. As the Latinist and medievalist Anders Piltz explains,

> In comparison with today, the period of scholasticism was, seen as an information system, a relatively closed world. A limited number of classical texts were available and the prospects of discovering more authors or texts were relatively limited. The texts that had been inherited were incorporated into a canon [a body of works accepted as authoritative] because of their intrinsic value, a canon of knowledge and wisdom that *every individual with any claim to education should know, or of which he should at least know the main outlines.*[49]

For the best and brightest students, an advanced degree in theology was the surest gateway to the upper levels of the church in northern Europe. Canon law was also a very promising avenue of advancement for ambitious young men: the day-to-day duties of the senior clergy consisted almost entirely of ecclesiastical administration, for which canon law was held to be the most suitable qualification.[50] In Italy, on the other hand, a degree in civil law was the key to lucrative employment in a great many fields.

Some schools (e.g., the proto-university of Salerno, located south of Naples and the University of Montpellier, west of Marseilles) specialized in medicine, which was also taught in other universities. Discussing the career choices open to students who grew bored at the University of Paris with its endless wordy exercises in grammar and dialectical reasoning, John of Salisbury tells us that "Others went to Salerno or Montpellier and became clients of the physicians."[51]

However, since it took more than seven years fully to qualify as a doctor of medicine at Montpellier, aspiring physicians often chose other, quicker routes into medical practice.[52] In both France and Italy between the twelfth and fifteenth centuries, and almost certainly long thereafter as well, fewer than half of the medical practitioners plying their trade had taken any medical courses at a university. The remainder were non-university graduates, e.g., surgeons (a skilled and organized craft), barber-surgeons, pharmacists, herbalists, midwives, or local men and women admired for their holiness or wisdom. Given the very rudimentary state of medical knowledge in the universities and elsewhere, medieval patients must have been badly served by most practitioners. A man who held a medical degree from a fine university was no more likely to effect a cure than his less educated rival.[53]

To see what academic life was like for a medieval student, let us look at the seven liberal arts (*artes liberales*), which formed the basis for most university studies. These arts were grammar, rhetoric, dialectical reasoning, music, astronomy, geometry, and arithmetic. They were called the "liberal" arts (from *liberalis*, which has its roots in the Latin word *liber*, meaning "free") because they were held to be the proper course of study for free, i.e., non-servile, men. They were considered qualitatively different from and, indeed, much superior to the manual or mechanical arts and also to the practical and more mundane arts of law and medicine.

A detail of Andrea da Firenze's late fourteenth century painting *The Triumph of St Thomas Aquinas* gives us a listing of the authoritative thinkers most closely associated with the seven liberal arts and whose work (with one obvious error) therefore had to be studied with the utmost care. Here is a lightly edited version of that listing[54]:

Grammar	Priscian: Roman grammarian, sixth century CE (Common Era)
Rhetoric	Cicero: Roman lawyer, orator and statesman, first century BCE (before Common Era)
Dialectical reasoning	Aristotle: Greek philosopher who invented formal logic, fourth century BCE
Music	Tubal-cain: Biblical metalworker erroneously identified with music
Astronomy	Ptolemy: Greek astronomer, second century CE
Geometry	Euclid: Greek mathematician, third century BCE
Arithmetic	Pythagoras, Greek philosopher and mathematician, sixth century BCE

The first three of these liberal arts were the verbal arts of the *trivium*, a term which meant "the three roads" to knowledge. These roads were grammar, rhetoric, and dialectical reasoning. Latin grammar was the bedrock on which medieval education rested: scholarly Latin was, with isolated exceptions, the only language of university instruction. A treatise on education, written in 1252, instructs parents that from the springtime of a boy's seventh year until the end of his fourteenth year ("when the light of reason begins to shine"), grammar must be his chief focus of study. Grammar was held to discipline the mind and the soul at the same time and to be the gateway to all advanced linguistic subjects — rhetoric, logic, and the study of classic literature and the Scriptures.[55] As a mnemonic for schoolboys puts it,

> Gram loquitur; Dia vera docet; Rhet verba colorat; Mus canit; Art numerat; Ge ponderat; Ast colit astra.

> [Grammar speaks; dialectical reasoning teaches truth; rhetoric adorns words; music sings; arithmetic counts; geometry measures; astronomy studies stars.][56]

The fourth-century Latin encyclopedist Aelius Donatus was the author of *De partibus orationis ars minor* ("*The lesser art, concerning the parts of grammar*"). It became one of the most widely used texts of the medieval period. Using a format suitable for young students just beginning to study grammar, Donatus asks and answers in simple, clear terms:

> How many parts of speech are there? Eight. What? Noun, pronoun, verb, adverb, participle, conjunction, proposition, interjection. On the noun: What is a noun? A part of speech with case signifying a person or thing specifically or generally. How many attributes does a noun have. Six. What? Quality, comparison, gender, number, form, case.[57]

We can easily imagine the master putting each of these questions to a classroom full of students, and the students collectively chanting the answers aloud. Donatus offers many such exercises. Here is another one:

MASTER: What is irony?
STUDENTS: Irony is the trope [figure of speech] which uses the opposite of
what is being referred to....[58]

Medieval rhetoric was a complex discipline that is difficult to define and summarize succinctly. During the Middle Ages it drew heavily from the works of Marcus Tullius Cicero. His ideal of a truly learned man (*doctus orator*) was one who combined in his own person an extensive knowledge of all the sciences plus a wide experience of the problems of everyday life.[59] Cicero's own expertise in language and in Latin composition became the role model for medieval students. His elementary work, *De inventione* (*On Invention*), became in the Middle Ages the most widely used guide to Latin. Students were encouraged to pursue their own academic work by striving for eloquence, a subject which Cicero held to be of the greatest importance. As he says in *De Oratore* (*On the Orator*), which is a detailed treatment of rhetorical doctrines,

> Illa vis autem eloquentiae tanta est, ut onmium rerum, virtutum, officiorum omnisque naturae, quae mores hominum, quae animos, quae vitam continet, originem, vim mutationesque teneat, eadem mores, leges, iura describat, rem publicam regat, omniaque, ad quamcumque rem pertineant, ornate copioseque dicat.

> [Eloquence is so powerful that it embraces the origin and operations of all things in the world, all the virtues, duties, and natural principles related to the manners, minds, and lives of mankind. Eloquence also determines customs, laws, and rights, controls government, and expounds on every kind of topic in a polished and refined manner.][60]

Medieval rhetoric was traditionally held to consist of five parts: arrangement, delivery, invention, style, and memory.[61] In practice, it had several separate but overlapping facets. These were oratory; poetry; drama; preaching; and, perhaps the most important in practical terms, *dictamen* (also known as *ars dictandis*). This last discipline was the art of drafting accurate, well-phrased letters, official correspondence and all other forms of literary composition in Latin and in accordance with complex rules and forms.[62] Once they left the university and were looking for jobs, former students would have had much more need for *dictamen* than for any other aspect of rhetoric. The reason was that, as A. B. Cobban, a modern scholar, explained,

> The supranational character of papal affairs demanded the services of a far-flung network of highly trained notaries and the formulation of the most exacting business methods. It was essential that extreme care be taken in the drafting of official documentation, as [any] error or exploitable loophole might have the most serious repercussions in a society whose rights derived from the

written word. The instrument at hand was *dictamen* and its specialized off-shoot relating to the craft of the notary, the *ars notaria*. The demand created by the papal curia for graduates trained in *dictamen* and/or the *ars notaria* was paralleled by that of the imperial chancery and by royal administrations all over Europe wherever the civil law prevailed.[63]

A good example of how a medieval instructor taught *dictamen* at the beginner's level can be seen in this version of a "Dear Father, please send money" letter. The teacher's comments are shown in bold italics:

> To his father H., C. [the student] sends due affection. ***This is the salutation.*** I am much obliged to you for the money you sent me. ***This is the captatio benivolentie*** [i.e., an insert designed to show appreciation and to put the recipient into the right frame of mind]. But I would have you know that I am still poor, having spent in the schools what I had, and that which recently arrived is of little help since I used it to pay some of my debts and my greater obligations still remain. ***This is the narration.*** Whence I beg you to send me something more. ***This is the petition.*** If you do not, I shall lose the books which I have pledged to the Jews [the moneylenders of the Middle Ages] and shall be compelled to return home with my work incomplete. ***This is the conclusion.***[64]

Dialectical reasoning was based on Aristotelian logic, which was considered so important by the universities that in the thirteenth century it held a dominant place in the courses at Paris, Cambridge and Oxford leading to the BA degree. It was a three-step method of logical investigation involving (1) theses (propositions), (2) antitheses (counter-propositions), and then, ideally, (3) a synthesis of these opposing points of view. As used by Socrates, this process could show that a given thesis led to a logical contradiction; if so, that thesis must be invalid.

The four remaining — and more advanced — liberal arts were the mathematical arts of the *quadrivium* ("the four roads"): music, astronomy, geometry, and arithmetic. All were based on the Greek theories of these disciplines. To these we shall now turn.

Medieval universities approached music strictly in mathematical terms, e.g., by studying the Pythagorean theory of music as described by Boethius (c. 480–c. 524), a Roman scholar, philosopher and statesman whose work on music and arithmetic deeply influenced the medieval universities. This theory of music was based on ratios of the numbers 6, 8, 9, and 12: that is to say, it was based exclusively on what was termed "mathematical science."[65] As Cassiodorus, a near contemporary of Boethius explained,

> Mathematical science is that science which considers abstract quantity. By abstract quantity we mean that quantity which we treat in a purely speculative way, separating it from its material and other accidents [that is, from its other

qualities], such as evenness, oddness, and the like. It has these divisions: arithmetic, music, geometry, astronomy. Arithmetic is the discipline which treats of numbers in their relation to those things which are found in sounds. Geometry is the discipline of immobile magnitude and of forms. Astronomy is the discipline of the course of the heavenly bodies.[66]

Remarkably, it was not necessary for a medieval student to be able to play, sing or compose to be considered a fully qualified musician.[67]

Beginning in the tenth century, European scholars discovered, thanks to Muslim Spain, the Greek astronomical instrument known as the astrolabe. This was a kind of primitive computer that could, among other things, solve problems in spherical trigonometry of astronomical interest without the need to use calculations.[68] It became so famous in learned circles that, as mentioned earlier, Abelard and Heloise named their son "Astrolabe."

In the Middle Ages, the word "geometry" had many different meanings and does not lend itself to simple definition today. It had three branches: practical geometry (e.g., surveying), constructive geometry (used in architectural design and by masons in building houses, etc.), and theoretical geometry.[69] To teach this latter and rather abstract discipline, the Schoolmen reached for graphic, dramatic examples that would be easy for students to remember.

A textbook of 1496, for example, asks, "What is a body?" The answer is: "Length combined with width and depth." To make these abstractions clear, the book contains a drawing of a nude man who is standing upright and has been transfixed by three long spears. The accompanying text graphically instructs the student:

> Imagine a spear which pierces the skull and comes out through the anus. This measures length. A second spear goes in through the chest and out through the back and this measures depth. A third spear goes in through one side and out through the other and this measures width.[70]

The medieval concept of *arithmetica* did not involve computations but rather the study of the theories underlying numbers, i.e., a philosophical analysis of number, unity, equality, ratio, and proportion. In modern mathematics, this kind of number theory is referred to as the philosophy of number. Medieval mathematics thus did not deal with addition, subtraction, multiplication and division. These utilitarian aspects of mathematics were lumped together by medieval thinkers as *computus* or algorism, a corruption of the name of the Arab scholar al-Khwarizimi, whose *Treatise on the Calculation with Hindu Numerals* was translated into Latin in about 1143.[71]

Study requires sustenance, so let us now look at meals at the medieval university. Even though they had to get up very early, students often began the day without any breakfast. In a contract written in 1286, the rector of a church in Bologna agreed to feed two relatively prosperous German students, who were lodging with him, as follows. At around 10:00 A.M. they would get "good bread and good wine." The daily bread ration ranged from about three to four pounds. Each day the students were also entitled to about one pint of wine, usually diluted with water. Fruit or cheese would normally be provided as well.

Dinner was a thick soup with soaked bread and sometimes meat in it. This meal was served at 4:00 P.M. in winter and at 5:00 P.M. in summer. If the students had to attend university courses in the evening, dinner would be served later. The Sunday meal was the culinary highlight of the week—a big event, with plenty of meat and lots of undiluted wine. John of Garland assures us in 1241 that even impoverished students could be sure of having enough to eat while they were at the university. Green vegetables, broad beans and wine were relatively cheap in the markets and with a little patience and ingenuity could be combined into nourishing meals.[72]

A medieval university did not have a fixed location, that is, a formal campus. Students were usually taught in private houses or in halls rented for that purpose. It was not until the fifteenth century that universities began to equip themselves with handsome, substantial buildings.[73] The classroom of the medieval university was sparsely furnished and very simple. It had a chair for the master, benches for the students (sometimes with desks where they could stack the manuscripts containing the texts they studied) and a few cupboards along the walls. In winter, the floor was strewn with rushes to help keep feet warm but there was no fireplace.[74] At first students took notes on wax tablets and did their best to keep up with the lecturer's flow of speech. When they fell behind, they might respond by hissing, groaning, or throwing stones to try to make him speak more slowly.[75]

A good example of how medieval students took notes are a student's cramped, detailed notes from a lecture on Aristotle's *De Anima* (*On the Soul*), which was given at the University of Uppsala (Sweden) in November or December 1482.[76] Using a kind of university shorthand, these notes are written with a quill pen in black ink on one page of paper. The original is preserved in the library of the University of Uppsala but it is, alas, too dark and too illegible to be reproduced here. It consists of three parts:

• The text of the book itself (*litera*), i.e., which appears as very widely spaced lines of thick black script.
• The lecturer's explanations or glosses (*glossae*) on individual words and phrases. These take the form of comments added above the text lines but

in much finer script. To insert these glosses, the student simply turned over his quill pen and wrote with the narrow back of the quill.

• The substance of the lecture itself (*commentum*) was closely written in the margin adjacent to the relevant parts of the text.

Students also used editorial notations used to help keep track of their work. For example, *Sube et maxie* (short for *Substantie autem maxime*) meant that the commentary that follows refers to a section that begins with these words.

Jean de Jandun (c. 1286–1328) was a French philosopher living in Paris. He had studied at the University of Paris and earned his master of arts degree there at the Collège de Navarre (founded by Jeanne de Navarre, queen of France in 1305), where he lectured on Aristotle. He said that to be in Paris was to exist in an *absolute* sense; to live anywhere else was to exist only in a *relative* sense.[77] Perhaps as a diversion from endless disputations over Aristotelian thought, in 1323 he wrote *De laudibus Parisius* (*A Treatise in Praise of Paris*), which describes medieval university life in the most glowing terms. It was probably the first tourist guide to Paris. Here is an excerpt from this work:

> Dans la ville des villes, à Paris, dans la rue dite du Fouarre, non seulement on enseigne les sept arts libéraux mais, de plus, la clarté très agréable de toute lumière philosophique, répandant les rayons de la pure vérité, illumine les âmes capables de la recevoir. Là aussi l'odeur la plus suave du nectar philosophe réjouit l'odorat apte à recueillir une émanation si délicate. Les merveilles des principes divins, les secrets de la nature, l'astrologie, les mathématiques et les ressources salutaires que procurent les vertus morales, y sont dévoilés aux regards. Là se réunissent en foule les savants maîtres qui enseignent non seulement la logique, mais encore toutes les connaissances qui préparent aux sciences plus élevées....[78]

> [In Paris, the city of cities, not only are the seven liberal arts taught in classrooms all along on the rue du Fouarre /in old French, "fouarre" means "fodder" and refers to the rushes scattered on the floor, where students sat during their lessons/ but, moreover, the clarity of all philosophic knowledge, shining in beams of pure virtue, illuminates the souls of those who are capable of receiving it. There the sweet scent of philosophic nectar pleases the refined nose that can perceive such a delicate emanation. There, too, the marvels of divine principles, the secrets of nature, astrology, mathematics, and the salutary resources that generate moral virtues are all unveiled for study. Professors gather in crowds and teach not only logic but also all the other branches of knowledge that prepare the student for more advanced studies....]

We do not have accurate records of how many hours a day the average student spent in the classroom. A good guess is that he had to attend a maximum of three lectures a day, each one apparently lasting from between an hour and a half to two hours. In addition, there were various kinds of less formal but nevertheless mandatory supplementary exercises in the form of disputations, repetitions, and oral instruction of the catechism. What is clear is that students had a very full schedule. A typical academic day seems to have run as follows:

- Rise at 4:00 A.M.
- Faculty of Arts lecture at 5:00 A.M. This faculty derived its name from the seven liberal arts: the *trivium* (grammar, rhetoric, and dialectic reasoning) and the *quadrivium* (music, astronomy, geometry, and arithmetic). At the canon law school of the University of Paris (and presumably at the Faculty of Arts as well), lectures by the professors were delivered without notes and, in the predawn darkness, without any light either.[79] Since it was impossible for students to take their own notes without any light, they tried to memorize the gist of what the master said. Martino de Fano, a legal scholar of the thirteenth century, gave this helpful advice to his students: "And finally, as you lie in bed or walk about the street, go over what you have learned and say, 'Today I have learned so many laws, and these are the opening words of each.'"[80] A good memory was a critically important asset for medieval students. A 1490 textbook on the art of memory (*ars memorativa*) gives a table containing illustrations of 25 real or mythical animals. The author, Jacobus Publicus, claims that, using this table and three similar ones, the reader will be able to keep 100 different things in his head in correct order.[81]
- Mass at 6:00 A.M.
- Breakfast 8:00 A.M.—10:00 A.M. (9:00 A.M.—11:00 A.M. in Lent)
- Formal debates before the noon meal
- Repetitions (these formed the component chapters of a manuscript book) and lectures from 3:00 P.M.— 5:00 P.M.
- Disputations from 5:00 P.M. to 6:00 P.M.
- Repetitions after the evening meal
- Bed at 9:00 P.M.[82]

We cannot discover precisely what courses medieval students had to take and pass to qualify first for the bachelor of arts degree and then for the master of arts degree (*magister artium*), but it is certain that careful study of the *quadrivium*, coupled with heavy doses of the "three philosophies" (natural, moral, and metaphysical), were required. In Paris, the first official provisions for the BA degree date from 1252; those of Oxford followed soon after.[83] At medieval universities, qualifying for this degree was not child's play. It required four years of intense and expensive study.

To give us some idea of its demands, Rashdall offers a partial list of the *chief requirements* for the BA degree at Oxford in 1268. This list has been annotated and edited for the sake of clarity but it is still quite complicated. In the interests of brevity we will not try to explain all of its contents in detail. However, some explanations will be necessary and have been added here. They appear in indented italics to set them off, visually, from the rest of the text. As thus revised, Rashdall's list reads as follows[84]:

For BA Four years of study for "determination" [equivalent to achieving the BA degree]. To have heard [that is, to have attended classes which covered a given subject]:

1. The Old Logic [a subdivision of Aristotle's works], i.e., Porphyry's *Isagoge*, the *Categoriae* and *De Interpretatione* of Aristotle, the *Sex Principia* of Gilbert de la Porrée, twice; and the Logical works of Boethius (except *Topics*, book iv), once.

   To give an example of the inherent difficulty of some of these works, let us consider the first one, Porphyry's Isagoge. Porphyry (c. 233–c. 309) was a Neoplatonic philosopher best known for his Introduction (Isagoge) to Aristotle's Categories, which was a primer on logic. One of the most fundamental and most difficult philosophic questions of the Middle Ages was the problem of universals. The Stanford Encyclopedia of Philosophy *explains that this problem focuses on how universal cognition of singular things is possible. It asks:*

   > How do we know, for example, that the Pythagorean theorem holds universally, for all possible right triangles? Indeed, how can we have any awareness of a potential infinity of possible right triangles, given that we could only see a finite number of actual ones? How can we universally indicate all possible right triangles with the phrase "right triangle"? Is there something common to them all signified by this phrase? If so, what is it, and how is it related to the particular right triangles? The medieval problem of universals is a logical, and historical, continuation of the ancient problem generated by [Plato].[85]

   Porphyry raised the problem of universals in a passage which Rashdall describes as having played "a more momentous part in the history of thought than any other passage of equal length in all literature outside the canonical Scriptures."[86] Porphyry wrote to his pupil Chrysaorius:

   > *Since to teach about Aristotle's* Categories *it is necessary to know what genus and difference are, as well as species, property, and accident [these are the five components of the philosophic concept of "substance"], and since reflection on these things is useful for giving definitions, and in general for matters pertaining to division and demonstration, therefore I shall give you a brief account and shall try in a few words, as in the manner of an introduction, to go over what our elders said about these things. I shall abstain from deeper enquiries and aim, as appropriate, at the simpler ones.[87]*

   These "deeper enquiries," Porphyry warns his student, involve such ques-

tions as "whether genera and species exist as substances, or are confined to mere conceptions; and if they are substances, whether they are material or immaterial; and whether they exist separately from sensible objects, or in them immanently. This sort of problem is very deep, and requires a more extensive investigation."[88]

2. In the New Logic (another subdivision of Aristotle's works), Aristotle's *Priora Analytica, Topica, Sophistici Elenchi,* twice; *Posteriora Analytica,* once.

In addition, to have studied:

(1) Grammar, i.e., Priscian, *De constructionibus,* twice; Donatus, *Barbarismus,* once.

(2) Natural Philosophy (*philosophia naturalis*: the objective study of nature and the physical universe), i.e., Aristotle, *Physica, De Anima, De Generatione et Corruptione Animalium.*

To have responded [debated] *de Sophismatibus* for a year or have heard the *Posteriora Analytica* twice, instead of once.

To have "responded to the question" [this academic exercise required a student to play an active role in a logical disputation].

In practice, the student spent his first two years of the BA program listening to lectures and attending disputations (*disputatio*).[89] There were three kinds of lectures. The first were the formal "ordinary" lectures delivered by a master. He would first read the text aloud and then explain its important points. These lectures were given in the morning. The second kind were the simpler "extraordinary" lectures, given by masters in the afternoon to cover less essential law texts. The third type were the elementary "cursory" lectures given by bachelors in the afternoon as part of their own training as apprentice masters. These supplemented the ordinary lectures.[90]

Detailed regulations issued by a German university (Leipzig) in 1471 discussed "Rules for Attending Lectures and Writing Exercises." The university ordered that

> The procedures shall be as follows: whoever attends any lecture or aspires to a degree in arts, except for mathematics, *logica Hesbri* [the works in logic by the Oxford logician, philosopher, and chancellor William of Heytesbury, c. 1313–1372], and the *politica* [Aristotle's *Politics*], is obliged to follow diligently the book that is assigned, in such a way that he has either his own or a borrowed text of the lecture with him at all times during the lecture (no more than two or three students may used the same text at one time). Moreover, unless he has a legitimate excuse, he cannot miss any lecture which he ought to hear, or fail to be present for any exercise, commencing from the third lecture or exercise on. As far as possible, he is not to distort, by word or idea, the meaning of the lecture or exercise. Finally, he must not schedule two lectures or two exercises for the same hour.[91]

Disputations were oral debates, usually held once a week. They followed the rules of Aristotelian logic. There were masters' and bachelors' disputations. The disputations themselves were on logic or on topics drawn from the three philosophies. In the second two years of a four-year BA program, students had to take part in the disputations themselves. In so doing, they had to reply to "objections" in logical disputations and, as noted earlier, to "respond to the question." To do so effectively, students had to be bright and able to read, understand, and speak Latin.

To qualify for the MA and a license to teach, a student had to study for three more years if he had already "determined" and for eight years if he had not. The graduate curriculum was not easy. It included Aristotle; Augustine of Hippo (354–430), whose prolific writings helped set the agenda for almost every theological debate in the Middle Ages; seven classic works from the liberal arts; and one book in each of the "three philosophies." After he had received his MA, a student could specialize if he wished. A medical degree required a total of six years of study; civil law, four years; canon law, five years; and theology, four or five years.[92]

A word is needed here about one of the most important medieval textbooks, the *Four Books of Sentences* (*Sententiarum libri IV*), which was written by Peter Lombard (c. 1095–1160), bishop of Paris. After studying law at Bologna in his native Italy, he went to France to study theology, chiefly at Paris, where he would teach for almost 20 years. In about 1145, he became a *magister* at the cathedral school of Notre-Dame in Paris. The *Sentences* (a better translation might be "maxims"), completed around 1150, earned him the honorific title of "master of the *Sentences*" (*magister sententiarum*).

This celebrated book was not an original work but rather a *summa* (a comprehensive summation) of Christian doctrine presented in four long chapters. It was an exceptionally handy collection of the maxims (*sententiae*) of Augustine and other fathers of the church, (i.e., the most senior and most respected Christian authors), together with the opinions of various medieval masters, all arranged in a systematic treatise that was easy for university students to use. Now university students would not have to read the entire works of a given author to understand his teachings but could grasp the core of them easily by reading the excerpts so thoughtfully provided by Lombard.

Not surprisingly, the *Sentences* was an unqualified success: indeed, from the 1220s until the sixteenth century it was the standard textbook of theology used at all major medieval universities. Newly minted masters had to lecture on it (and other subjects as well) for two years before being allowed either to leave the university and look for a job elsewhere or to enter a higher academic faculty for advanced studies. Many hundreds of scholars wrote commentaries on it. With the exception of the Bible itself, it is said that no work of Christian literature has been commented on more extensively.

The *Sentences* covered the whole sweep of Christian thought up to that time. It begins with evidences for the existence of God and of the Trinity (Book I). It then moves on to address creation and the doctrine of the angels (Book II), Christology (Book III), and the sacraments (Book IV). In Book IV, Abelard was probably the first to insist that there were only seven sacraments and to explain the dogmatic matters to be discussed under each one.

His book remained very popular in the universities but some later commentators felt that Lombard was on shaky theological ground. For example, in 1240, shortly after he became bishop of Lincoln (an office that carried with it the responsibility for what was taught at the University of Oxford) the great scholar Robert Grosseteste protested against the university's decision to teach the *Sentences*, rather than the books of the Bible, in the morning. Grosseteste argued that since the Bible was the foundation stone of Christian theology, it should be taught during the best hours, i.e., the morning hours, of the day.[93] In a similar vein, Roger Bacon, the Oxford teacher whose achievements will be described later, would complain in 1267 that lectures on the *Sentences* were more popular than those on Scriptural subjects themselves.[94]

Before the appearance of the printed book in the last quarter of the fifteenth century, students had to use manuscript books provided by stationers (*stationarii*). Certain stationers held the original, university-approved copies (*exemplaria*) of teaching texts, which had been corrected and approved by the professors. These stationers copied the texts and, for a fee, loaned them to be recopied by scribes. This was done as follows: the original copies were unbound and loaned out for copying in fascicles (parts of a book) known as *peciae* ("pieces"). Not all manuscript books for school use were subject to the *pecia* system but many medieval universities used the *pecia* system from the thirteenth century on. The earliest tariff on this system lists for rent copies of 138 different manuscript books.[95] The *pecia* system is described in more detail in Appendix 4.[96]

Not all students were dirt poor. In "The Miller's Tale," Chaucer introduces us to Nicholas, a well-to-do "clerk," i.e., a student, who has a taste for and the means to enjoy the good life. This young man has completed the first part of a liberal arts education, i.e., the *trivium*, and is now boarding with an ugly old miller, who has recently married a beautiful, sexy, 18-year-old wife. It does not take much imagination to guess what eventually happens, especially since Chaucer describes the student as being very good looking. This is what we learn:

This clerk was cleped hende Nicholas.
Of derne love he koud, and of solas;
And thereto he was sly and full privee,
And like a maiden meeke for to see.
A chambre had he in that hostelry–
Alone, withouten any compaignye–
Full fetisly y-dight with herbes swoote;
And he himself as sweete as is the roote
Of licoris or any setewale....
And thus this sweete clerk his timie spente,
After his freendes' finding and his rente.[97]

[This clerk was known as clever Nicholas.
He knew of secret love and of its satisfaction;
And, moreover, he was sly and very discreet,
And like a maiden, meek in appearance.
He had a room in that inn,
Alone, without any company,
Very elegantly strewn with sweet-smelling herbs;
And he himself smelt as sweet as the root
Of licorice or a ginger-like herb....
And so this sweet student spent his time
Living on his friends' money and on his own income.][98]

Now, with this overview of medieval universities behind us, we are
ready to look carefully at the earliest university — the University of Bologna.

II

The University of Bologna

Private law schools, often specializing in Roman law, i.e., civic law, flourished in Bologna, probably because the city was so conveniently located on the trade routes of northern and central Italy. As early as 1119, the city was being described as *Bononia docta* ("Bologna the learned").[1] In the 1130s law was being taught there by individual masters, who did not follow a set curriculum but who simply taught as they saw fit.[2] Bologna always took pride in its mastery of the law. The university would later make this proud boast:

> Petrus ubique Pater
> Legum Bononia Mater.

[Rome, symbolized by the apostle Peter, is known everywhere as the father of the law; Bologna is the mother.][3]

During his pontificate (1159–1181), Pope Alexander III vigorously encouraged the teaching of law, a policy which helped to consolidate Bologna's position as the most important European center for the study of Roman and canon law.[4] The first mention of an order by a papal legate regarding the welfare of the students and masters of Bologna comes in 1176–1177. The pope forbade them, under pain of excommunication, to entice landlords by offering them above-market rents to get lodgings for themselves in the residence halls (*hospita*). He also prohibited students and masters from applying for already-occupied lodgings before expiration of the current leases.[5]

It is impossible to say precisely when the University of Bologna began. The university asserts a traditional birth year of 1088 but this claim is seriously disputed by scholars. What is clear is that Bologna is now considered to be the oldest university in the world, if only by a slight margin. By about 1200 the private law schools, which focused on the study of Roman and canon law, had coalesced into a university. At first it had no fixed location: lectures were usually held in the great halls of convents. (Although "convent" is now used to refer to an establishment of nuns, its broader meaning is not gender-specific. In this broader sense, a convent is simply a local community or house of a religious order or congregation.)

Bologna was at that time a small but vibrant city of about 10,000 souls. It did not engulf the university but instead gradually took on a new and more distinctive character from the influx of students and masters.[6] The University of Bologna became the prototype of the "students' university" of southern Europe, that is, one run mainly by the students (by the student guild)—not by the masters, who were merely employees hired by the students on annual contracts. Only in the examinations (always oral, never written) of candidates for degrees did the authority of the masters reign supreme; in other matters, the students had full control.[7] The masters, however, always had a college of their own, which held a monopoly on the power to "make" new masters, i.e., by awarding advanced degrees.[8]

Technically speaking, there was not just one but several "universities" coexisting at Bologna. Each faculty, e.g., law, arts, and medicine, was divided into two universities: the *universitas citramontanorum* ("this side of the mountains") for students from the Italian peninsula, and the *universitas ultramontanorum* ("beyond the mountains") for students from the lands across the Alps. Professors had their own corporation, known as the *collegium doctorum*.

In contrast, the University of Paris was the model for the "masters' university" of northern Europe, one where the masters, not the students, played a leadership role. Thus Bologna and Paris represent two archetypal universities. In fact, Rashdall describes them as the only *original* universities: by this he means that all their successors copied them in one way or another.[9] In practice, many later universities were influenced in various ways by Bologna *and* Paris.

In 1155, the Holy Roman Emperor Frederick I Barbarossa issued the *Authentica Habita*, an edict designed to protect university students at Bologna and elsewhere in his Lombard kingdom. By this time, the fame of Bologna as a center for legal studies had already spread far and wide. Its students came not only from Italy but also from other lands beyond the Alps. Frederick's decree was couched in general terms and did not mention Bologna specifically but it may have been issued at the request of the law professors at

Bologna. The emperor probably expected that a center for the study of Roman law would provide him with an ideological base for his expansionist policies and would help him reject papal claims of supremacy.[10] Inserted into the *Codex* (legal code) of Justinian and confirmed by the pope, over time the *Authentica Habita* came to have great importance. Indeed, it provided the base for juristic interpretations that ushered in the concept of a *privilegium scholarium* (scholarly privilege), similar to the older *privilegium clericorum* (clerical privilege).

As a result, students throughout the Lombard kingdom would now have formal rights and privileges. The *Authentica Habita* was hailed as a guarantee of academic freedom.[11] In it the emperor decreed, among other things:

> Nous promulguons donc une loi générale et valable éternellement pour que désormais nul ne soit assez audacieux pour oser faire quelque tort aux étudiants. Qu'ils ne souffrent aucun dommage pour la défaillance de quelqu'un de la même province, ce qui est arrivé en vertu d'une coutume perverse, à ce qu'on m'a reporté. Ceux qui auront négligé de réparer ces torts seront considérés comme des corrupteurs de cette constitution et du temps présent.... Les recteurs des divers lieux exigeront d'eux la restitution *au quadruple de l'intégralité.*[12]

> [Therefore we promulgate a law, applicable universally and eternally, so that nobody will dare to cause any harm to students. Let them not suffer any damage caused by a fault of somebody of the same province, as happened in connection with some perverse {i.e., now discarded} custom, and as was reported to me. Those who fail to repair those damages will be considered violators of this legislation and of the present government.... The rectors of the various establishments shall insist on *quadruple repayment of the total fine.*]

Student life in Bologna (and elsewhere as well) almost always began with a journey, often a long and difficult journey. Over time this adventure became known as the "academic pilgrimage" (*peregrinatio academica*). Physically fit travelers could walk 20 to 25 miles a day under good conditions; horsemen could travel 30 to 40 miles in the same period; well-mounted professional couriers might cover as many as 60 miles a day.[13]

To get an idea of how much time was needed for long distance travel in the Middle Ages, we can note that it took Sir Richard Guylforde, an English religious pilgrim bound for Jerusalem, a total of 37 days to get from Rye on the English coast to Venice. His journey included 26 days of overland travel, 6 days by water, and 5 days' rest. This was par for the course. Richard Torkyngton, a similar English pilgrim headed for Jerusalem, needed about the same amount of time (38½ days) to get from England to Venice via Germany: 23 days overland, 8 by water, and 7½ days' rest.[14]

The handful of students lucky enough to live in a university town could of course continue to live at home but all the others had to spend days or even several weeks en route to their universities. Those coming from such distant places as Scandinavia, Scotland and Germany had to cross saltwater or scale mountains. Even in summer, crossing the Alps to get to Bologna was not easy. Writing in 1438, a Portuguese traveler left us this account:

> The next day I arrive at the foot of the St. Gotthard Pass, high in the Alps. It was the end of August, when the snow melts in the great heat, making the crossing very perilous. An ox, accustomed to the ways, goes in front drawing a long rope. To this a trailer is attached, on which the passenger sits, holding his horse behind him by the reins. In this way, if any accident happens, only the ox is imperiled.[15]

To economize and protect themselves from any landlords, shopkeepers, tavern keepers, stationers, booksellers, and masters who tried to exploit them — and to protect themselves from the city of Bologna itself, which wanted to prevent students and masters from leaving Bologna and moving to other cities — the students began to group themselves into self-governing "student nations" based on their geographic origins.

Toward the end of the twelfth century, these student nations slowly federated themselves into two *universitates* (student corporations similar to medieval trade guilds) — one for foreigners coming from beyond the Alps and one for Italians who were not from Bologna itself. Eventually, in Bologna there would be 14 student nations for the foreigners and 3 for the Italians. Officially, the masters were not part of these *universitates*. Instead, they organized themselves into two doctoral colleges — one for canon law, the other for civil law — and took charge of the examinations (which, as stated earlier, were oral, not written) and the grading.[16]

By about 1200 the collegial doctoral examinations given by law teachers in Bologna had become the core around which the professorial legal community began to crystallize. Pope Honorius III ruled in a bull of 1219 that no one might teach in Bologna unless he had first received a license from Archdeacon Gratia of Bologna, who was required to make a careful examination of the candidate's qualifications. Modern scholars have disputed whether this bull marked the beginning of the archdeacon's control over the teaching license at Bologna or whether it was merely a reaffirmation of an existing policy. The middle-of-the-road position adopted by Rashdall's editors, F. M. Powicke and A. B. Emden, was that

> We are justified, in view of the canonical tradition of the episcopal jurisdiction over scholars recognized by the *Authentica Habita* of Frederick I ... in concluding that the masters in the twelfth century were not altogether free from ecclesiastical authority.[17]

What is clear is that on the day of his coronation (22 November 1220), the Holy Roman Emperor Frederick II promulgated a constitution entitled *De statutis et consuetudinibus contra libertem Ecclesiae editis*. This safeguarded the immunities and privileges of the clergy, including students. The emperor ordered the jurists of Bologna to insert it into the great *corpus*, or body, of Justinian's Roman law. (Jurists are those who have a thorough knowledge of the law. They are not to be confused with *jurors*, i.e., members of a jury.)

In the 1220s, the city of Bologna was so pleased by the prosperity and fame flooding into it — thanks chiefly to the university — that it even considered putting some of the most famous law teachers on the city's payroll. Supporters of this idea argued that having a predictable and guaranteed income would encourage these masters to stay in Bologna, rather than looking for better-paid jobs elsewhere. If they stayed, it was held, their presence would ensure a constant flow of good quality law students into Bologna from abroad, thus guaranteeing the city's continuing popularity. This proposal was eventually adopted — but not until about 1280, by which time towns and public authorities elsewhere in Italy, as well as in Spain and southern France, had already begun this practice.[18]

Papal interest in the new universities continued unabated. In 1234, Pope Gregory IX ordered an expert canonist to assemble a new collection of decretals that would bring together all of the relevant papal and conciliar (church council) law since the time of Gratian (d. before 1160), a famous legal scholar at Bologna. (A decretal was a written reply by the pope to a question about church practice that had been referred to him; today this kind of papal document is known as a rescript.)

The resulting compilation of nearly 2,000 decretals is formally known as the Gregorian decretals (*Decretales Gregorii IX*) and informally as the *Liber extra* because the measures it contained lay outside of (*extra*) Gratian's own work. The pope sent it to the law faculties at Bologna and Paris with instructions that they were to teach it as the official law of the Roman Church. Remarkably, this same compendium would remain in force for Roman Catholics until 1918.[19]

By the middle of the thirteenth century the city of Bologna was playing a very active role in university affairs. It granted students the right to compensation for damage suffered in riots or fires, reduced prices for rents and food, and gave them a legal status similar to that enjoyed by the citizens of Bologna. At the same time, however, it also influenced the election of rectors and made nonclerical students subject to civil law in criminal cases.[20]

When its statutes were formally issued in 1252, the University of

Bologna was finally stabilized as an educational and scholarly institution. Law students there needed enormous amounts of patience and self-discipline. In civil, i.e., Roman, law, the most important texts were Emperor Justinian's collation of laws: the *Institutiones*, *Codex*, *Digestum*, and *Novellae*. The *Digestum*, a monumental collection of interpretations and commentaries by Roman jurists, which defines fundamental concepts of Roman law, was the subject of regular lectures at Bologna. Here, for example, are some of the carefully drawn legal distinctions that appear in its opening pages. They have been lightly edited and broken into short segments for ease of reading:

> Public law [*ius publicum*] is the legislation which refers to the Roman state; private law [*ius privatum*] on the other hand is of value to the individual. Common law contains statutes about sacrifices, the priesthood and civil servants. Private law can be divided into three parts: it comprises regulations based on natural law and regulations governing the intercourse of nations and of individuals.
>
> Natural law [*ius naturae*: natural law was held to be virtually "God-given" and thus, unlike "positive law," i.e., manmade law, it was not easy to change] is what is taught to all living creatures by nature itself, laws which apply not only to mankind but to all living creatures on the earth, in the heavens or in the seas....
>
> International law [*ius gentium*] is the [commonly recognized set of] laws applied by every nation in the world.... Civil law [*ius civile*] does not deviate completely from natural law but neither is it subordinate to it.... It is either written or unwritten....
>
> *Justice is the earnest and steadfast desire to give every man the rights he is entitled to.* [This justly famous medieval definition of justice comes from the classical jurist Ulpian, who stated: *Iustitia est constans et perpetua voluntas ius suum cuique tribuendi.*[21]] The injunctions of the law are these: live honestly, do no man injury, give to every man that he is entitled to.
>
> Jurisprudence [*ius prudentia*] is knowledge of divine and human things, the study of right and wrong.[22]

How was law taught at Bologna? The answer: a master would carefully read an approved legal textbook to his students — word by word, line by line — and would painstakingly explain the meaning and application of every sentence. Medieval law students had to memorize the opening words of enormous numbers of laws and to be able to recall them immediately and in proper order to keep up with the lecturers, who would refer to them quickly and without pausing. When, as often happened, law students felt that the master was lecturing too rapidly, by their groans, sighs or body language they would beg him to slow down.

To make sure that no part of a legal text would remain unexamined, law books were divided into a number of parts (*puncta*) and stated the days on which each part should be explained. The earliest *puncta* are those of Bologna, dating from 1252.[23] Odofredus de Denariis, one of the renowned glossators (scholars who commented on and annotated the texts of the law), left us this excellent description of how he taught a legal text at Bologna in about 1250:

> First, I shall give you the summaries of each title before I come to the text. Second, I shall put forth well and distinctly and in the best terms I can the purport of each law. Third, I shall read the text [aloud] in order to correct it. Fourth, I shall briefly restate the meaning. Fifth, I shall solve conflicts, adding general matters (which are commonly called *brocardica*) and subtle and useful distinctions and questions with the solution, so far as Divine Providence shall assist me. And if any law is deserving of a review by reason of its fame or difficulty, I shall reserve it for an afternoon review session.[24]
>
> I shall always begin the *Old Digest* [part of the *Corpus iuris civilis*, the body of Roman law as codified by the Emperor Justinian in the sixth century] on or about the octave of Michaelmas [which marked the feast of St. Michael the Archangel] and finish entirely, by God's help, with everything ordinary and extraordinary [i.e., two different kinds of lectures], about the first of August. Formerly the doctors did not lecture on the extraordinary portions; but with me all students can have profit, even the ignorant and newcomers, for they will hear the whole book, nor will anything be omitted as once was the common practice here. For the ignorant can profit by the statement of the case and the exposition of the text, the more advanced can become more adept in the subtleties of questions and opposing opinions. And I shall read all the glosses, which was not the practice before my time.[25]

Masters at Bologna were initially paid by the students themselves; thus the students had the upper hand in financial terms. (As noted earlier, at Paris the masters had the upper hand.) The masters feared student boycotts of their classes because these would reduce or perhaps end their salaries. Even in normal times, students were not reliable employers: Odofredus complained that "scholars are not good payers because they wish to learn but they do not wish to pay for it; all want to learn, no one wants to pay the price."[26]

By 1269 Bologna had 1,464 students, most of them studying law.[27] Strikes and cessations of lectures were not uncommon. They were caused both by academic discord and by unforeseen external events — civil unrest, reactions to controversial papal policies and fear of the plague. During the thirteenth and fourteenth centuries, the university went on strike on at least 13 occasions; there were also about 6 stoppages due to plague.[28] Students and masters alike were quick to threaten to go on strike and to migrate to rival cities if conditions in Bologna displeased them.

The right to strike strengthened the university's hand *vis-à-vis* the townsmen. "Town and gown" is a term traditionally used to describe the two communities of a university town. "Town" refers to the nonacademic population. "Gown" refers to the clothing of a university student and thus connotes the university community as a whole. The last important town-gown collision at the University of Bologna during the Middle Ages occurred in 1321. It centered around the execution of a student who had tried, with the help of some other students, to abduct a notary's daughter from her father's house. To show their anger at his execution, many students and professors moved to Sienna and refused to return to Bologna until a town-gown reconciliation was worked out a year later.[29]

One of the most distinguished Latinists at Bologna was Gasparino da Barzizza (1359–1431), a grammarian and teacher noted for introducing a new style of epistolary Latin inspired by the works of Cicero. The first humanist to spend significant time teaching at a university, he taught rhetoric, grammar, and moral philosophy, with the goal of reviving Latin literature. Gasparino was at the University of Bologna from 1421 to 1428, where his mastery of law, mathematics and literary abilities was so remarkable that he later became secretary to Cardinal Albergati, bishop of Bologna, and then secretary at the papal chancery in Rome. Politian, a scholar who taught Greek and Latin at Florence after 1480, described Gasparino's achievements with wonderment: "It is better to be silent about him," Politian wrote, "than not to say enough."[30]

III

Legal Scholars at Bologna

As promised in the Preface, in this chapter we will begin introducing some of the men and women who played pivotal roles, directly or indirectly, in medieval universities, chiefly in Bologna, Paris and Oxford. Eight candidates from Bologna now stand before us. In rough chronological order they are: Pepo (c. the last quarter of the eleventh century), Irnerius (c. the end of the eleventh century), Gratian (d. before 1160), Bulgarus (d. c. 1167), Tancred (d. c. 1236), Accursis (d. 1263), Giovanni d'Andrea (d. 1348), and Oldradus da Ponte (d. after 1350).

Pepo

We have no firm dates or reliable details on the earliest law professors at Bologna. The first of them is said to have been a little known scholar named Pepo, described as "the bright shining light of Bologna" (*clarum Bononiensium lumen*). He presented himself to the Holy Roman emperor Henry IV (r. 1084–1105) as an expert on Roman law. In this capacity, he may have also taught law at Bologna in the last quarter of the eleventh century.[1] Aside from these tidbits, we know nothing more about him.

Irnerius

Legend has it that Pepo instructed Irnerius, a less elusive figure who taught law at Bologna either toward the end of the eleventh century or in the first half of the twelfth century. Irnerius (his name is also spelled Guarnerius or Warnerius) is reported to have drawn crowds of students to the law school at Bologna, even from the lands across the Alps. As the demand for trained judges and administrators increased in the late eleventh century, Bologna became the center of European legal scholarship. Its prestige became so great that, beginning in the thirteenth century, law professors insisted that they be addressed as *domini* (lords). In their own eyes, at least, the subjects they had mastered and now taught made them, according to a contemporary chronicler, "the fathers and brothers of princes."[2]

Hailed by later commentators as the "lamp of the law" (*lucerna iuris*) because of his knowledge, Irnerius is traditionally credited with restructuring the *Corpus iuris civilis* and to have begun the process of "glossing" the *Corpus* by commenting on it following the rules of dialectical reasoning.[3] He is reported to have begun as a teacher of the liberal arts, to have studied law in Rome, and to have conducted diplomatic missions for the countess of Tuscany and for the Holy Roman emperor Henry V.

Irnerius is said to have been instrumental in establishing the preeminence of Bologna as the major center for legal studies in Europe. We do not know the year when he began to teach at Bologna or precisely what and how he taught there.[4] Some legal historians, however, credit him with the innovative idea of treating law as being separate, conceptually, from either ethics or logic. This meant that he could theorize about justice in the abstract — without getting bogged down immediately in the ethical or logical implications of the case at hand. He did not ignore ethics and logic but seems to have treated them separately from justice.[5]

Gratian

Gratian was a twelfth-century canon lawyer at Bologna who has variously been described as a monk, a bishop, a lawyer or an academic teacher of the law.[6] Little is known about his life but it is clear that in about 1140 he wrote or compiled a famous work on canon law, the *Concordia Discordantium Canonum (The Concord of Discordant Canons)*, which became known simply as Gratian's *Decretum (Decretum Gratiani)*.[7] The *Decretum* contains some 3,945 excerpts drawn from a wide range of religious and secular sources. To these authoritative texts (*capitula*), Gratian added his own comments (*dicta*), in which he tried to smooth out the conflicting opinions advanced by the revered authorities he quoted.[8]

Gratian has been called "the father of scientific canon law."[9] One of his achievements was to define canon law as being independent of theology. What this meant in practice was that the jurist, who exemplified human law, was charged with judging only human *acts*, not human *intentions*. The great Italian poet Dante thought that Gratian had earned a place in paradise for thus having separated "l'uno e l'altro foro," i.e., for dividing the inner forum of conscience from the outer forum of acts.[10]

The *Decretum* quickly became the basic canon law textbook of law schools of Europe. Indeed, it has been said that, before Gratian, canon law did not exist as an academic subject.[11] Throughout the Middle Ages and, for the Catholic Church until 1917, it would remain a definitive work on ecclesiastical law. It offered a way to resolve, via dialectical reasoning, some of the questions on which religious or political authorities often differed, e.g., "Should priests read profane [secular] literature as well as religious literature?"

Gratian approached this problem by marshalling authorities on both sides. First, he presents the conclusion favored by the anti-secular camp: "From all which instances it is gathered that knowledge of profane literature is not to be sought after by churchmen." He then balances this with the view of the pro-secular camp:

> But, on the other hand, we read that Moses and Daniel were learned in *all* the wisdom of the Egyptians and Chaldeans.... In Leviticus also we are ordered to offer up to the Lord the first fruits of honey, that is, the sweetness of human eloquence. The Magi, too, offered the Lord three gifts, by which some would have us understand the three parts of philosophy.[12]

Gratian then goes on to quote Pope Clement and other theologians to the effect that knowledge of secular writings is in fact necessary if we are to understand sacred scriptures. Maintaining an evenhanded approach that will spare him the wrath of both camps, Gratian reaches the unassailably mild conclusion that "priests must not be ignorant."[13]

Modern scholars who believe that Gratian was a law teacher can point to some of the 36 fictitious cases listed in the second recension (i.e., an authoritative text) of the *Decretum*. If he was indeed a professor, he used vivid examples, as any good teacher would, to catch and hold the interest of his students. The following case study from the *Decretum* has been edited to improve the flow of the text. A certain "Master Rolandus" was an early Bolognese law teacher who commented in detail on the *Decretum*.[14] Although his peers held him in low esteem (one of them said that he was nothing but a pompous, lazy drunk), we shall rehabilitate him here by borrowing his name for use in this case study:

> A bachelor [let us call him Master Rolandus] wanted a wife and children, so he married a prostitute. She was the daughter of a serf and the granddaughter

of a freeman. Although her father wanted her to marry another man, the grandfather decided that she should marry Rolandus instead — only in order to control her sexual appetites. She could not have children because she was infertile. When Master Rolandus discovered this, he made love to his own maid in hopes of having children. Later, after he had been convicted of adultery for this act and had been punished, he asked another man to rape his wife so that he could divorce her. [See the questions below for an explanation of this point.] After the rape and the divorce, Master Rolandus married a non–Christian woman — but only on the condition that she convert to Christianity.[15]

Gratian then poses eight questions but does not give us any answers to them. Probably in this way he was trying to stimulate thought and discussion among law students. His questions are:

Is it lawful for a man to marry a prostitute? If she is married only to control her sexual desires, does she deserve to be called a wife? Whose judgment should she follow — that of her free grandfather or her servile father? Was Master Rolandus allowed to conceive children with a maid while his wife was still alive? What happens if, due to being raped, the wife of Master Rolandus is proven "to have lost her virtue" and to have become promiscuous? Can an adulterous man divorce his adulterous wife? May a man marry again while his divorced wife is still alive? Can a Christian man marry a non–Christian woman under the condition cited above?[16]

Gratian himself did not make many direct references to Roman law in the original version of the *Decretum*. Later writers, however, added about 150 canons (legal rules) to his book, including many taken from Roman texts, and also incorporated into it procedural systems borrowed from Roman law. They thus provided what David d'Avray, a modern scholar, has aptly called "the 'software' for a hierarchy of working Church courts."[17]

This "software" proved to be useful from its very beginnings. The canonists began to borrow legal ideas from the secular lawyers, and *vice versa*. A symbiotic relationship eventually grew up between these two "learned laws," a relationship that was so useful for both parties that scholars now speak of the "reception" of Roman law by the canonists. This meant that canonists could now accept Justinian's *Corpus iuris civilis* (*Body of civil law*) as a supplemental source of canon law and could use it when traditional canonical sources were lacking.[18] These two laws thus became interdependent: in fact, law students needed to master *both* of them to be sure of earning a good living. As a result, handbooks on civil law for canonists and on canon law for laymen were in great demand and were eagerly consulted.[19]

Bulgarus

The "Four Doctors"— the most famous twelfth-century jurists of the University of Bologna's law school — were Bulgarus, Martinus Gosia, Hugo de Porta Ravennate and Jacobus de Boragine. Bulgarus (d. c. 1167) emerged as the leading figure. His commentary, *De Regulis Juris*, is regarded as a model of legal excellence.

In Bulgarus' era, mock trials in the law school involved three fictional characters: Titius, his wife Seia, and Titius' adversary, Seius. Bulgarus brought these mythical figures to life. We learn, for example, that "Seia, Titius' wife, lived in fear of the strokes and blows he dealt her so generously (possibly because she spoke so often to strange men.)"[20] Titius and Seius, for their part, found themselves at odds because they interpreted an agreement in conflicting ways, namely:

> Titius gave all his possessions to Seius on the condition that the latter provide him with food. In doing so, Titius did not think about the offspring that were later to arrive. Seized with misgivings, Titius asked that the possessions that he had given away on certain conditions (the provision of food) be returned to him, believing that he had the right to change his mind. Seius, however, challenged this, saying that Titius had no right to alter things, especially as both parties were bound by an agreement and that he had met all its stipulations fully.[21]

Bulgarus settled this theoretical case by holding that the gift of the possessions could not be retrieved, but if the size of the transfer had not been specified, Titius — when he became a father — could have claimed in the children's name, but not in his own name, one quarter of their inheritance.[22]

Tancred

Scholars who wrote commentaries on the law of decretals were known as decretalists. This title first appeared at the University of Bologna, where decretals were used as texts in the canon law course. One of the most famous decretalists was Tancred (c. 1185–1236), archdeacon of Bologna. Born in Bologna, he remained there, except when professional duties called him elsewhere, throughout his life.

By 1214 he had earned the position of master of decrees (*magister decretorum*) at Bologna and was teaching canon law there. Later he became a canon of the city's cathedral and was named archdeacon in 1226. Three successive popes (Innocent III, Honorius III, and Gregory IX) commissioned him to undertake diplomatic and judicial papal missions. He also served as an advocate in the church courts. Despite this busy schedule, Tancred produced a steady stream of judicial works. He is best known today for his manual of ecclesiastical procedural law, the *Ordo iudicarius* (1214–1216), which, together with his work on marriage and other subjects, received a ready acceptance among teachers of canon law.[23]

Accursis

Known as the "idol of the glossators," Accursis (d. 1263) studied and taught law at Bologna for more than 40 years. His major work was the *Glossa ordinaria*. Consisting of more than 96,000 glosses it made available to others the great wealth of Roman law scholarship.[24]

Giovanni d'Andrea

One of the last great figures of the classical age of canon law, which extended between 1140 and 1375, was Giovanni d'Andrea (c. 1270–1348), who was also known as Johannes Andreae. He was a married lay professor of decretals at the University of Bologna, where he earned his doctorate between 1296 and 1309 and where in 1317 he drafted the statutes by which the university was governed. He spent virtually all his professional life teaching at Bologna — from 1301/1302 until his death from the plague in 1348 — except for teaching twice in Padua (from 1307–1309 and again in 1319).

Among his most important works were extensive commentaries on all the official collections of decretals. His most influential book, *A treatise on war, reprisals and the duel*, was used by later writers as the foundation for the modern theory and practice of international law. Giovanni's cumulative legal output was so voluminous that his contemporaries referred to him as *iuris canonici fons et tuba* ("the fount and trumpet of canon law"). Indeed, he is now regarded as the father of the history of canon law.[25] One of his daughters, Novella, is said to have been such an expert jurist in her own right that she was capable of replacing her father in the lecture hall.[26]

Oldradus da Ponte

Oldradus (d. after 1350) studied law at Bologna in the late 1280s and early 1290s. Later he served as a member of the household of Cardinal Peter Colonna, as a judge in Bologna, as a law teacher at the University of Padua, and, finally, as an advocate at the papal court in Avignon. The Florentine poet and scholar Francesco Petrarcha (1304–1374), known to the English-speaking world simply as Petrarch, described Oldradus as the most illustrious jurist of his age.[27]

Oldradus was the first medieval jurist to produce large numbers of *concilia*, which were detailed analyses of the law relevant to specific cases, and *quaestiones* (questions) in the same vein. While many *concilia* and *quaestiones* were based on actual cases, they were sometimes adapted for use in law schools or as models for jurists to study. The two examples used below have been shortened and edited for purposes of clarity.

The first is Oldradus' *Concilium* No. 35 (c. 1350), which focuses on a marriage made under duress. The student is given the following information on this hypothetical case:

> A certain layman named Johannes, aspiring to marry a certain Margaret, even though he knew from her friends that she did not want to marry him, seized her violently and, though she was unwilling and inwardly resistant, through force and the threat of death he was able to carry her off and rape her repeatedly. Later, in the presence of certain other persons, he compelled her to utter the words of the marriage ceremony. Afterwards he held her, imprisoned and resistant, raping her again. For twelve days or thereabout he kept her shut in the house. She fled as soon as the opportunity arose and immediately protested publicly that she had never consented to this marriage. It is asked: is there a contract of marriage between them?

Oldradus' judgment is as follows:

> And briefly it must be said that given the facts above, no marriage was celebrated between these two people. The reason is that marriage is contracted through the legitimate consent of a man and a woman ... though these events took the form of a marriage contract, i.e., the words of marriage and the carnal joining, the substance of a marriage contract, namely, Margaret's consent, was absent. The aforesaid words and carnal joining cannot complete a marriage contract by themselves.... Margaret fled when she was able.... [I]n a marriage contract, consent ought to be free.... Here, however, it was not free, and only through force and threats could Johannes have intercourse with her. And therefore there was no marriage between them.[28]

In his *Questio* No. 92 (c. 1350), Oldradus addresses the question of the hypothetical guilt or innocence of a knight who lost a castle:

> A king was holding a castle and when he had a war with his enemies, he made an agreement with a certain knight that, in return for a payment, the knight would guard it. That knight gave custody of the castle to a certain person. Through that person's fault, the enemies came and occupied the castle. Now it is asked whether the knight would be held liable.

After looking at this case from several different legal angles and exploring it at length, this was Oldradus' conclusion: "According to the law of the nobles of our land: if the knight gave custody to another noble, he is not held liable; if to a non-noble, he is held liable."

This finding, Oldradus said, is consistent with the *ius commune*. He is referring here to the "general law." This was the combination of Roman law, canon law and medieval law which was taught in the universities between the eleventh and sixteenth centuries and which formed the common law of continental Western Europe — but not that of England, which, as mentioned earlier, had a common law all of its own.[29]

IV

The University of Paris

As early as 1119 a loose conglomeration of monastery schools and the cathedral school of Notre-Dame existed in Paris. The growth of this academic community was so rapid that when John of Salisbury returned there in 1164 after an absence of 16 years he could write to his friend Thomas Becket, archbishop of Canterbury:

> Quand j'ai vu l'abondance de vivres, l'allégresse des gens, la considération dont jouissent les clercs, la majesté et la gloire de l'église entière, les diverses activités des philosophes, j'ai cru voir, plein d'admiration, l'échelle de Jacob, dont le sommet touchait le ciel, et était parcourue par des anges en train de monter et descendre. Enthousiasmé par cet heureux pèlerinage, j'ai dû avouer: le Seigneur est ici et je ne le savais pas. Et ce mot du poète m'est venu à l'esprit: "Heureux exil que celui qui a cet endroit pour demeure."[1]
> ["When I saw the abundance of provisions, the elation of the people, the consideration which the students enjoyed, the majesty and the glory of the whole of the Christian church, I seemed to see, full of admiration, Jacob's ladder, whose summit touched heaven, and was covered by angels climbing and descending it. Filled with enthusiasm by this happy pilgrimage, I had to confess: the Lord is here and I did not know it. And this saying of a poet came to my mind: 'Happy is the exile who has this spot for his abode!'"]

It has been joked that Paris became the capital of France mainly because of the king's lost baggage. In 1194, the official records of France, which were being carried in the wartime baggage train of King Philip II Augustus (r. 1180–1223), were captured by the English when Richard the Lionhearted defeated Philip in battle. The French king decided to safeguard the most important documents and registers in the future by storing them in a fixed, secure location. Understandably, he chose Paris, the biggest city of his realm and his favorite royal residence, for this site.[2]

By around 1200, the University of Paris had emerged from the conglomeration of monastery schools and the cathedral school of Notre-Dame mentioned earlier. The majority of students entering the university's faculty of arts were only 14 to 16 years old; the law students, medical students and theological students were about four or five years older.[3] There was no such thing as a "typical" student. Instead, five different types of university students can be identified.[4]

The first was the average young man matriculating (being formally accepted) at a university for the first time. Typically, he came from what in modern Western countries today we would call a middle-class family. As Rashdall says,

> The vast majority of scholars [students] were of a social position intermediate between the highest and the very lowest — sons of knights and yeomen, merchants, tradesmen or thrifty artisans, nephews of successful ecclesiastics, or promising lads who had attracted the attention of a neighbouring abbot or archdeacon.[5]

In academic terms, this student was not especially gifted and was not destined to be a high achiever. Indeed, he would leave his university after spending only one and a half years there, simply "being" rather than studying. He did not plan to take any examinations or to earn any degree: the universities termed him *scholaris simplex* ("simple student"). He and his kind constituted fully 50 percent of the student body and were undoubtedly responsible for most of the rowdy behavior so criticized by townsmen and for which students were so rarely punished. In 1355, for example, three students were expelled from the Collège de Navarre in Paris for having attacked their professor on a street in broad daylight. The *parlement* (the parliament of medieval France), however, ordered the Collège to reinstate them.[6]

The second type of student had greater ambitions. His goal was the *baccalarius artium* (bachelor's degree), which he could earn by studying with a master for two to two-and-a-half years. He would then be 16 to 19 years old. Bachelors of arts accounted for about 20 to 40 percent of the student body.

The third type of student aimed for the master of arts degree. When he received it, he would be 19 to 21 years old and would then have to teach for two years. If he did not leave the university immediately after that, he would go on to study in the higher faculties of medicine, theology, or law (canon or civil). He and his colleagues comprised 10 to 20 percent of the student body.

The fourth type of student was dramatically different from all the others: he was the student of rank. Private tutors had already brought him up to the master's degree level. He might appear at the university with a retinue of his own servants; socially, he would be most at ease with his peers in the law faculty. He expected to receive from the university the customary privileges accorded to the nobility and he did receive them: the university was honored to count among its students a man of such distinguished social standing.

The fifth and final type was the advanced specialized student. He wanted to earn a licentiate in medicine, theology, or canon or civil law (or both). Such a degree would give him a license to teach (*licentia docendi*) in his own faculty. As early as 1212–1213, masters at Paris had the right to hold examinations and recommend students to the chancellor of Notre-Dame for this license. The chancellor was required to confer the degree on any qualified candidate without making him pay additional fees or swear oaths.[7] If the advanced specialized student could afford it, he would study for the doctorate. By a reform of 1366 the complete course for a doctorate in theology was extended over a period of 16 years; this was reduced by only 1 year under statutes promulgated in 1452. Thus by the time an advanced specialized student had earned the doctorate he would be in his late 20s or early 30s.[8] Such exceptional students constituted a tiny fraction of the whole student body: only 2 to 3 percent, for example, in the German universities.

No reliable figures are available but it is estimated that in about 1200 the nascent University of Paris had a population of between 2,500 and 5,000 students.[9] As was the case in Bologna, students in Paris found that a collective organization, i.e., a *universitas*, gave them some protection from townsmen who tried to take advantage of such a captive market. This problem would persist in various forms throughout the Middle Ages.

A late but extreme example is the case of John Bilneye, an ex-academic who had gone into local politics and had become a landlord to Cambridge students. He was soon involved in a bitter dispute with the university over the use of his hostel. When students wished to rent rooms in it, he turned them down on the spurious grounds that he planned to live there himself. The university complained that he was thereby violating the agreed rental procedures. Tempers grew so heated that at one point a group of students marched to Bilneye's house and threatened him with death. In 1420, the university drew up a formal list of 25 complaints against him, accusing him of perjury, of challenging the authority of the chancellor with a force of 100 armed men, and of repeatedly violating both the law and the statutes of the university itself.[10]

The first recorded town-gown brawl in Paris occurred in 1200. Some details have been lost but according to a contemporary account this riot began in a tavern, where the servant of a noble German student, who was bishop-elect of Liège, was attacked.[11] The students who were present retaliated by beating the aggressor so severely that they left him "half-dead." The provost of Paris (the chief dignitary of that city) responded to this breach of the peace by leading an armed band of citizens in a raid on a German student hostel. In the fight that followed, some students were injured and several were killed, including the bishop-elect himself.

The university masters appealed to the French king, Philip II Augustus, for redress. He granted it quickly, fearing that if he did not do so the masters would go on strike and might even leave Paris permanently, taking their students with them and setting up a university somewhere else. The king thereupon sentenced the provost to life imprisonment — subject to an unusual provision. The provost would be allowed to put his innocence to the test by submitting to the ordeal by water or by fire.[12] If convicted by the ordeal, he would be hanged; if acquitted, he would be banished from Paris. As it turned out, the provost was spared either outcome: he broke his neck while trying to escape from prison.

Stern punishments were handed out by the king to the other offenders. The houses of those who had fled from the forces of law and order were destroyed. The riotous students who had been captured were sentenced to the same fate as the provost — unless they could persuade the injured students to intercede for them. The injured scholars did indeed ask that their fellow students be spared the provost's sentence and that they be flogged instead. This request was denied, however, as being detrimental to the king's prestige.

The outcome was that the king issued a charter, which stipulated that any students arrested by royal officers must be handed over to an ecclesiastical rather than to a secular judge. The ranking townsmen of Paris had to swear to respect student privileges. Each new provost was required on taking up his office to swear, in the presence of scholars assembled in one of the churches of Paris, to respect these same privileges. This was the origin of the role of the provost of Paris as the Conservator of the Privileges of the University.

When defendants were accused of violating any privileges granted to them by the king, their cases would be tried in the Paris court over which the provost presided. For the further protection of the students, it was decreed that trial by battle or by ordeal would be refused to prisoners charged with assaulting students. Finally, Paris students were protected from arrest at the hands of secular justice.

The king's decisions made it clear that the rights of the student would be protected in the future. A royal document to this effect stated:

> Afin que ces décisions soient soigneusement gardées et renforcées à perpétuité dans la stabilité de droit, nous avons ordonné que notre prévôt et le peuple de Paris confirment par serment qu'ils observeront en toute bonne foi ces choses vis-à-vis des écoliers.[13]
>
> [So that these decisions will be carefully safeguarded and strengthened in perpetuity in the body of the law, we have ordered that our provost and the people of Paris confirm under oath that, in all good faith, they will abide by these provisions *vis-à-vis* the students.]

The king was well disposed toward the young university chiefly because he had a vested interest in promoting the economic, social, political and academic development of the city of Paris. This royal benevolence would be of utmost importance in the rise and survival of the university as a center of academic freedom. The king was also aware that it was the church, not his own regime, that would be responsible for supervising students and masters. The church would have to make sure that their ideas and behavior did not get out of hand and threaten either the doctrines of Christianity or the established social order.[14]

Pope Innocent III (1198–1216), himself a graduate of Bologna, was very active on the educational front. His 1207 decretal *Tuae fraternitatis* authorized clerics (i.e., students) who were studying at a center of learning far from their benefices to continue drawing income from these benefices while they were away. In 1208–1209, the pope officially recognized the academic statutes of the University of Paris. The fourth Lateran Council (1215) strengthened medieval education by reiterating Alexander III's order of 1179 that cathedral churches must open free schools for impoverished students. Innocent III confirmed the right of the scholars of Paris to appoint their own representatives when legal cases arose. He also interpreted and guaranteed the regulations that the Paris masters of theology, canon law and arts had sworn to obey. Finally, he established the policy that any student expelled from the university could be readmitted later if he made suitable amends. These rules were embodied in two decretal collections, *Compilatio III* (1210) and *Compilatio IV* (1215–1216), which were sent to masters and students and which were to be observed both in and out of the classroom.[15]

The University of Paris grew very quickly. The Franciscan friar and theologian Guillaume le Breton tells us that, as early as about 1210,

> Never before in any time or in any part of the world, whether in Athens or in Egypt, had there been such a multitude of students. The reason for this must be sought not only in the admirable beauty of Paris, but also in the special

privileges which King Philip and his father before him conferred upon the scholars.[16]

This was not a unique occurrence but the beginning of a long-running trend. We learn that in Paris by about 1285,

> Clerc vienent as estudes de toutes nations
> Et en yvier s'asanlent par plusuers legions:
> On leur lit et il oient pour leur instructions;
> En esté s'en retraient moult en leurs regions.[17]

[Clerks of all nations come to study, and in winter assemble in their legions; they are lectured to and listen for instruction, and then in summer many go back to their homes.]

There were two substantive reasons for the popularity of Paris. The first was that thanks to the administrative reforms set in motion by King Philip II Augustus after 1190, Paris had become the royal capital, and a very lively one at that. As the French medievalist Jacques Verger remarks, "La naissance de l'université se situe très précisément dans un contexte d'exaltation politique de la ville de Paris." ("The birth of the university took place, very precisely, in the context of the intense political excitement of the city of Paris.")[18]

The second reason for the growth of the university was personal. Paris offered young men adequate living conditions and a plethora of ways to satisfy their intellectual, career, and even their sexual ambitions. Very few of the students had ever lived away from home before. Some of them happily devoted themselves to the literary and academic offerings of Paris. By 1323 there were 28 booksellers in Paris, not counting the keepers of numerous open-air bookstalls. When the rector of the University of Paris attended the Foire du Lendit (the most important fair in Paris, held for 15 days in June) in an official capacity, it was to buy parchment for university use.[19] Richard de Bury (1286–1345) — a bishop and bibliophile who will be discussed later — had this to say about the city:

> O Holy God of Gods in Sion, what a mighty stream of pleasure made glad our hearts whenever we had leisure to visit Paris, the paradise of the world...! There are delightful libraries, more aromatic than stores of spice; there abundant orchards in all manner of books ... there, indeed, opening our treasures and unfastening our purse strings we scattered money with joyful heart and bought books without price.[20]

The least self-disciplined and least ambitious university students, however, steered well clear of libraries and booksellers. Instead they happily threw themselves into the carnal pleasures of Paris. We have much contemporary evidence for this latter course of action. The French priest and later

Cardinal Jacques de Vitry was a severe moralist. He remembered what Paris was like when he was a student there from about 1205 to 1210. He writes:

> The city of Paris ... drifted in the shadows enveloped in many crimes and perverted by innumerable abject [acts].... Like a scabious she-goat and like a soft ewe, it corrupted many of the newcomers who flowed in from all parts with its ruinous example.... Simple fornication was held to be no sin. Everywhere, publicly, close to their brothels, prostitutes attracted the students who were walking by on the streets and the squares of the city with immodest and aggressive invitations. And if there were some [students] who refused to go in [with them], they called them sodomites, loudly and behind their backs.[21]

The cardinal also had little good to say about the students themselves:

> Almost all the students at Paris, foreigners and natives, did absolutely nothing except learn or hear something new. Some studied merely to acquire knowledge, which is curiosity; others to acquire fame, which is vanity; others still for the sake of gain, which is cupidity and the vice of simony [buying or selling a church office or ecclesiastical preferment]. They wrangled and disputed not merely about the various sects or about some discussions, but the differences between the countries [i.e., the student nations] also caused dissentions, hatreds and virulent animosities among them and they impudently uttered all kinds of affronts and insults against one another.
>
> They affirmed that the English were drunkards and had tails; the sons of France [were] proud, effeminate and carefully adorned like women. They said that the Germans were furious and obscene at their feasts [celebratory academic dinners]; the Normans, vain and boastful; the Poitevins, traitors and always adventurers. The Burgundians they considered vulgar and stupid. The Bretons were reputed to be fickle and changeable, and were often reproached for the death of [King] Arthur. The Lombards were called avaricious, vicious and cowardly; the Romans, seditious, turbulent and slanderous; the Sicilians, tyrannical and cruel; the inhabitants of Brabant, men of blood, incendiaries, brigands and ravishers; the Flemish, fickly, prodigal, gluttonous, yielding as butter, and slothful. After such insults from words they often came to blows.[22]

Amid this seeming chaos, however, order reigned. The English cardinal Robert of Courson, formerly a master at Paris and now a papal legate, drew up in 1215 the first statutes for the University of Paris. Among other things, they established teaching programs and procedures, regulated academic customs at official meetings, confirmed rules for examinations for the teaching degree, stressed that masters must exercise jurisdiction over students, and stated that candidates for a master's degree in arts had to have studied for six years (this was later reduced to four years or even less) and to be at least 20 years old.[23]

Three brief quotations from the cardinal's statutes describe the books that a student had to study to qualify for a master's degree in arts[24]:

- "The treatises of Aristotle, on logic, both the old and the new, to be read in the schools in the regular [i.e., in the advanced "ordinary" lectures] and not in the extraordinary [elementary] courses."
- "The two Priscians, or at least the second, are to be read in the schools in the regular courses." [The first 16 books of Priscian's *Institutiones Grammaticae* were known as the *Priscianus major* or *magnus*. The last 2 books were termed the *Priscianus minor*.]
- "On the feast-days [there were about 100 of them a year] nothing is to be read except philosophy, rhetoric, *quadrivialia* [books relating to the *quadrivium*], the Barbarisms [the third book of the *Ars major* of Donatus], the Ethics [Aristotle's *Nichomichean Ethics*], if one so chooses, and the fourth book of the Topics [of Boethius]. The books of Aristotle on Metaphysics or Natural Philosophy, or the abridgements of these works, are not to be read...."

Between 1220 and about 1260, the University of Paris gradually developed the institutions it would retain until the end of the Middle Ages. These were[25]:

- From 1220 on, a constitution for the student nations. There were four nations in the arts faculty: the French, including the Latin peoples; the Normans; the Picard, including the Low Countries; and the English, comprising the English, the Germans and others from northeastern Europe.
- From about 1240 on, a rector, elected from the masters of the faculty of arts, which was the lower faculty.
- From about 1260 on, three higher faculties: theology, canon law, and medicine, each with its own dean and statutes.

Rashdall mentions that, at least initially, the University of Paris "lived upon its misfortunes."[26] The first town-gown disturbance (1200) had resulted in the university receiving its first charter from the king. Later, an incident in which the chancellor was mistreated had produced the first batch of papal privileges for the university. Finally, a tavern brawl of 1228–1229 ended with the university outmaneuvering the monarchy itself.

This brawl occurred during the carnival season, when some students went into a Paris tavern in the neighborhood of Saint-Marcel and, according to the English monk and chronicler Matthew Paris, "by chance found good and sweet wine there." (All the quotes used here come from Matthew Paris.[27]) At the end of their drinking session, they quarreled with the innkeeper over the bill. Heated words were spoken. Insults soon led to blows: ears were pulled and hair was torn. The innkeeper called in his neighbors, who beat the students severely and forced them to leave.

But this was hardly the end of the matter. The next day the first group of students, now reinforced by other students armed with swords and sticks, broke into the tavern, beat up the innkeeper and his friends, opened the wine taps and left them flowing, and then, "flown [filled] with insolence and wine," spilled out into the street and began to pester peaceable citizens, men and women alike. It was not long before the forces of law and order arrived. Matthew Paris recounts that the queen, "with female impulsiveness," had ordered the provost and his mercenary bodyguard to punish the perpetrators of this outrage. By mistake, however, the bodyguard attacked a party of innocent, unarmed students, who were peacefully enjoying their holiday outside the city walls. In the ensuing fracas, several of these students were killed.

The masters of the university responded to this excessive use of force by going on strike and suspending their lectures. Their complaints to the bishop and to the papal legate, Cardinal Romano, fell on deaf ears: the ecclesiastical authorities wanted to punish the university for its independence and excesses. Indeed, four years earlier the papal legate himself had been mobbed by students during a dispute involving the university's seal.

When the masters found that their strike was having no impact on church authorities, they proclaimed that if justice was not done within one month, they threatened to close the university for as long as six years. They proved true to their word: most of the masters and students did indeed leave Paris. Many of them accepted an invitation from Henry III of England, where they resumed their studies at the new universities of Oxford and Cambridge. Others moved to the smaller universities or cathedral schools of France, e.g., Toulouse, Orléans, Reims, and Angers.

Although Cardinal Romano himself was still quite hostile to the university, Pope Gregory IX finally came to its defense. Alarmed that the prestige and commercial prosperity of Paris would suffer unless the university was reopened, the pope recalled his legate and ordered the king and Queen Mother to punish the offenders. The pope also issued several bulls clarifying and upholding the privileges of the university, which he fondly referred to as "wisdom's special workshop."[28] Protracted university-church negotiations were undertaken but it was not until 1231 that the masters and students were finally back in Paris again.

In this connection, the pope's most important bull was *Parens scientiarum* (1231), which served as the charter of the University of Paris. It was, indeed, the university's Magna Carta because it gave papal sanction to the university's all-important right to strike. The bull provided that in retaliation for any outrage committed on a scholar and not redressed within 15 days, the Parisian masters could suspend their lectures, thus shutting down the university. In addition, *Parens scientarum* confirmed other privileges, for example:

• The right of the university to establish its own statutes
• The right to punish transgression of these statutes itself[29]
• The right to have criminal cases tried by ecclesiastical courts

It also confirmed the university's authority to make statutes and to expel students who refused to abide by them.[30] The poetic, evocative language of this bull reflects the affection that Gregory IX himself surely felt for the University of Paris. Here are its opening words:

> Paris, mère de sciences [*Parens scientiarum*], brille, chère à nos cœurs, comme une seconde Cariath Sapher, la cité des lettres; grande assurément, elle fait encore attendre d'elle, généreusement, de plus grandes choses par les espoirs placés dans ses maîtres et ses élèves ; en elle, en effet, comme en une officine particulière de la sagesse, l'argent trouve l'origine de ses filons et l'or le lieu dans lequel il est forgé selon le rite.... C'est ici qu'est extrait de la terre le minerai de fer et que, tandis qu'est affermie la fragilité humaine, il devient le bouclier de la foi, la glaive spirituel et toute l'armure chrétienne, solide contre les puissances aériennes [des démons].[31]

> [Paris, mother of the sciences [*Parens scientiarum*], shines, dear to our hearts, like a second Cariath Sapher, the city of letters [this ancient "city of the book" or "city of the scribe" is mentioned several times in the Old Testament]; grand as she is, the university will attain yet greater heights built on the hopes placed in her masters and students; she is an exceptional headquarters of wisdom, a rich seam of silver and the place where gold is forged according to rites.... It is here that iron ore [factual knowledge, figuratively speaking] is extracted from the earth and which, while shoring up human weaknesses, becomes the shield of the faith, the spiritual two-edged sword and the Christian armor, proof against the powers of the air [demons].]

The dramatic growth of the University of Paris did not escape in-house criticism. The French theologian and poet Philippus de Grevia became a *magister* there in 1206 and served as the university's chancellor from 1218 to 1236. He was also a spokesman for the interests of the church, whose power to supervise scholarly studies had been diminished by the growth of the university. Philippus argued the university was actually *hindering*, not helping, the cultivation and transmission of scholarly knowledge. He complained to his colleagues:

> At one time, when each *magister* taught independently and when the name of the university was unknown, there were more lectures and disputations and more interest in scholarly things. Now, however, when you have joined yourselves together in a university, lectures and disputations have become less

frequent; everything is done hastily, little is learnt, and the time needed for study is wasted in meetings and discussions. While the elders debate in their meetings and enact statutes, the young ones organize villainous plots and plan their nocturnal attacks.[32]

Despite these self-serving protests, Philippus could not turn the clock back: the university was such a good idea on so many fronts that it would become a centerpiece of medieval life. The University of Paris itself would go from strength to strength. In contrast to Bologna, where canon and civil law was the most important discipline, the faculty of arts came to occupy a dominant position at the University of Paris. It was larger than the combined faculties of theology, law and medicine. By 1249 there was a single rector of the four student nations. He headed the faculty of arts and was the leading figure in the guild of masters. He summoned and presided over university meetings, directed university finances and was the university's representative to the nonacademic world.

Despite these powers, however, the rector could never act in a dictatorial manner because he held office only briefly (for periods of time ranging from one month to three months) and was accountable both to his fellow masters and to the student nations.[33] In hopes of reducing the number of contested elections for rector and the students' defiance of the rectors and of university rules, the papal legate Simon de Brie tried in 1266 to extend the rector's statutory term in office to six weeks. He failed in this effort; the dispute would simmer on for another 15 years.

During the thirteenth century, the University of Paris would become the most important university in the world. Its recruiting area would extend far beyond the frontiers of France itself—into the British Isles, Germany, Denmark and the Low Countries.[34] In the mid–thirteenth century, however, the independence of the masters of this university faced a serious challenge from the mendicant orders (i.e., the friars), notably the Dominicans and the Franciscans. The basic issue here was that each order had its own hierarchy of schools, ranging from the elementary to the advanced levels, and each wanted to retain control of its own monastic students sent to the university.

The University of Paris earned such an outstanding reputation as a center for theology that the most able friars were sent there for advanced study. Indeed, its prestige and influence were so great that the medieval University of Paris has no parallel in any modern university in the West today.[35] The mendicant orders did not want to integrate with the university. They refused to let their students take the mandatory arts course of the university, arguing that, thanks to their earlier studies, these very bright students had already mastered its substance and that they must now be shielded from the secular knowledge which was the hallmark of the faculty of arts.

Without going into all the details, we can briefly trace the main outlines of this quarrel. In the first place, by avoiding inception (in this context, the procedure by which the masters' guild regulated admission into its own ranks), the mendicants also avoided taking the customary oath to abide by the statutes of the university. The masters' guild argued that it had the right to demand an oath of obedience from all students who wanted to enjoy university privileges. The friars replied, in effect, that they did not plan to submit to the authority of the guild and, moreover, that they wanted to be governed only by their own superiors, not by the secular masters of the University of Paris.

Another contributing factor here was the jealousy of the regular (non-mendicant) masters. As the modern French scholar Jacques Verger explains, beginning as early as the 1230s

> Les écoles dominicaines et franciscaines eurent grand succès; enthousiasmés à la fois par la qualité de l'enseignement et la vie évangélique des frères, beaucoup d'étudiants rallièrent les nouveaux ordres. Ce succès suscita le mécontentement des autres professeurs que, de plus, constataient que les nouveaux venus, tout en appartenant à l'université, continuaient à dépendre avant tous de leurs ordres respectifs et, refusant les contraints de la solidarité universitaire, ne s'associaient guère à la défense des privilèges et de l'autonomie. Dans les années 1250, à Paris, les séculiers lancèrent l'offensif contre les écoles des Mendiants pour tenter de les chasser de l'université ou, au moins, d'y réduire fortement leur place....[36]
>
> [The Dominican and Franciscan schools enjoyed great success: filled with enthusiasm both by the quality of teaching and the evangelical lifestyle of the friars, many students rallied to the new orders. This success aroused the ire of other professors, who took note of the fact that the newcomers, while belonging to the university, continued as a priority to depend on their respective orders. Refusing to accept the constraints of university solidarity, they made little effort to defend the university's privileges and autonomy. In the 1250s, the secular masters went on the offensive against the mendicants — to try to drive them away from the university or at least to reduce significantly their influence....]

Struggles with the mendicants seesawed back and forth for many years. Pope Innocent IV had inclined toward the masters' point of view but his successor, Alexander IV, firmly sided with the mendicants in his bull of 1255, *Quasi lignum vitae.* Alexander IV wanted to treat the university not as an independent body of scholars but simply as a tool of papal policy. He felt that the mendicants should be able to veto any proposal by the secular masters to go on strike. Only after his death in 1261 did a compromise seem possible and it would not be until 1318 that the masters would feel strong enough to require the friars to swear an oath of obedience to the University of Paris. In the end, the friars would agree to this demand without too much opposition. Although this dispute would surface again at Paris in later years (though with less intensity), the independence of the University of Paris, especially its right to strike, for the moment survived intact.[37]

On the intellectual front, during the thirteenth century the University of Paris had gradually been absorbing Aristotle's philosophy, thanks to translations and commentaries by the Muslim philosopher Averroës (1126–1198), who is known in the Islamic world as Ibn Rushd. He had the greatest admiration for Aristotle, writing that

> I consider that the man was a rule and exemplar which nature devised to show the final perfection of man.... [T]he teaching of Aristotle is the supreme truth, because his mind was the final expression of the human mind. Wherefore it has been well said that he was created and given to us by divine providence that we might know all there is to be known. Let us praise God, who set this man apart from all others, and made him approach very near to the highest dignity humanity can attain.[38]

Averroës wanted to rescue Aristotelian thought from the misrepresentations of earlier translators. His own translations and commentaries on Aristotle, however, turned out to be very divisive within the medieval Christian context. For example, he argued that since God was the Prime Mover, He was entirely separate from the world and did not play any providential role within it.[39] Nevertheless, Averroës' translations and commentaries proved to be so impressive that Christian scholars simply could not ignore them. These scholars had only two choices: either they could accept these ideas as authoritative because of the mastery and the excellence of Averroës' work, or they could reject them because their implications ran counter to Christian doctrine.[40]

There were four such implications:

- The world is eternal and will never end.
- There is one all-embracing intellect for the whole of mankind, not a large number of individual (personal) intellects.
- Free will and free choice do not exist.
- The soul cannot suffer the punishments of hell because it, too, is destroyed when the body perishes.[41]

By the late 1260s two well-known Paris masters — Siger of Brabant and Boethius of Dacia — had been strongly influenced by such Averroistic interpretations of Aristotle. They in turn put forward theses which — while brilliantly reasoned from a philosophic, i.e., Aristotelian, point of view — ran seriously afoul of church teachings. As a result, 13 of these theses were formally condemned in 1270 by Stephen Tempier, then bishop of Paris and formerly a professor and chancellor of the University of Paris.[42]

This drastic step did not restore orthodoxy, however, so in January 1277 Pope John XXI charged Bishop Tempier with inquiring into the source of the heretical ideas still said to be circulating at the university.[43] Three months later, in March 1277, the bishop made public a list of 219 condemned theological and philosophical theses. It is unclear whether Bishop Tempier was acting in response to the pope's request or whether he had already decided to launch this campaign on his own. In any case, the 219 theses covered a broad swath of Christian thought: the nature of philosophy; the nature of God; divine knowledge and omnipotence; angelology; God's absolute power; the eternity of the world; human intellect, freedom, and free will; the nature of the Eucharist; morality; and reward and punishment in the life to come.

Because these theses expressed points of view that ran counter to the revealed truths of Christianity, Bishop Tempier marked each one of them with the notation "error." Anyone teaching or listening to these heretical ideas would be excommunicated unless he or she appeared before the bishop or the chancellor, within seven days, for appropriate correction. Bishop Tempier did not make specific accusations over this issue but laid out the problem in general terms without naming names. He wrote:

> Un rapport réitéré, venant de personnes éminentes et sérieuses, animées d'un zèle ardent pour la foi, nous a fait savoir qu'a Paris, certains hommes d'étude ès arts, outrepassant les limites de leur propre faculté, osent exposer et disputer dans les écoles, comme s'il était possible de douter de leur fausseté, certaines erreurs manifestes et exécrables, ou plutôt des mensonges et des fausses déraisons, contenues sur le rouleau ou les fiches en annexe de la présente lettre....[44]
>
> [A repeated report from eminent and serious people, who are motivated by an ardent zeal for the faith, have given us to understand that at the University of Paris certain men in the arts faculty, overreaching the limits of their own faculty, have dared to reveal and to argue about in their schools (as though it was possible to doubt their falsehood) certain manifest and execrable errors, or rather lies and false conclusions, which are listed in the annex to this letter.]

It now seems likely that these theses originally came from Greek or Islamic sources. Bishop Tempier explicitly noted that the scholars whose errors he was condemning had drawn their inspiration from "pagan writings," e.g., from Aristotle via Averroës.

The University of Paris continued to flourish. In 1292 Pope Nicholas IV confirmed that it was now — and had long been — a *studium generale* (or *studium* for short: the terms are used interchangeably). This meant that it was a full university in the modern sense of the word. Three important privileges flowed from this fact:

A *studium generale* was an institution of higher learning that had been confirmed or, more rarely, founded by a broadly based and widely respected authority. Many universities just "grew" but some had a clearly discernable beginning. The first imperial university was set up in Naples in 1224 by the Emperor Frederick II. In 1244 or 1245 Pope Innocent IV founded a *studium generale* in the papal curia in Rome. Both popes and emperors, being (in theory, at least) unchallenged in their respective fields enjoyed what scholars have called "universal status." For this reason, the rights and duties of the *studium generale* were considered to have universal status as well. That is to say, they took precedence over and transcended the rights and duties of such lesser religious and political institutions as churches, dioceses, towns, principalities and states.[45]

Beneficed clergy, i.e., students drawing an income from a benefice, who were studying at a *studium generale* and were perforce absent from their home dioceses could continue to draw this income while at the university.

In addition, beneficed clergy enjoyed the privilege of the *ius ubique docendi* ("license to teach anywhere"), a papal permission establishing that once they had received a degree from a *studium generale* it was valid everywhere in Christendom. In theory, they therefore had the right to teach in any other university without having to take further qualifying examinations.[46] The power to confer this right was a vital privilege of the medieval university; in practice, however, many universities (e.g., Montpellier and Orléans) continued to impose their own examinations on those who graduated from other institutions before these newly arrived scholars were allowed to teach.[47]

The University of Paris had its rogues as well as its scholars. In 1329 Jean le Fourbeur ("John the rascal"), a student at the arts faculty of the University of Paris, was arrested and jailed for raping a woman named Symonette. The arrest was carried out under the authority of the bishop of Paris, Hugh of Besançon, a former professor of canon law. This case is interesting because it revolves around two conflicting claims: papal authority vs. a higher good. A key question was the legality of a fine imposed on the bishop, in contravention of the university's privilege of immunity from such fines.[48]

Details of this case have been lost but it is clear that Jean le Fourbeur claimed to be innocent of the rape and had initially been released into the custody of his master, in accordance with a long-standing scholarly privilege. Not long thereafter, however, Jean was arrested — presumably because he had by then been found guilty of the rape — and was imprisoned until he could pay the stiff fine of 400 Parisian pounds, which had been imposed by a subordinate of the bishop for this offense. The fine was soon paid and Jean was permitted to return to the University of Paris.

There was, however, a catch (a hidden difficulty) in this case: the University of Paris enjoyed a papal immunity from fines. As soon as he was released, Jean raised the immunity issue with his master and with other masters. As a result, the bishop himself had to appear at a meeting of the general congregation of the university, where he swore that he knew nothing about the immunity and that inquiries should be directed to his subordinate, who had handled all aspects of Jean's case.

After confirming that Jean was again a student in good standing, the university then summoned the bishop's subordinate to appear and requested him either to return the 400 pounds or give a good explanation why he should not. The subordinate appeared before the university congregation as requested but argued that since Jean had been found guilty and that since the rape had taken place in a different diocese, there was no reason to return the money.

Asserting his scholarly status, Jean then offered to submit to punishment for his crime, but not by paying a fine. At another meeting of the university congregation, held early in 1330, the rector read a statement and petition, both prepared by Jean, in which Jean claimed to be a student in good standing and asserted that the bishop and his men had extorted payment from him by force and by threats. The congregation then decided that since Bishop Hugh himself had sworn an oath to support and defend the university, he was now guilty of perjury, disobedience and rebellion. An open letter was drafted to church prelates, setting forth the facts of the case as understood by the university and condemning the bishop for his actions and for his failure to return the money.

Bishop Hugh, however, knew his canon law. He sent a petition to the papal court asking whether he — a bishop charged by the church with punishing wrongdoers in his own diocese — should be handicapped in that task by an oath sworn to the university *before* he became bishop. He argued that if the charge of perjury was going to be raised every time a case arose involving a student, there was no way he would be able to punish immoral behavior in his flock. Pope John XXII was persuaded by this defense and released the bishop from his oath to the university.

Now it was the university's turn to take up the legal cudgels. It argued that the real issue at stake here was not Jean's crime or the 400 pounds but rather the privileged exemption from episcopal authority that Pope Gregory IX had granted to the university nearly a century before, i.e., in 1231. Bishop

Hugh had argued for the higher good, i.e., his duty to care for the faithful, but the university rested its own case solidly on papal authority. The university claimed that Bishop Hugh was not only failing to obey his oath to the university but that he was also acting in direct opposition to a papal privilege. If Hugh's action was not overruled, the university asserted, the legal standing of all other papal exemptions would be undermined as well.

After more than a year of legal wrangling, the university finally won the battle. Reaffirming the university's exemption from fines by reason of papal privilege, John XXII decided that the papal-authority argument prevailed over the higher-good argument. In 1331 he therefore ordered Bishop Hugh to repay the 400 pounds. This was soon done and the case was closed. No further action was taken against Jean. He was indeed guilty of raping Symonette but in the end he escaped any punishment because he was clever enough to take advantage of the law as it applied to the University of Paris. As for Symonette herself, she was never directly involved in the legal battle between the university and the bishop; she dropped out of sight and nothing more is known about her.

In another example of medieval justice as it affected university life, in 1380 the University of Paris brought suit against Hugues Aubriot, *prévôt* of Paris (the senior royal official of the city). He was convicted and imprisoned because his troops had manhandled the rector of the university and had violently dispersed and robbed students who had simply tried to participate in the funeral procession of King Charles V. According to the formal complaint filed by the university, among other things, the *prévôt*

> ... chassa injurieusement le recteur et puis le prit par le menton en leu disant du mal de que cela irait encore plus mal avant le soir, le menaçant très fortement ... aussi plusieurs de ses sergents et autres frappèrent plusieurs coups sur le dit recteur ; et le dit prévôt dit ses mots: » Tuez, tuez tout; au recteur, au recteur! »... Et not contents de ces choses, les sergents et d'autres de la compagnie du dit prévôt emportèrent plusieurs capes, housses, manteaux, houppelandes, barrettes, ceintures, bourses, couteaux, or et argent monnayé de plusieurs des dits suppliants....[49]
>
> [The *prévôt*] injuriously chased the rector and then grabbed him by the chin, threatening him that he would get even harsher treatment before evening.... Many sergeants and others struck the rector several times, while the *prévôt* encouraged them by shouting, "Kill, kill everybody! Go for the rector!" ... Moreover, not content with the damage they had done, the sergeants and others then stole from the students their capes, habits, overcoats, hats, belts, knives and money....]

When it was not dealing with such small-scale transgressions, the University of Paris, and especially its chancellor, Jean Gerson, played a key role in major political and legal matters, e.g., helping to resolve the Great Western Schism of 1378–1417. Since 1305 the pope had resided at Avignon but later moved back to Rome. In 1378 the archbishop of Bari was elected as Pope Urban VI. He proved so hostile to some of the long entrenched and powerful cardinals, however, that they elected one of their own colleagues as a rival pope — Pope Clement VII — and set him up in Avignon.

In earlier times the church had been "universal," i.e., united and centralized under one pope. As a result, it had been extremely influential in medieval society. With the schism, however, there were suddenly two (and later three) rival popes — one in Rome (Urban VI), the other (Clement VII) in Avignon in southern France — each with his extensive cast of cardinals, bureaucrats, offices and supporters. The third pope was Alexander V of Pisa (r. 1409–1410), who was succeeded by John XXIII (r. 1410–1417).

On an international level, the Great Western Schism proved to be extremely divisive. Eight European powers — France, Aragon, Castile and Léon, Cyprus, Burgundy, Savoy, Naples, and Scotland — sided with Clement VII of Avignon. Ten others — Denmark, England, Flanders, the Holy Roman Empire, Hungary, northern Italy, Ireland, Norway, Poland, and Sweden recognized Urban VI of Rome. This fragmentation of traditional support for a "universal" papacy greatly weakened it in the long run by exposing it to the unrelenting pressures of rising regional powers.[50]

The schism also posed the most serious problems on the personal level — not only for the faithful (it was joked that, as long as there were two rival popes on earth, no dying person had the slightest chance of entering heaven) — but also for the university students themselves. Medieval universities were required to send to the pope the time-honored *rotuli* (petitions for benefices) for their students. The question immediately arose: to which pope should these *rotuli* be sent? The gifted chronicler Froissart recounts that

> When the King of France was informed [that there were now two rival popes], he was greatly surprised at first. He called together his brothers, the chief barons, the prelates and the rector, masters and doctors of the University of Paris to consider which of the two popes he should recognize. It took some time to decide the matter, for many of the clergy were at variance, but finally all the French prelates favoured Clement, as did the King's brothers and the greater part of the University of Paris.
>
> [Froissart then describes which pope was favored by the various European powers.] In this way the Christian kingdoms were at variance over the two popes and the churches were also divided. The greater number were for Urban, but the richest in terms of revenue gave their full allegiance to Clement.[51]

Since the issue was still unresolved, in 1393 the king of France asked the University of Paris to find a way to end the imbroglio. The university

appointed a commission of 54 professors, masters and doctors to make recommendations in a letter to the king. Their letter was a long one but it made
three recommendations: mutual abdication, arbitration, or a general council. To quote from the letter itself:

> "The first way [i.e., the first alternative]. Now the first way to end the schism
> is that both parties should entirely renounce and resign all rights which may
> have or claim to have to the papal office...."
>
> "The second way. But if both cling tenaciously to their rights and refuse to
> resign, as they have done up to now, we would propose the way of arbitration.
> That is, that they should together choose worthy and suitable men, or permit
> such to be chosen in a regular and canonical way, and these shall have the full
> power and authority to discuss the case and decide it, and if necessary and
> expedient, and approved by those who according to the canon law have the
> authority [i.e., the cardinals] they may also have the right to proceed to the
> election of a pope."
>
> "The third way. If the rival popes, after being urged in a brotherly and
> friendly manner will not accept either of the above ways, there is a third way
> which we propose as an excellent remedy for this sacrilegious schism. We mean
> that the matter shall be left to a general council. This general council might be
> composed, according to canon law, only of prelates, or, since many of them are
> very illiterate [i.e., they could not read Latin fluently] and many of them are
> bitter partisans of one or the other pope, there might be joined with the
> prelates an equal number of masters and doctors of theology and law from the
> approved universities. Or if this does not seem sufficient — there might be
> added besides one or more representatives from cathedral chapters [a cathedral
> chapter was an association of clerics of a given cathedral who helped the
> bishop administer the diocese] and the chief monastic orders, in order that all
> decisions might be rendered only after most careful and mature deliberation."[52]

None of these three options was accepted immediately. Gradually, however, "the third way" mentioned above, which became known as the conciliar movement or conciliarism, gathered momentum. It held that the final
authority in spiritual matters lay not with the pope but with the membership of the church itself, as articulated by a general council of the church.
One of the most prominent advocates of conciliarism was Jean Gerson
(1363–1429}, who as noted earlier was chancellor of the University of Paris
and a renowned theologian in his own right.

Gerson's parents were very devout peasants who had 12 children, 7 of
whom would devote themselves to the religious life. As an exceptionally
promising lad, he was sent to the famous Collège de Navarre at the University of Paris at the age of 14. Five years later he obtained the degree of licentiate of arts and began to study theology. By this time the University of Paris
had risen to enormous importance: it held a central position in the world
of the church, maintained close ties with the royal court and enjoyed the

protection of the French kings. These kings frequently used academic the-ologians as their personal confessors and sought the university's advice on matters of state.[53]

Gerson's great abilities quickly caught the university's attention. He was elected twice as proctor (official representative) for the French student nation, i.e., the association of French-born, French-speaking students at the uni-versity. An even higher honor was soon bestowed on him. The chancellor brought him to Avignon to help represent the university in a canon law case involving a recent doctoral graduate who had been condemned by the fac-ulty of theology because he had taught that the Virgin Mary, like other mor-tals, was born with original sin. Gerson and other university delegates personally believed in the immaculate conception (the doctrine that Mary, the mother of Jesus, was conceived without original sin), but they success-fully rested their case not on theology but on legality, i.e., on the legal right of the university to test the orthodoxy of its teachers as it saw fit.

Gerson became a doctor of theology in 1394 and at the early age of 32 he was elected chancellor of the university three years later. In this capacity he wanted to reform the program of studies by cutting back the arid, para-lyzing intricacies of scholastic thought and by injecting some evangelical and pastoral warmth into university teaching. Although he personally approved of the scholastic method, he was highly critical of the undisciplined lectur-ers who gave scholasticism such a bad name. Here, for example, are some of his satiric comments on a lecture given by a Spanish Dominican from the faculty of theology. Gerson says of this speaker:

> Possessed by some spirit he "pours forth sound without sense" (as Vergil says of the Sybil). So barbarous was his teaching, so confused and inane his speech, that you would hardly credit him with a human intellect.... Our subtle theolo-gian made the desired impression: with obscure and complex words, intelligi-ble neither to himself nor to others, he filled the ears of his audience and won their admiration. Prick up your ears, students and scholars. Such deep and profound doctrine — unlike any you have ever heard before, I believe! Give this man his due applause — he is a messenger of divine counsel. No, rather hiss him off the stage.... It is out of ignorance that monstrous and chimerical fictions such as these arise; ignorance is the origin of that high-sounding but nonsensical stuff that is noised about.[54]

Despite such acid comments, Gerson remained totally committed to the intellectual power and social mission of the university. Indeed, he claimed in *Vivat Rex*, a famous speech he gave in 1405, that through its fac-ulties the university represented all human knowledge. Gerson said of the university:

... avisez bien son estat et sa composicion.... Regardes la faculte de medicine : elle cure et gouverne la vie corporelle. Regardez philosophie morale, ethiquez, yconomiquez, politiquez, de quoy traictent les ars et le droict et loys, et vous trouverez que par cez deux facultez est gouverne la vie civile et politique. Theologie, c'est de certain, gouverne la vie espirituelle, divine et catholique.[55]

[...Note well its status and its composition.... Look at the faculty of medicine: it cures and governs corporal life. Look at moral philosophy, ethics, economics, politics, and at what motivates the arts, jurisprudence and the laws. You will find that these two faculties govern civil and political life. What is certain is that theology governs the spiritual, divine and Catholic life.]

Moreover, he added, since it recruited its members from every country and every region, the university was a microcosm of the whole society and thus was the best possible interpreter of the common good.[56] As he asked, rhetorically, in *Vivat Rex,*

Maiz en la fin l'Universite ne represente elle pas tout le royaulme de France, voir tout le monde, en tant que de toutes partes viennent ou pouent venir suppoz pour acquerir doctrine et sapience?[57]

[But, in the end, doesn't the university represent the whole kingdom of France — indeed, the whole world — in that from all parts people come or can come to it to learn Christian doctrine and wisdom?]

Notwithstanding the high marks he won in other fields, Gerson's greatest achievement was helping to resolve the schism. Thanks to his untiring efforts, in 1409 the Council of Pisa deposed the two reigning popes (Benedict XIII and Gregory XII) and elected Alexander V in their place. But since neither Benedict nor Gregory acknowledged the council's authority to depose them, there were now three popes, each of whom claimed to head the church. In a sermon preached after the end of the Council of Pisa, Gerson claimed an ambitious role for the University of Paris: it would act as mentor to the king of France and help him reunite the church.[58]

In 1417 Gerson and his fellow reformers convened the Council of Constance. It removed Pope John XIII, who had succeeded Alexander V; the other two popes resigned. The council then ended the schism by electing a new pope, Martin V, who was officially accepted as pope in 1418. It also passed two decrees designed to prevent another schism. The first was *Sacrosancta,* which established that a council had power over a pope in all matters pertaining to faith and to the reformation of the church (e.g., schism). The second decree was *Frequens,* which required that a council be called every 10 years.[59]

In his own treatise *De potestate ecclesiae* (*On Ecclesiastical Power*), written between 1391 and 1415, Gerson depicted the pope as being (here we will use modern terminology) simply a constitutional monarch who was subject to a church council. The Council of Constance, Gerson argued, had thus done no more than restore the papacy to its proper role in medieval life.

When it was not bringing popes into line, the University of Paris was trying to control its own unruly students. During the fifteenth century it passed many laws hoping to discipline the students called *martinets* ("swallows"), who roamed at large in the town, sleeping by day and plundering the inhabitants by night. These ne'er-do-wells must have been well known to the French lyric poet François Villon (1431 – d. after 1463), who was without doubt the most famous *criminal* graduate of the University of Paris in medieval times. He was a well-educated man who voluntarily and unswervingly took to a life of criminal excess. Villon killed a priest, consorted with thieves and prostitutes, spent time in prison, was sentenced to be "hanged and strangled." He managed to talk his way out of this penalty, however, and instead was permanently banished from medieval Paris. He thoroughly enjoyed his notoriety, writing that after his death,

> Au moins sera de moy memoire
> Telle qu'elle est d'un follastre.[60]

> [At least there will be a memory of me
> As one who was a merry madcap.]

Villon's story is quite remarkable. Villon's father died while his son was still young.[61] Canon Guillaume de Villon, chaplain of Saint-Benoît-le-Bientourné and later professor of canon law at the University of Paris, raised the boy, gave him his last name and arranged for his education. Villon was a very intelligent young man and was a good student when he applied himself to his studies. The records of the faculty of arts of the University of Paris show that in 1449 he received the degree of bachelor of arts, and in 1452, that of master of arts. The lure of the roistering life of Paris was so great, however, that he remained there after graduating, though without any visible means of support, and in the process fell into bad company.

His first serious run-in with the law came in 1455.[62] The self-serving account he gave to the police ran along the following lines. At about 9:00 P.M. on the fifth of June of that year, he was peacefully sitting on a stone bench in the Rue St. Jacques, just below the belfry of St. Benoît-le-Bientourné. With him were two friends — Giles, a priest, and Ysabeau, a young woman. Along the street came another priest, Philippe Sermoise, accompanied by a clerical friend, Jehan le Mardi. Villon claimed to have arisen courteously when the two men approached the bench and asked Sermoise, "Good brother, why are you so angry?" Villon offered Sermoise a seat but instead Sermoise replied, "By God I have found you and will heat your ears!"

We do not know what had enraged Sermoise but it is clear that he then pulled out a dagger and slashed Villon's upper lip, causing blood to flow. Acting purely in self-defense (or so he claimed), Villon then drew his own dagger, stabbed Sermoise in the groin and, seeking safety from his badly wounded assailant, dashed into the cloisters of St. Benoît. Sermoise, waving his bloody dagger, ran after him. Villon stooped, picked a heavy cobblestone, turned, and smashed it into Sermoise's face. The police carried Sermoise to a nearby prison, where he received rudimentary first aid. They asked him "whether, if he died from his wound, he wanted a hue and cry raised against Villon" (i.e., whether he wanted Villon to be arrested). The priest said "No" and pardoned and forgave Villon.

Moved to a hospital, Sermoise died not long thereafter. Villon was summoned to appear before the royal tribunal but, probably fearing that he had a weak case, he had already fled to a hideout near Paris run by the Coquillards, a band of hardened criminals who used a street jargon that law-abiding citizens could not understand. Since he failed to appear before the tribunal, he was banished from Paris. But because Sermoise had publicly forgiven him, Villon managed to obtain a royal pardon in 1456 and was able to return to his beloved Paris.

This is not the place to chronicle Villon's many other crimes and adventures. Suffice it to say that for the rest of his life he continued to share, in full measure, the excesses and tribulations of the underclass in fifteenth-century Paris. After his repeated stints in jail, the authorities wanted to wash their hands of him for good: he was therefore condemned to be *pendu et étranglé* (hanged and strangled). So many of Villon's criminal friends had been executed in this way that he pays ironic tribute to them in his famous *Ballade des Pendus* (*Ballad of the Hanged Men*).

Here are two of its stanzas, given first in medieval French and then in modern English:

> Frères humains qui après nous vivez,
> N'ayez les cuers contre nous endurcis,
> Car, se pitié de nous povres avez,
> Dieu en aura plus tost do vous mercis.
> Vous nous voiez cy attachez cinq, six:
> Quand de la char, que trop avons nourrie,
> Elle est pieça devoree et pourrie,
> Et nous, les os, devenons cendre et pouldre.
> De nostre mal personne ne s'en rie:
> Mais priez Dieu que tous nous absouldre!
>
> La pluye nous a buez et lavez,
> Et le soleil dessechiez et noircis;

Pies, corbeaulx nous ont les yeux cavez,
Et arrachié la barbe et les sourcis.
Jamais nul temps nous ne sommes assis;
Puis ça, puis la, comme le vent varie,
A son plaisir sans cesser nous charie,
Plus becquetez d'oyseaulx que dez a couldre.
Ne soiez donc de nostre confrarie;
Mais priez Dieu que tous nous veuille absouldre![63]

[My brothers who live after us,
Don't harden your hearts against us too,
If you have mercy on us now,
God may have mercy upon you.
Five, six, you see us, hung out to view.
When the flesh that nourished us so well
Is eaten piecemeal, ah, see it swell,
And we, the bones, are dust and gall,
Let no one make fun of our ill,
But pray that God absolves us all!

The rain has soaked us, washed us: skies
Of hot suns blacken us, scorch us: crows
And magpies have gouged out our eyes,
Plucked at our beards, and our eyebrows.
There's never a moment's rest allowed:
Now here, now there, the changing breeze
Swings us, as it wishes, ceaselessly,
Beaks pricking us more than a cobbler's awl.
So don't you join our fraternity,
But pray that God absolves us all.][64]

Villon was very lucky. In 1463 the *parlement* of Paris granted his appeal that the death sentence be commuted to banishment from Paris for 10 years. At this point, then 32 years old, he disappears from the historical record. Perhaps to make up for his crimes, Villon has left us some very fine work. Indeed, one of the most famous lines of European secular poetry is his rhetorical question *Mais où sont les neiges d'antan?* ("Where are the snows of yesteryear?") — a question that nostalgically evokes the fleeting beauty of lovely women.[65]

The happy era of relative autonomy for the University of Paris slowly drew to a close, beginning in the late thirteenth century. This process moved toward a climax in the mid–fifteenth century, when in 1446 Charles VII ordered that all legal disputes relating to the University of Paris were to be settled by the *parlement*, not by the university itself. The king's power over the university was growing. In the fifteenth century the university became increasingly vulnerable to monarchial control because in the choppy political waters of the time it proved itself pacifistic, indecisive, inept and, above all, chiefly concerned with protecting its own privileges.[66] A last straw came in 1446, when as Rashdall reports,

> The university asserted that two doctors, on a frivolous complaint (*pro casu levi*) made by a former housemate of one of them, had been imprisoned by the Provost of Paris. They were claimed both by the university and by the bishop, and the Parlement intervened between the two claimants. This action raised the whole question of privilege.... The records of the proceedings in congregation give an excellent impression of the outraged dignity of the university, *alma mater Parisiensis* [our mother, the University of Paris.][67]

Charles VII did not want the *parlement* to waste its time — or to waste his own time — on such trivial claims of privilege. In 1446 his prosecutor issued this royal statement:

> To the king in his kingdom, where he is emperor and not subject to any man, it belongs — and not to the pope or any other — to create corporate bodies. He has created the university and endowed it with privileges, as was meet. And the university is his daughter, bound to him in reverence, honor and subjection.[68]

Six years later, in 1452, acting on behalf of the king the papal legate Cardinal Guillaume d'Estouteville pushed through a *réforme générale* (a general reform) of the statutes of the University of Paris. By that time Paris was becoming the largest medieval university in the world: an incomplete inventory of 1464 suggests a university population of about 3,000 students, masters and other personnel directly connected with the university.[69] The cardinal's centralizing efforts began to undermine the status of the university as a self-governing international institution and prepared the way for its final subjection to monarchial control.

In 1474 the king ordained that the rector of the University of Paris must always be a French subject. When the university refused to obey this order, the current (non–French) rector was forced to resign and all the university's privileges were suspended. They were restored only when a new French rector had been installed.[70] The final blow to the university's freedom of action finally came in 1499, when Louis XII rescinded the university's right to go on strike. This step reflects the evolution — or the decline — of the University of Paris from a relatively independent *studium generale* to an institution forced to bow to royal commands.

After 1499 the university would no longer be able to wield its most powerful weapon: going on strike, i.e., suspending lectures and encouraging students and masters to leave Paris for greener academic pastures elsewhere. The king's edict thus marks the culmination of the university's gradual transition from a semi-autonomous, broadly based, international institution to a more dependent and more insular national institution that was increasingly subject to the king's control.

As stated earlier, the year 1500 will be taken here as marking the end of the Middle Ages. Political society in its modern form, symbolized by the powerful, well-organized nation-state, had by then made its initial appearance in Western Europe. Nearly all the principal states now had new universities of their own. These did not "grow" spontaneously but were purposively founded by emperors or popes. In practice, these new universities depended heavily on local secular authorities for their administration, operation and support.[71] The long era of the medieval university's relative independence was finally over.

V

Three Scholars and a Heretic (or a Saint)

The noteworthy people of this chapter are all associated, directly or indirectly, with the University of Paris. The three scholars are Thomas Aquinas, Bonaventure of Bagnoregio, and Siger of Brabant. Our heretic (or saint) is Joan of Arc.

Thomas Aquinas (c. 1225–1274)

An Italian philosopher and theologian in the scholastic tradition, Thomas Aquinas was one of the greatest theologians of the Middle Ages. He set himself the task of reconciling Aristotle's thought with the tenets of Christianity.[1] His development of a carefully structured, logically organized hierarchy of knowledge within a Christian framework was a remarkable intellectual achievement. Not only was Aquinas brilliant but he was also a prodigious worker.

The infamous Dominican inquisitor and prolific author Bernard Gui assures us that when working in his monastic cell Aquinas could dictate to three or four secretaries on different subjects at the same time — even, it was said, continuing to dictate briefly *in his sleep* — when he was so tired that he fell asleep in the middle of a sentence.[2] His written output was enormous: it runs to 34 volumes in one modern edition. He was also a full-time teacher, conducting about two disputations a week during the regular term and, during the Christmas and Easter holidays, supervising many *disputationes de quodlibet* ("whatever you like," i.e., free-ranging discussions on any philosophical or theological subject).[3]

Aquinas' career was relatively short in terms of years but, intellectually, it was meteoric. Born in about 1225 into a family of minor nobility living near Aquino in the Kingdom of Sicily, he began his early education at the age of 5 at the great Benedictine monastery at Monte Cassino. A very bright lad, in about 1235 he entered the University of Naples, joined the Dominican order in about 1242 at the age of 17, and in 1244 was sent to the Dominican school in Cologne, Germany. There he studied under a celebrated philosopher-theologian, Albert the Great (Albertus Magnus, d. 1280), who was lecturing on philosophy and theology and who introduced Aquinas to Aristotelian thought.

Aquinas was a quiet, simple, modest, heavy-set man. His fellow students, thinking that he was also stupid, nicknamed him "the dumb Sicilian ox." But when he proved himself exceptionally able in the cut-and-thrust of dialectical debates, Albert rebuked these students, telling them: "You will call him a 'dumb ox,' but I declare to you that he will yet bellow so loud in doctrine that his voice will resound through the whole world."[4] This indeed proved to be the case.

In 1245 Aquinas went with Albert to the University of Paris, where three years later he graduated with a bachelor of theology degree. He then returned to Cologne, where he was appointed second lecturer and *magister studentium* (head of the student body). After studying there with Albert for several more years, he returned to Paris for a master's degree (received in 1252) and a doctor of theology degree (received in 1256) and began to lecture on theology in Paris, Rome, and other Italian towns. He moved to Rome in 1261 at the invitation of Pope Urban IV and then lectured in Bologna and Paris.

In 1272 the Florence chapter of his order empowered him to begin a new *studium generale* at a location of his choice. Later, at the instigation of the chief of his order and Charles I, king of Sicily, he was installed in the professor's chair at Naples. In 1274 Pope Gregory X directed him to attend the Second Council of Lyons and, if possible, to settle the differences between the Greek and Latin churches. Falling ill en route, Aquinas died at the Cistercian monastery of Fossa Nuova. His remains now rest in the Church of the Jacobins in Toulouse, France.

Aquinas' most important work, begun in 1273 but still unfinished when he died at the age of 49 in 1274, was the *Summa theologica*. This work, often called the *Summa* in short, is not light reading, being lengthy and complicated, but we can get a feel for its contents and tone by looking at two of its features.

The first feature is how Aquinas handles *quaestiones*. The initial *quaestio* in the *Summa*, entitled "On theology, its nature and the extent of its validity," is divided into 10 articles. The second of these articles is: "Is theology a science?" In the following lightly edited account of the *Summa*'s answer to this question, the italicized phrases reflect the standardized format Aquinas uses. He says:

The second question is dealt with thus:
   It would appear that theology is not a science.

(1) Every science starts with self–evident principles. But theology starts with the articles of faith, which are not self–evident.... Theology is therefore not a science.
(2) *Furthermore*: science does not deal with [contingent] details. Theology however does deal with details such as the behaviour of Abraham, Isaac and Jacob and the like. Therefore theology is not a science.

Against this however there are the words of Augustine.... "Only those things are included in this science that inspire, nourish, safeguard and strengthen our faith." This refers to no other science than theology. Therefore theology is a science.
   I answer: one must admit that theology is a science. But *it should be understood* that there are two kinds of "science"....
   On the first point: it should be said: the basic propositions of every science are either self–evident or derived from the information yielded by some higher science. As has been shown, this latter is true for theology.
   On the second point: details are used in theology not as chief objects but either as illustrative examples from real life ... or to endorse the authority of those who have helped to convey the divine revelation which is the basis of the Bible, and therefore of theology.[5]

The second feature of the *Summa* is one of its most famous: the *quinquae viae* ("Five Ways"), i.e., Aquinas' five arguments for the existence of God.[6] They can be summarized as follows. Following the same rigorous format used in other parts of the *Summa*, Aquinas begins with two formal objections to the proposition that God exists:

The first Objection is that if one of two contrary concepts is infinite, the second concept would be altogether destroyed. The word "God" means that He is of infinite goodness. If He existed, there would be no evil discoverable, but there is indeed evil in the world. Therefore God does not exist.
   The second Objection is that it is superfluous to suppose that a given phenomenon, e.g., the world, which can be explained by a few principles, should instead be explained by many principles. The world can be explained by two only principles — nature and human reason. Accordingly, there is no need to posit any other principle, i.e., the existence of God.

Aquinas then presents his own views. He first quotes God on God's own existence: "I am Who I am" (Exodus 3:14) and then states that the existence of God can be proved in five ways. Paraphrased and edited for the sake of brevity but using Aquinas' own words wherever possible, his five "arguments" are:

1. *The argument from motion*: In the world, it is certain that some things are in motion. It is impossible that a thing should be both mover and moved, i.e., that it should move itself. Whatever is in motion must therefore have been put in motion by something else. But this process cannot go on indefinitely because there would be no "first mover" (*primus motor immotus*) and, consequently, no later mover — as a walking stick moves only because it is put in motion by the hand of the walker. Therefore it is necessary to arrive at a "first mover," i.e., one which is put in motion by no other mover. This first mover is God.

2. *The argument from causality*: In the world we can see that there is a chain of cause and effect. It is impossible for a thing to be the cause of itself: to do so, it would have to exist prior to itself, which is impossible. It is therefore necessary to admit the existence of a first cause, which we call God.

3. *The argument from possibility and necessity*: We find in nature that it is simultaneously possible for things to be and not to be: things can be generated and then corrupted, so that they both *are* and *are not*. But it is impossible for these things always to have existed: that which can "not be" at some time does not exist. If everything can "not be," then at one point nothing would have existed. If this had been the case, then nothing would exist now: that which exists now exists only thanks to something already existing. If at one point nothing was in existence, it would have been impossible for anything to exist; even now, nothing would exist — which is absurd. Therefore, all beings are not merely *possible* but there must also be something the existence of which is *necessary*. We must therefore postulate the existence of a being having of itself its own necessity — not receiving it from another, but rather causing in others their own necessity. This being is God.

4. *The argument from gradation*: Some beings are more good or less good; more true or less true; more noble or less noble; etc. "More" and "less" reflect in their different ways the maximum, e.g., a thing is said to be hotter according to how close it approaches maximum hotness. The maximum in any genus is the cause of all that genus: for example, fire, which is the maximum heat, is the cause of all hot things. Therefore there must be something which is to all beings the cause of their being, goodness, and every other perfection. This we call God.

5. *The argument based on the governance of the world*: Things which lack intelligence, i.e., natural bodies, act for an end: they always, or nearly always, act in the same way, in order to obtain the best result. It is clear that they do so not by chance but by design. Whatever lacks intelligence cannot move toward an end unless it is directed by some being endowed with knowledge and intelligence — as an arrow is shot at its target by the archer. Thus some intelligent being exists by whom all natural things are directed toward their end. This being we call God.

Aquinas ends his commentary on the existence of God by replying to the two objections he raised at its beginning. Regarding the first objection, he says that since God is infinitely good, he can allow evil to exist but that out of it He can produce good. Regarding the second objection, he concludes that just as whatever is done involuntarily by nature must be traced back to God as its first cause, so too whatever is done voluntarily by human beings must be traced back to some higher cause than human reason, i.e., God.

Bonaventure of Bagnoregio (c. 1217–1274)

Bonaventure was a Franciscan friar, a mystical theologian, a master of theology at the University of Paris, and the cardinal bishop of Albano. He became one of the most prominent men in medieval Latin Christianity.[7] As minister general of the Franciscan order, he steered the Franciscans along a moderate but highly intellectual course that made them the most prominent order in the church until the coming of the Jesuits.

His theology was highlighted by a creative attempt to integrate faith and reason. He conceived of nonintellectual material creatures, e.g., animals, as "footprints" (vestiges) of God. Reason shows us that God is the ultimate cause of the world, which He created at a first moment of time. Intellectual creatures (human beings) are the images and likenesses of God; reason leads us to understand Him as the illuminator of knowledge and the source of grace and virtue. Finally, our study of Being will show us that God is the absolutely perfect Being, whose essence entails His own existence. God is also an absolutely *simple* being and is the one that causes composite beings (i.e., all other beings) to exist. Bonaventure teaches that Christ is the "one true master," who offers knowledge — which is first based on faith but is then developed by rational understanding. At the end of this process, the believer can hope for mystical union with God.

Born in Tuscany in about 1217, Bonaventure recounts that as a child he was miraculously cured by the intervention of St. Francis of Assisi soon after the latter's death in 1226: "When I was a boy, as I still vividly remember, I was snatched from the jaws of death by his invocation and merits."[8] Bonaventure matriculated as a layman in the arts faculty of the University of Paris in 1235 and received his master of arts degree in about 1243. He joined the Franciscan order in 1243 or 1244, using the name "Bonaventure" to celebrate his good twofold fortune — first thanks to St. Francis and then thanks to Alexander of Hales, an inspiring teacher at the University of Paris.

Bonaventure remained at the University of Paris from 1243 to 1248, attending lectures and disputations in theology. He received his license to teach (*licentia docendi*) in 1254 and for the next three years he discharged the three duties of a master: lecturing on the Bible, engaging in disputations, and preaching. Later, Pope Alexander IV directed the secular masters of the University of Paris to accept both Bonaventure and Aquinas as masters of theology; they were so accepted in 1257. By that time, Bonaventure had been appointed minister general of the Franciscan order.

Between 1257 and 1266 he traveled by foot through France and Italy, returning to Paris in 1266 to defend the Franciscan friars there from attacks by conservatives in the theology faculty and by radicals in the arts faculty. When the papacy itself lay vacant from 1268 to 1271, papal electors are said to have offered the papacy to Bonaventure, but he declined this honor and suggested Teobaldi Visconti instead. After Teobaldi was elected as Pope Gregory X, he made Bonaventure a cardinal in 1273.

Bonaventure died the next year and was hailed by his contemporaries as "a man eminent for his knowledge and eloquence, a man outstanding for his sanctity and acknowledged for the excellence of his life, both religious and moral."[9] He wrote extensively, always on religious subjects: the critical edition of his works (*Opera omnia*) fills 10 volumes. He did his best to reconcile the diverse and not infrequently conflicting traditions of medieval theology and Aristotelian thought.

Siger of Brabant (c. 1240 — between 1281 and 1284)

Siger of Brabant was a professor of philosophy at the University of Paris and a strong advocate of the new understanding of Aristotle made possible by Latin translations of Greek and Arabic philosophic works. He had come to Paris in the 1250s to study the liberal arts, supported by a benefice from Liège. Siger found the works of Aristotle, as interpreted by the Spanish Muslim commentator Averroës, so inspiring that Siger's own teachings began to run directly counter to Christian doctrines. He rejected, in short, the orthodox efforts to reconcile Christian and Greek philosophy. As a result, both Bonaventure and Aquinas denounced him.

As mentioned earlier, in 1277 Bishop Tempier of Paris condemned many of Averroës' philosophic propositions. This was a blow that ended Siger's academic career. More specifically, Siger was held to have fallen into four doctrinal errors. These involved his views on divine providence; on the eternity of the world (Siger held that God did not create the world because it has always existed); on human intellect (he believed that a single intellect is shared by all mankind); and on moral freedom.[10]

Siger was later stabbed to death by his own secretary, a cleric who had gone mad, but his fame as someone who openly spoke his mind has lived on. With his poet's eye, Dante imagined Siger in Paradise, seated at the side of Thomas Aquinas and in the company of other great Christian thinkers. Dante wrote:

> This is the eternal light of Siger
> Who, when he lectured on the rue du Fouarre,
> Syllogized unwelcomed truths.[11]

Joan of Arc (c. 1412–1431)

Known in her own time — and still known in France today — as *La Pucelle* (the Maid), Joan is the national heroine of France because of the enormous courage she showed in 1431 during her trial and execution as a relapsed heretic. The University of Paris was not officially in charge of this trial and execution but its influence on the whole process was enormous and is worth discussing in some detail.

Acting under what she believed was the direct guidance of heavenly voices, Joan, a simple peasant girl, led the French army to victory at Orléans and thus defeated the English campaign to conquer France during the Hundred Years' War. Her life ended tragically (she was burned at the stake) but it has inspired a flicker of humor. As the Irish comic dramatist George Bernard Shaw (1856–1950) put it in his splendid play, *Saint Joan*, she was "judicially burnt for what we call unwomanly and insufferable presumption ... there were only two opinions of her. One was that she was miraculous: the other was that she was unbearable."[12]

In 1430, while fighting a rear-guard action to protect French soldiers who were forced to retreat from the English, Joan was captured by the Burgundians, who were allies of the English. Many Frenchmen believed that the future of France would best be served not by the failed Valois dynasty, which had produced the mad king Charles VI (r. 1380–1422), but by the dukes of Burgundy, who in contrast now ruled one of the most powerful and culturally advanced states of Europe.[13] The Burgundian chronicler Chastellain recorded Joan's capture in these words:

> The Maid, going beyond the nature of womankind, performed a great feat and took much pain to save her company from loss, staying behind like a chief and like the most valiant member of the flock.... An archer [a Burgundian], a stiff

and very harsh man, angry that a woman of whom one had heard so much should have surpassed so many valiant men ... laid hold of her from the side of her cloth-of-gold doublet and pulled her from her horse flat upon the ground.[14]

As a result of the English occupation of Paris during the Hundred Years' War, some key faculty members at the University of Paris had been replaced by pro–English clergymen.[15] When news of Joan's capture reached Paris, these clergymen played a key role in arranging her transfer to the English and, later, in her prosecution. The University of Paris sent some of its best men to help cross-examine her. It assigned to its faculties the task of assembling and investigating the charges against her.[16]

Although Joan was technically a prisoner of war, she was also, more fatally, accused of heresy. On this basis, the university insisted that she be tried by a religious tribunal as a heretic. As a result, she was soon in the hands of the pro–English bishop of Beauvais, Pierre Cauchon (c. 1371–1442), in whose diocese she had been captured. In 1431 she was forced to stand trial before a church court, an ordeal that lasted four months (from 9 January to 30 May 1431). See Appendix 5 for two letters of 21 November 1430 from the University of Paris: the first to Bishop Cauchon, the second to the English king Henry VI.

Many if not most of Joan's judges were graduates of the University of Paris.[17] Bishop Cauchon, the formidable prosecutor at the 1431 trial, had been trained as a canon lawyer at the university. He became its rector in 1403 after a brilliant academic career and was later further honored by receiving the title of Conservator of the Privileges of the University. (As mentioned earlier, students in medieval universities enjoyed certain exemptions from the jurisdiction of the ordinary civil courts. These privileges were safeguarded by a conservator.) Nearly all of Joan's French judges were beholden, directly or indirectly, to the English, who were her mortal enemies.[18] Bishop Cauchon himself was a strong partisan of England's interests in France during the latter years of the Hundred Years' War.

Pro–English theologians from the University of Paris were consulted near the end of her trial, ostensibly to provide an unbiased second opinion. The verdict was of course a foregone conclusion. Her judges and the 39 assessors unanimously agreed that she was a relapsed heretic who must be handed over to the secular arm, i.e., to the civil authorities, and be put to death. Although this handing over was a critical legal step (only the secular arm, not the church itself, could carry out a sentence of execution on a condemned heretic), this was not done in Joan's case. She was immediately burned at the stake in the public marketplace at Rouen on 30 May 1341. To ease her last moments, Friar Isambart de la Pierre found a cross in a nearby church and held it up so that Joan could see it. He later reported that Joan,

> Being already surrounded by the flame, never ceased to the end to proclaim and profess in a high voice the holy name of Jesus, imploring and invoking without cease the aid of the saints of paradise, and again, which is more, while surrendering her spirit and letting her head fall, she uttered the name of Jesus as a sign that she was fervent in the faith of God.[19]

Joan's ashes were collected and were thrown into the Seine to make sure that no remains survived and could be venerated later on as relics. Many spectators believed that Joan was innocent. Jean Tressard, secretary to the king of England, exclaimed in great agitation when he returned from the execution: "We are all ruined, for a good and holy person has been burned."[20] Both a cardinal and a bishop were said to have wept bitterly.[21] Joan's executioner, Geoffroy Thérage, later told his friends that "he had a great fear of being damned, [because] he had burned a saint."[22] A few days after Joan's death an Englishman who had been present remarked in sorrow: "La brave femme. Que n'est-elle anglaise!" ("The courageous woman. She could have been English!"—said with a touch of regret that she was not.)[23]

The French regained control of Paris in 1436 and the English were gradually driven out of northern France in the early 1450s. Joan's trial was investigated by the pro–French inquisitor-general and other clergymen in 1450, 1452, and 1455–1456. During this process, a number of those who had taken part in the first trial confirmed that the information about Joan that had been sent to the theologians of the University of Paris had been deliberately falsified. These eyewitnesses said that the verdict was predetermined and was based on fabricated charges.

In 1455 the inhabitants of Rouen revolted against their English overlords. The forces of the French king, Charles VII, were able to enter the city unopposed. For political reasons, both Charles VII and the pope wanted to clear Joan's name and to reward the people of Rouen. They thus approved a second — posthumous — trial, which is known as the "nullification trial." The University of Paris did not play any direct role in this second trial, although a number of its theological advisers were graduates, faculty members, or officials of the university. Such men included Robert Ciboule (rector in 1437), Guillaume Bouillé (rector in 1439), Jean de Montigny (dean in 1445), and Jean Bouchard (rector in 1447).

The new trial began in Paris in 1455 and ended in Rouen in 1456. The court interviewed 115 witnesses, many of whom had participated in the first trial. It concluded that the first trial had been procedurally flawed from the outset. These legal shortcomings included the following[24]:

- Joan had been put into an English military prison run by men, rather than into an ecclesiastical prison guarded by women.
- The interrogation procedures and the evidence amassed against her fell far short of legal norms.
- Joan was condemned solely on the basis of her interrogation in Rouen: nothing was ever *proven* against her.
- She was denied any legal or other counsel.
- In his haste to get rid of her, Bishop Cauchon failed to obtain the necessary death sentence from a secular court: he simply sent her from his own ecclesiastical court directly to the stake.

Ostensibly because of these legal irregularities, the second trial declared the first trial to be null and void. Joan, now dead for 25 years, was at last fully acquitted. She was canonized in 1920.

VI

The University of Oxford

Rashdall believed that advanced studies at Oxford began in the wake of a quarrel between King Henry II and his archbishop of Canterbury, Thomas Becket, in 1167.[1] This spat led to a temporary ban on English scholars going to Paris for their studies, which in turn, according to Rashdall, forced English masters and students to settle in Oxford. Later scholars, however, have argued that Rashdall's thesis is too radical to reflect accurately the ups-and-downs of twelfth-century English educational life. They argue that students may first have gone to the long-established and well-regarded cathedral school of Lincoln instead.[2]

Oxford (its name means "oxen ford") was at first no more than a small provincial town located on the River Thames. Its later population in medieval times of 4,000 to 6,000 souls would never rival London's 40,000 people but by the 1180s Oxford was growing considerably in stature. Most importantly, it had become the headquarters of the royal administration and the seat of the church courts. These two developments encouraged some of the learned lawyers, i.e., men skilled in both canon law and civil law, to set up shop in Oxford and to begin teaching law there. They were so successful that, within a decade, Oxford's law school was the only one in England that was able to attract students from abroad.[3]

A university was in existence at Oxford by about 1200. It received its first papal statutes, which granted scholars clerical immunity from secular arrest, in 1214. Even in these very early years, Oxford is thought to have had more than 2,500 students. The new university made a major contribution to the economic life of the city because of the scholars' needs for food, shelter and supplies. In 1244 King Henry III gave the chancellor of Oxford wide jurisdictional powers, putting him in charge of such practical matters as judging cases of debt, setting rents for student lodgings, hiring horses for university purposes, resolving breaches of contract, and regulating the purchase of foodstuffs in a lawsuit where one of the parties was a member of the university. Moreover, in 1238 the king gave the university the power to supervise trade in foodstuffs within the city of Oxford.[4]

The pattern of study and graduation at Oxford (and, for that matter, at Cambridge as well) was based on the Parisian model. The pace of academic life in the English universities, however, was less hurried than in Paris. Except for the town-gown problems discussed below, Oxford seems to have enjoyed a relatively placid evolution. It did not involve itself very deeply in controversial political affairs. Perhaps as a result, it benefited from the consistent support of the English king and of the papacy.[5]

There were two reasons for the town-gown problems that appeared in Oxford at an early date. The first was that many citizens resented the clerical status of the scholars, which made them a privileged body within the city, freed them from the normal constraints of justice, and gave them the powerful protection of the chancellor's court. The second was the highly visible degree of involvement the university had in the economic and environmental affairs of the city. In 1339, for example, under pressure from the university the butchers who skinned animals were forced to conduct their bloody trade outside the city walls. In the same vein, the university called for regular cleaning of the streets and for separate prison accommodation for women.[6]

In 1209, a killing of a townswoman, accidentally committed by an Oxford student with a bow and arrow, led the authorities to arrest some of his colleagues. Two or perhaps three of these students, who in fact had nothing to do with the townswoman's death, were hanged under the orders of the mayor and the king. This unjust and draconian punishment prompted the masters to go on strike and to leave Oxford, followed by their pupils. Both were protesting the king's violation of the rights of the clergy (*privilegium fori*). After fleeing from Oxford, they settled in Cambridge and, in effect, founded a new university there between 1209 and the 1220s.[7] It followed the academic patterns set by Oxford and Paris. In 1254 the University of Oxford received from Pope Innocent IV confirmation of all its "immunities, liberties, and laudable, ancient and rational customs, and approved and honest constitutions."[8]

Eleven of the 39 self-governing colleges of the University of Oxford today were founded between 1261 and 1448. They are still the most visible reminders of the medieval university. Because Balliol College is such a good example (today it is one of Oxford's most popular colleges, measured in terms of the number of students who want to enter) its earliest history is worth recounting here.

Sir John de Balliol was one of the most loyal lords of King Henry III of England during the Barons' War of 1258–1265. John was married to a Scottish princess, Dervorguilla of Galloway; their son, also named John Balliol, would be King of Scots from 1292–1296. Sir John was a very rich man with extensive estates in England and France.[9] Although the earliest history of the college lies more in the realm of legend than historical fact, it is said that Balliol had frequent and violent differences of opinion with Walter Kirkham, bishop of Durham.

Balliol was temperamentally inclined to use force to get his way. Kirkham, described as "little in body but great in mind," was no shrinking violet either. Their problems came to a head at some point between 1255 and 1260, when Kirkham excommunicated a few of Balliol's men because, on Balliol's orders, they had taken over lands that Kirkham claimed belonged to the church. In revenge, Balliol waylaid the bishop and his entourage. Legend has it that he either assaulted Kirkham physically or otherwise subjected him to some kind of indignity. Balliol also kidnapped a few of the bishop's men. The surviving records about this incident are murky; the truth of the matter, if it ever could be known, might turn out to be less dramatic. It does seem, however, that Kirkham formally complained to Henry III about the mistreatment allegedly inflicted on him by Balliol.

The king responded with a writ condemning the attack in the strongest terms. The bishop demanded that suitable reparations be made immediately. Balliol had no choice but to surrender himself to the authorities. There is no hard evidence about what happened next, but rumor had it that Balliol was required to prostrate himself before the doors of Durham Cathedral, where Kirkham publicly chastised him. As a further penance, the bishop also ordered Balliol to perform a substantial act of charity.

To comply with this latter demand, in about 1263 Balliol founded a hostel in Oxford for 16 impoverished scholars and left money for this purpose in his will. It was not until 1282, however, that his widow Dervorguilla provided endowments and statutes (the latter based on Parisian models) for what would become Balliol College. Today it is arguably the oldest of Oxford's colleges.[10]

Queen's College at Oxford also has an unusual history. It was founded in 1341 by Robert de Eglesfield, whose statutes decreed that 12 scholars, representing the 12 apostles, were to dine on three sides of a rectangular table, representing the Last Supper, and must wear blood- red robes, symbolizing the Crucifixion. Members of Queen's College had an ample domestic staff at their beck and call. These included, in addition to the ordinary servants, a treasurer's clerk, a butler, a cook, a scullion, a baker, a brewer, a miller to grind wheat, a boy to help wherever an extra pair of hands was needed, a barber, a gardener, a washerwoman, and a night watchman.

The only original statute still observed at Queen's College today is that dinner in the hall of the college is always announced with a trumpet. Another echo of the medieval past is preserved here as well. Each Christmas a Boar's Head ceremony is held to commemorate a student who, when studying Aristotle on a nearby hill, managed to save himself from a wild boar by stuffing his manuscript book down the beast's throat.[11] To demonstrate further the persistence of Oxford's traditions, we can remember that the English poet and critic Matthew Arnold's description of the university — as seen from Boar's Hill — has become its most famous evocation. In his poem *Thyrsis* (1866), Arnold said of Oxford:

> And that sweet city with her dreaming spires,
> She needs not June for beauty's heightening.[12]

There is another side of the Oxford coin, however. One of the most candid and unflattering sketches of Oxford students is that left to us by Richard de Bury (1281–1345). Richard studied at Oxford and was chosen to be tutor to Prince Edward of Windsor, who afterward became King Edward III. He was a gifted official and with the support of the king rose rapidly through the ranks, becoming bishop of Durham in 1333, high chancellor of England in 1334, and treasurer in 1336. Richard was also a bibliophile and in about 1345 he wrote the *Philobiblon*. This work describes his love of manuscript books and gives us a damning picture of how the careless student, perhaps a *scholaris simplex*, treated them. It tells us:

> But the race of scholars [students] is commonly badly brought up, and unless they are bridled in the rules of their elders they indulge in infinite puerilities. They behave with petulance and are puffed up with presumption, judging of everything as if they were certain, [but] they are altogether inexperienced.
>
> You may happen to see some headstrong youth lazily lounging over his studies, and when the winter's frost is sharp, his nose running from the nipping cold drips down, nor does he think of wiping it with his pocket-handkerchief until he has bedewed the book before him with the ugly moisture. Would that he had before him no book, but a cobbler's apron!
>
> His nails are with fetid filth as black as jet, with which he marks any passage that pleases him. He distributes a multitude of straws, which he inserts to stick out in different places, so that the halm [stalks] may remind him of what his memory cannot retain. These straws, because the book has no stomach to

digest them, and no one takes them out, distend the book from its wonted closing, and at length, being carelessly abandoned to oblivion, go to decay.

He does not fear to eat fruit or cheese over an open book, or carelessly to carry a cup to and from his mouth; and because he has no wallet at hand he drops into books the fragments that are left. Continually chattering, he is never weary of disputing with his companions, and while he alleges a crowd of senseless arguments he wets the book lying half open in his lap with sputtering showers. Aye, and then hastily folding his arms he leans forward on the book, and by a brief spell of study invites a prolonged nap; and then, by way of mending the wrinkles, he folds back the margin of leaves, to the no small injury of the book.[13]

Perhaps it was louts like this one who were responsible for the most famous case of town-gown friction at Oxford — the St. Scholastica's Day Riot. It began on 10 February 1355, when some Oxford students were served such foul wine at a tavern that they threw both the wine and its container at the barkeeper's head. This assault and its aftermath triggered a three-day riot, during which students were mustered at the University Church of St. Mary the Virgin. This church was the center of university life. It housed the university's library and provided a fitting setting for lectures and academic ceremonies.

During the riot, six Oxford students were killed and many others were injured. The upshot was that the mayor and aldermen of Oxford were arrested, the sheriff was removed from office, and the university's powers over the town were increased. Even more remarkably, for the next 470 years, i.e., until 1825, the mayor and the corporation of Oxford would be forced to parade at an annual St. Scholastica's Day service at the church of St. Mary the Virgin *to do public penance for their offences to the students in 1355.*

By the first half of the thirteenth century, Oxford had achieved a European-wide reputation for excellence in mathematics and the natural sciences.[14] Its fame would increase even further as it became a center for theological discussions. Oxford's growing renown was based in large part upon the *corpus* of newly available Aristotelian learning, which had been translated into Latin and thus became available to European scholars beginning about 1150.

A high point for Oxford came in 1379 when William of Wykeham, the wealthy bishop of Winchester and the high chancellor of England, founded what is popularly known as New College (its official name is the College of St. Mary). One of the most famous of the Oxford colleges, it is a milestone in England's collegiate history because of its grand scale and its functionally planned quadrangle buildings.[15] Today Wykeham is hailed as the creator of English collegiate architecture.[16] He also coined the college's motto:

"Manners Makyth Man." This was revolutionary at the time because it was written in English (rather than in Latin) and because of its social implications. The motto implies that the true measure of an individual's worth is not birth or property but how well he or she behaves toward other people.

In the statutes drafted for his new institution, Wykeham explained that the Black Death and the tides of war, commerce and industry had led to a decline in the number of students and thus to a shortage of well-educated clergy. He hoped that New College would help correct this situation. Indeed, his college of 70 students nearly doubled the number of students then living in Oxford's secular colleges. Most New College students studied theology but some of them were permitted to study Roman and/or canon law to prepare themselves for positions in ecclesiastical courts, administration or royal government. Wykeham, however, had another and more personal reason to found New College: in keeping with medieval practice, he wanted to establish a chantry for the intercession of his soul. In his thoroughgoing way he even specified which psalms and prayers the clergy (also part of his foundation of the college) and students were to use throughout each day.

New College is historically important, too, because the tutorial system began there: in 1379 money was allocated for the payment of tutors (*informatores*). Today, undergraduates at both Oxford and Cambridge are still taught by tutorials. This challenging system involves a very small number of students (from one to three) meeting with a college fellow who is a specialist in their subject. They must communicate and defend their own ideas orally, as well as critique those of the other students, and discuss them with the college fellow. This intellectual give and take creates a learning situation that is highly effective. There is no place to hide; students cannot remain passive, as they can and often must do during a standard lecture course.

It should be noted that the common law of England was not taught in English universities, although Roman (civil) and canon law were. There is no single, clear answer why this was the case. Dr. Paul Brand, Senior Research Fellow and Academic Secretary at All Souls College, Oxford, explains the situation in these words:

> In so far as medieval universities were primarily intended to produce graduates who would be of service to the church, Roman law and canon law were the obvious subjects to study since they helped create trained canon lawyers. One might also say that medieval university teaching was in all cases based on understanding and glossing books of authority: there were no such books to provide the basis for teaching the common law. The third thing one might say is that the heart of the English legal system and of the nascent legal profession lay in London. Neither Oxford nor Cambridge was sufficiently close to London to be a convenient location for teaching young lawyers.[17]

To learn how the common law of England was taught, we may consult Chief Justice John Fortescue, an eminent English jurist. Writing in 1470, he describes the educational institution (*studium pupplicum*) in the western suburb of London where English law was taught. This was not a full-fledged university but rather what we might call a training school for the legal profession. It consisted of 10 or more lesser "inns" (known as Inns of Chancery), which taught students the basics of the law, and the four larger and more prestigious Inns of Court (Lincoln's Inn, Inner Temple, Middle Temple, and Gray's Inn), which provided advanced legal instruction.[18] These inns also served, in effect, as finishing schools for young aristocrats. As Fortescue explains,

> In these greater Inns, indeed, and also in the lesser, there is besides a school of law a kind of academy of all the manners that nobles learn ... the knights, barons and the greatest nobility of the kingdom often place their children in these Inns of Court, not so much to make the law their study (having large patrimonies of their own) but to form their manners.[19]

Toward the end of the Middle Ages, the University of Oxford was graced by two of Europe's finest medieval architectural and scholarly monuments: the Divinity School (built 1427–1488) and Duke Humphrey's Library (built 1444–1488). To these we must turn.

The Divinity School, a masterpiece of Late Gothic architecture, is the most beautiful medieval building still standing in Oxford. It is also the oldest surviving building erected separately for a purely university purpose, namely, to house the lectures and disputations of the theology faculty. It was the university's first examination school: here (until the nineteenth century) the professor of divinity supervised the oral examination of candidates. Its elaborate fan-vaulted ceiling, highlighted by 455 bosses carved with the initials or arms of those who contributed to the cost of construction, is simply magnificent and is well worth a visit.

The first library for the university itself (as distinct from the libraries of its component colleges) was begun in about 1320. It was housed in a modest room in the heart of Oxford's academic quarters, close to the schools where lectures were given. This room is still in use as a vestry and meeting room for the nearby University Church of St. Mary the Virgin.[20] Begun with funds supplied by the bishop of Worcester, Thomas de Cobham, this little library was still unfinished when he died in 1327.

In 1444 the university decided to build a new library — to be known as Duke Humfrey's Library — directly over the Divinity School. It was designed to house the priceless collection of more than 281 manuscripts that had been donated to the university by Humfrey, duke of Gloucester, the younger brother of King Henry V. Because of chronic shortages of funds, the new library was not opened until 1488. In addition to the usual contents of medieval libraries it had Greek and Latin classics, along with some works of Italian humanist scholars. It was magnificently restored by Thomas Bodley (1545–1613), an English diplomat and scholar who had been educated at Oxford's Magdalen College (founded in 1458, it is pronounced "maudlin") and who was Merton College's first lecturer in Ancient Greek. The Bodleian Library now contains about 7,500,000 volumes. Rashdall says of it:

> It is the first irruption of the full-blown Italian Renaissance into Oxford, and no doubt helped on that spontaneous grouping after an improved Latinity, and a more literary education which, at Oxford as at Paris, prepared the way for the men of the Renaissance proper — the wandering Greeks and the Northern scholars who had studied in Italy.[21]

VII

Luminaries at Oxford

We shall now look briefly at the lives and works of five remarkable scholars who taught at the University of Oxford in medieval times. In chronological order they are: Robert Grosseteste, Roger Bacon, John Duns Scotus, William of Ockham, and John Wycliffe (also spelled Wyclif and in several other ways).

Robert Grosseteste (c. 1175–1253)

Robert Grosseteste became the leading figure in the growth of scientific studies at Oxford. He was an English scholastic philosopher, theologian, bishop and polymath (a person of encyclopedic learning) who introduced European thinkers to Greek and Arabic philosophical and scientific writings via his Latin translations of their works. He received his higher education at Oxford, where he studied law, medicine and the natural sciences. Rashdall says of him that "His writings show a range and versatility rare indeed among medieval doctors [i.e., scholars]: he was a French poet, an agriculturalist, a lawyer, a physician and a preacher."[1]

Grosseteste also devoted himself to geometry, optics and astronomy. His most famous scientific text was *De luce* (*Concerning Light*), in which he argued that light was the basis of all matter. In optics he experimented with mirrors and lenses. He held that experimentation must be used to verify a theory by empirically testing the results of its predictions. In an astronomy text he stated that the Milky Way was the fusion of light from many small stars that were close together. In his work *De Iride* (*On the Rainbow*) he wrote:

This part of optics, which when well understood, shows us how we may make things at a very long distance off appear as if placed very close, and large near things appear very small, and how we may make small things placed at a distance appear any size we want, so that it may be possible for us to read the smallest letters at incredible distances, or to count sand, or seed, or any sort of minute objects.[2]

Grosseteste was chancellor of Oxford from about 1215 to 1221. Beginning in 1229 or 1230 he was the head of the Franciscan school at Oxford and lectured on theology. The Franciscan chronicler, Thomas of Eccleston, recorded that his teachings were of great benefit to the order. Grosseteste also wrote a commentary on Aristotle's *Posterior Analytics* and *Physics*, as well as many treatises on scientific subjects. He became bishop of Lincoln in 1235 and held that that post until his death in 1253. Known as a brilliant but highly demanding leader of the church, he insisted that all his clergy be literate and have some training in theology. (Many rural parish priests in the Middle Ages had only enough Latin to stumble through the Mass. Very few of them had ever studied theology as an academic disciple.)

During this time he also translated Aristotle's *Nichomachean Ethics* from the Greek, making this important work available to the West in its entirety for the first time. He was one of the first Western scholars to argue that natural phenomena can be described mathematically.[3] Grosseteste worked hard to further his three main convictions: the supreme importance of saving souls; the need for a highly centralized and hierarchical church; and the superiority of the church over the state. These beliefs sometimes brought him into conflict with both the crown and the papacy.

He wrote more than 120 works and laid the intellectual foundations for two procedural principles which were of much use to science in the Middle Ages: applying mathematics to the natural sciences to describe and explain them, and using observation and experiment to test scientific hypotheses. The application of these principles shifted the medieval study of scientific data away from being merely an unstructured speculative exercise toward a mathematical inquiry based on repeatable cycles of observation, hypothesis and experimental verification.[4]

Roger Bacon (c. 1214–c. 1292)

Roger Bacon was Grosseteste's best student and is remembered by history as *doctor mirabilis* ("the wonderful doctor"). This English Franciscan friar, philosopher, medieval scientist, and theologian was one of the most famous men of his time. He was a major advocate of Aristotle and of experimental science. Bacon believed, for example, that "Mathematics is the door and the key to the sciences."[5]

He also broke new intellectual ground. In his time it was widely accepted that an idea could not be rejected *simply because it failed to meet the test of empirical proof.* Instead, conventional wisdom held that ideas were more real than any concrete examples of them. Such concrete examples, it was believed, were inherently unreliable, being subject to change, to decay and to imperfections. To base anything on them was thus very likely to lead thinkers into serious mistakes. Bacon, however, argued that theories prove nothing by themselves: they must be subjected to — and must be supported by — experimental science (*sciatica experimentalis*).[6]

Bacon was also convinced that the proper basis for a learned education was the study of ancient languages (chiefly Greek) and of mathematics. These disciplines, he argued, were the cornerstones of philosophy, theology, medicine and science. As Rashdall puts it with his usual felicity, Bacon believed that "Theology and philosophy must be studied philologically and historically: science must be studied mathematically and experimentally."[7]

Bacon earned a master's degree at Oxford between about 1228 and 1236, where he studied logic and natural philosophy and lectured on Aristotle. He moved to France in 1241 to teach at the University of Paris. Bacon returned to Oxford in 1247 and joined the Franciscans in about 1257, expecting to get a teaching position. He did not receive one, however, probably because in 1256 Richard of Cornwell became head of the academic side of the Franciscan order in England. Richard was very critical of Bacon's ideas. The end result was that Bacon was forced to end his studies at Oxford and to join a friary in Paris. He wrote bitterly of this experience: "They forced me with unspeakable violence to obey their will."[8]

For the next 10 years Bacon would have no personal contact with the outside world and could not publish anything, although he was permitted to correspond by letter. The tide turned for him when Pope Clement IV came to power. Recognizing Bacon's intellectual prowess, the pope sent him a letter in 1266, urging him to write down his ideas "without delay, and with all possible secrecy, without regard to any contrary precept of your Superiors or any Constitution of your order."[9] Bacon was so eager to get back to scholarly studies and teaching that in less than two years he wrote a seven-part encyclopedia, consisting of the *Opus Maidus* (*Great Work*, running to 840 pages), the *Opus Minus* (*Smaller Work*), and the *Opus Terbium* (*Third Work*).

Bacon wanted to explain to the pope why the sciences deserved a prominent role in university teaching and why they were equally important to the church itself. He brought scientific insights to bear on theological and philosophical issues. He even proposed a telescope, arguing that

> For we can so shape transparent bodies, and arrange them in such a way with respect to our sight and objects of vision, that the rays will be reflected and bent in any direction we desire, and under any angle we wish, we may see the object near or at a distance.... So we might also cause the Sun, Moon and stars in appearance to descend here below.[10]

In *Opus Maidus* he gave 42 degrees for the maximum altitude of the rainbow, which was the most accurate measurement made to that date. Because of the light they shed on medieval learning, Bacon's 1271 comments on learned matters (*Compendium Studio Philosophize*) are of no little interest. In it, he despairs of the parlous state of theological learning in his time. Never shy about voicing his own opinions, this is how he describes the current state of play in theology:

> For forty years past certain men have arisen in the universities who have created themselves masters and doctors in theology and philosophy, though they themselves have never learned anything of any account, nor will they or can they learn by reason of their position....
>
> There are boys who are inexperienced in the knowledge of themselves and of the world and of the learned languages, Greek and Hebrew ... who in many cases enter those orders [the Franciscan and Dominican orders] at or below the age of twenty years. This is the common course, from the English sea to the further confines of Christendom, and more especially beyond the realm of France; so that in Aquitaine Provence, Spain, Italy, Germany, Hungary, Denmark, and everywhere, boys are promiscuously received into the orders from their tenth to their twentieth year, boys too young to be able to know anything worth knowing....
>
> Many thousands become friars who cannot read their Psalter or their Donate [i.e., their Latin grammar: Donatus was the favorite grammarian of the Middle Ages] yet, immediately after their admission, they are set to study theology. Wherefore they must of necessity fail to reap any great profit ... so that they are become Masters in Theology and in Philosophy before being disciples [of experts]. Wherefore infinite error reigns among them.... [Bacon then goes on to deplore the almost universal ignorance of Greek and Hebrew in the orders and the universities and the low quality of the translations of Aristotle available then.][11]

Bacon had a nice sense of humor. He believed that theology should be taught by focusing on the sacred texts themselves, not on magisterial disputations and *quaestiones*. He complains that

> For the last fifty years theologians have been concerned mainly with *quaestiones*. This is made obvious by all the tractates and *summae* by every possible author which are so big and so heavy that you have to have a horse to carry them.[12]

VII. Luminaries at Oxford

Bacon had such a confident, far-ranging mind that it was easy for him to stray off the reservation of doctrinal thought. In fact, he was condemned by his own order in 1278 "on account of certain suspected novelties," a charge which probably refers to his interests in astrology and alchemy. He was imprisoned in a convent in Ancona, Italy, and held there in solitary confinement. In 1290, however, Raymond of Guarded became the new head of the order and released all the prisoners at Ancona. It is thought that Bacon was among them and that he returned to England soon thereafter. He died c. 1292, probably at Oxford, but was not forgotten. His work in the philosophy of language and the philosophy of nature would influence such fourteenth-century writers as Duns Scotus and William of Ockham.[13]

John Duns Scotus (1265/1266–1308)

Hailed as *doctor subtilis* ("subtle doctor") because of his complex, nuanced thought, John Duns Scotus was one of the most influential philosopher-theologians of the Middle Ages. He left his intellectual mark on a wide range of intractable subjects. These include the defense of the doctrine of the immaculate conception; logical issues in religious discourse; the problem of universals; divine illumination (the belief that humans need divine help to attain certain knowledge); and human will and human freedom (Scotus says that we all face *multiple options* at each moment of choice: we can decide to do *x* but we can also decide to do *y*).[14]

Scotus was a Scot, hence his nickname "Scotus." He began studying at Oxford in 1288 and in 1291 was ordained as a priest in the Franciscan order. While at Oxford he wrote commentaries on Peter Lombard's *Sentences* during the academic year of 1298–1299. Completing his studies there in 1301, he began lecturing on the *Sentences* at the University of Paris in 1302. Together with 80 other friars he was expelled from France in 1303 for taking the pope's side in a dispute with the French king over the taxation of church property to support the king's wars with England. However, he and his colleagues were allowed to return to Paris the next year. In 1304, too, he was named as the Franciscan regent master (i.e., a master who taught) in theology at Paris. For reasons that are now unclear, he moved to the Franciscan house at Cologne and began lecturing there in 1307. Scotus died in Cologne in 1308. His tomb in the Franciscan church there bears this succinct inscription:

Scotia me genius. Anglia me susceptive. Gallia me dacoit. Colonia me tenet.[15]
[Scotland bore me. England sustained me. France taught me. Cologne holds me.]

Scotus is justly famous for his lengthy, tightly reasoned contributions to natural theology, i.e., the attempt to prove the existence and nature of God without any recourse to divine revelation. His argument for the existence of God is so convoluted that to describe it here in any detail would impede the flow of the text. We will therefore do great violence to it by over-simplifying it greatly and distilling it into two fundamental points[16]:

- A "first cause" must exist, namely, a being that forms the first link in a chain of causality.
- This being is a preeminently excellent being. It is the primary being. It has intelligence and will. It is unique, i.e., there is only one such being. This being is God.

Scotus reveled in complicated thoughts that are quite difficult or perhaps impossible for non-philosophers to understand. For example, he invented the concept of "haecceity." As defined by the *Stanford Encyclopedia of Philosophy*, a haecceity is a non-qualitative property responsible for individuation.[17] That is to say, it is what is responsible for the special qualities, properties or characteristics of a thing which make it a *particular* thing. Haecceity is thus a person's or an object's *thisness*.

In an earlier chapter we noted that medieval nominalism was a school of thought which held that a universal concept such as "father" does not have any independent existence beyond the particular person it names. In direct contrast, medieval realism argued that universals do in fact exist outside the mind, i.e., they have an independent reality all of their own. Medieval realists believed that common (or shared) natures or essences are somehow divided into what Scotus calls "subjective parts." The *Stanford Encyclopedia of Philosophy* admits that "it is not easy to explain precisely what this divisibility amounts to" but it then goes on to quote Scotus on the problem of individuation. This quotation is reproduced below — not in hopes that the reader will be able to understand it but simply to demonstrate the intricacies of Scotus' thought. He wrote:

> Because there is among beings something indivisible into subjective parts — that is, such that it is formally incompatible for it to be divided into several parts each of which is it — the question is not what it is by which such a division is formally incompatible with it (because it is formally incompatible by incompatibility), but rather what it is by which, as a proximate and intrinsic foundation, this incompatibility is in it. Therefore, the sense of the questions on this topic [i.e., individuation] is: What is it in this [particular] stone, by which as by a proximate foundation it is absolutely incompatible with the stone for it to be divided into several parts which of which is this stone, the kind of division that is proper to a universal whole as divided into its subjective parts?[18]

Over the centuries the reputation of John Duns Scotus has had its ups and downs. By the mid–fourteenth century his school of thought was so influential that it formed part of the teachings of the Franciscan order. By the early sixteenth century, however, the epithet "dunce," which refers to the Scottish town of Duns where Scotus was born and raised, was used derisively to mean a person who was very slow-witted or stupid.

Scotus' intellectual subtleties and his strong defense of the papacy against the divine right of kings proved offensive to some of the later and more doctrinaire English reformers. For example, Thomas Cromwell was the English statesman and adviser to King Henry VIII who was responsible for drafting the legislation that formalized England's break with Rome. In 1535 Richard Layton, one of Thomas Cromwell's commissioners, wrote to his master from Oxford:

> We have set Dunce in Bocardo [a prison in central Oxford that predated the university], and have utterly banished him Oxford for ever, with all his blind glosses ... [At Oxford's New College] wee fawned all the greet quadrant Court full of the leafed [leaves] of Dunce, the wind blowing them into every corner.[19]

William of Ockham (c. 1285–1348)

The Franciscan philosopher, theologian and political commentator William of Ockham (his name can also be spelled Occam) was known as *doctor invincible* ("invincible doctor"). Today he is widely remembered for a pragmatic method of thought known as Ockham's Razor. He was a late scholastic thinker closely associated with nominalism. This school of thought is now of interest mainly to philosophers and historians but a related concept — the "law of parsimony" (*lex parsimoniae*) — still has many practical applications in the world today.

Together with Thomas Aquinas and John Duns Scotus, Ockham is one of the major figures of medieval thought. Ordained a sub-deacon in 1306, he studied theology at Oxford between 1317 and 1319 and lectured there on the *Sentences* of Peter Lombard, also setting down his commentaries in written form. His opinions, however, seemed to some senior members of the theological faculty to be heretical. The result was that Ockham had to leave the university without earning his master's degree in theology. He returned to the Franciscan convent in London, where he had undertaken his elementary education, and continued to study theology and logic.

In 1323 Ockham was called before the Franciscan province's chapter meeting in Bristol to defend his views. At about the same time, someone —

history does not reveal just who this was — reported to the papal court at Avignon that Ockham was teaching heresy. He was summoned to Avignon in 1324 to answer this charge.[20] There he became deeply involved in a dispute over Apostolic poverty, i.e., the question of whether individual Franciscans — and, indeed, the Franciscan order itself — were permitted to own property.

Michael of Cesena, the chief administrative officer of the order, had also been summoned to Avignon to explain his own views on this issue. Michael argued that since Christ and his apostles had renounced all property rights and ownership (which meant, by implication, that they had to beg for their daily bread), Franciscans should do likewise and should live only by begging and by accepting offerings from the faithful.[21] The pope rejected this point of view. Michael then asked Ockham to study three recent papal bulls on poverty. Ockham did so and concluded that they contained so many errors that the pope himself (John XXII) was a heretic. Moreover, continued Ockham, since the pope also categorically refused to change his mind even after it had been clearly proven that he was wrong, he had in effect abdicated his papacy and thus could no longer be considered to be the pope!

Fearing imprisonment and even execution for this radical anti-papal stance, on 26 May 1328 Ockham, Michael and a few of their followers — riding stolen horses under the cover of darkness — fled from Avignon to Pisa. Later they went to Munich, seeking permanent refuge with the Holy Roman Emperor Louis IV of Bavaria, who had his own political quarrel with the pope. Excommunicated by the pope for leaving Avignon without permission, Ockham remained unrepentant. His philosophy was never officially condemned as heretical, however, and he devoted the rest of his life to writing about political issues, e.g., the respective authority and rights of popes and kings. He died in Munich in 1348.

Today, usually without realizing it, many of us use Ockham's Razor in our daily lives when we look for the simplest explanation of any event. Although Ockham himself did not invent this concept and did not use this particular phrase, the underlying principle at play here is *Entia non sunt multiplicanda praeter necessitatem* ("Entities should not be multiplied beyond necessity"). Ockham's Razor is so called because it shaves off all unnecessary postulates and assumptions to reach the simplest possible explanation.

If, for example, you have been driving for hours at high speed along an Interstate highway in Nevada and have not bought any fuel recently, Ockham's Razor will tell you that the most likely explanation for why your engine is suddenly beginning to sputter is that you are running out of fuel. You do not need to look for complex and much less likely explanations, e.g., that a huge meteor has fallen into China's Gobi Desert and the prevailing westerly winds have filled the Nevada air with tiny dust particles that are now blocking the flow of air into the carburetor of your car.

Ockham's Razor has many other modern uses too. It underlies the KISS principle (Keep It Simple, Stupid). The medical principle of diagnostic parsimony is based on it, i.e., look for the simplest explanation or, as medical professors joke, "When you hear hoofbeats, think horses, not zebras." According to the great physicist Stephen Hawking, it even underlies the discovery of quantum mechanics.[22]

Two caveats, however, are necessary here. The first is that Ockham's Razor does not mean that the simplest explanation is always the best one: sometimes the best explanation turns out to be rather complicated. Thus a more precise formulation of Ockham's Razor is: "A theory should be as simple as possible, *but no simpler.*"

The second caveat is that Ockham's Razor has often been used to argue that God does not exist. This method of thought does not prove that God does *not* exist but it does suggest that, in the absence of truly *compelling* reasons to the contrary, one should not posit the existence of God. For this reason, Ockham earned a reputation in the late Middle Ages as the destroyer of Thomas Aquinas's synthesis of faith and reason.[23]

The fourteenth-century church felt threatened by some of Ockham's ideas, which it perceived as undermining its right to an exclusive mediating role between human beings and God. Ockham believed that the church did have such a role to play but that this role was not dogmatically set in stone. Instead, he argued that it was essentially an *artificial* arrangement. According to this point of view, the church could no longer legitimately depict itself as the sole passageway through which human beings had to pass en route to heaven, purgatory or hell. Needless to say, Ockham's ideas were not warmly received by a church that was then trying to shore up its own political and economic power against the rising nation-states of Europe and that wanted to fend off the growing secular challenges to its leadership.[24]

John Wycliffe (c. 1330–1384)

An English theologian and reformer who arranged for the first complete translation of the Bible into English and who vigorously urged the church to give up all its worldly goods, John Wycliffe was a precursor of the Protestant Reformation. Educated at Oxford and ordained in 1351, he was a fellow of Merton College in 1356 and a master of arts at Balliol College in 1360. He received his doctor of divinity degree in 1372. By 1374 he was deeply involved in church politics, e.g., papal taxes and appointments to ecclesiastical posts, and was writing treatises on divine and human "dominion," by which he meant the right to exercise authority and, indirectly, to hold property.[25]

Wycliffe argued that God is the only true source of dominion. If the men who exercise dominion on Earth are living in a state of mortal sin, their dominion is not genuine, i.e., it is invalid. Indeed, only the righteous have a legitimate claim to dominion, even if forces beyond their control prevent them from exercising it at any given time. Such bold patterns of thought eventually led Wycliffe to proclaim that since the church itself was sinful (this was an audacious and potentially heretical claim), it must surrender all its wealth and power to return to a holy state of evangelical poverty. According to him, such disendowment (stripping away the church's worldly goods) was clearly the duty of the state, that is to say, the king. Monarchy was for him the best form of government; kings must be obeyed because they are God's vicars on Earth and only He can depose them.[26]

By 1377 Wycliffe's influence in England was at its height. Parliament and the king both sought his opinion on whether England could refuse to send feudal payments to Rome; he assured them that such a refusal was lawful. The church was infuriated by Wycliffe's statements. Five papal bulls were issued against him, 24 of his conclusions were formally condemned, and Pope Gregory XI demanded that Oxford arrest him. The university, however, refused to take any action against its most famous scholar. The next year Wycliffe further offended the church by supporting the king in a case involving the right of sanctuary in a church. Wycliffe argued that the king's servants had the right to enter a sanctuary to bring a wanted man to justice — in this case, an insubordinate squire.

Settling down in his parish of Lutterworth, which was near Oxford, Wycliffe then began a carefully crafted, vitriolic assault on the established beliefs and practices of the church. As an advocate of predestinarianism (the belief that only a few saintly men and women are predestined to be saved), he did not hesitate to attack such major dogmas as transubstantiation — the belief that the bread and wine used in the Eucharist, i.e., in the Mass, is spiritually changed into the body and blood of Christ.

From 1380 to 1381 Wycliffe worked at Queen's College, arranging for two English translations of the Bible — one more idiomatic than the other. He believed that the Bible should be equally accessible to all, and the production by his followers of the "Wycliffe Bible" can be considered to be one of his major achievements. He also called for the founding of an order of Poor Preachers, who would convey Biblical truths to the common man in simple language. A heretical group, known as the Lollards, evolved from Wycliffe's teachings and actively propagated his views.

The new archbishop of Canterbury, William Courtenay (1347–1396), who was himself once chancellor of Oxford, soon took action against Wycliffe. In 1382 the archbishop had Wycliffe's 24 conclusions condemned by a council of theologians. Fearing for his own safety, however, Courtenay would not publish the condemnation at Oxford: "This is Oxford," he exclaimed, "[which will be] the University of heresies, if she will not allow orthodox truths to be published."[27] That same year Pope Gregory XI issued a blast against Oxford for sheltering Wycliffe. The pope's bull read in part:

> Gregory, bishop, *servus servorum dei* ["servant of the servants of God"], to his beloved sons the Chancellor and University of Oxford, in the diocese of Lincoln, grace and apostolic benediction. We are compelled to wonder and grieve that you, who, in consideration of the favors and privileges conceded to your University of Oxford by the apostolic see ... through a certain sloth and neglect allow tares [weeds] to spring up amidst the pure wheat [the church's dogmas] in the fields of your glorious University aforesaid; and what is still more pernicious, even continue to grow to maturity....
>
> It has come to our ears that John de Wycliffe ... has fallen into such a detestable madness that he does not hesitate to dogmatize and publicly preach, or rather vomit forth from the recesses of his breast, certain propositions that are erroneous and false ... we command your University with strict admonition, by the apostolic authority, in virtue of your sacred obedience, and under penalty of the deprivation of all the favors, indulgences, and privileges granted to you and your University by the said see, for the future not to permit to be asserted or proposed to any extent whatever, the opinions, conclusions, and propositions which are in variance with good morals and terms, even when those proposing strike to defend them under a certain fanciful wrestling of words or of terms. Moreover, you are on our authority to arrest the said John, or cause him to be arrested and to send him under a trustworthy guard to our venerable brother, the Archbishop of Canterbury, and the Bishop of London, or to one of them.[28]

Later in 1382 all of Wycliffe's writings were banned. His supporters at Oxford had to comply with the orthodox doctrines of the church or run the risk of severe punishment. Wycliffe himself suffered a stroke that impaired him physically but not mentally; he continued to write. Ordered by the pope to come to Rome to answer charges of heresy, Wycliffe refused to do so and remained unrepentant. He replied to the pope in 1384:

> And if I err in this sentence [i.e., in my conclusions], I will meekly be amended, yea, by the death, if it be skilful, for that I hope were good to me.

And if I might travel in my own person, I would with good will go to the pope. But God has needed me to the contrary, and taught me more obedience to God than to men.[29]

Felled by a second stroke, Wycliffe died at Lutterworth in 1384. The Council of Constance (1414–1418) condemned his writings and ordered that his books be burned and that his body be removed from consecrated ground. This order was confirmed by Pope Martin V and was carried out in 1428.[30] Wycliffe's fame, however, continued to grow after his death. He was hailed by sixteenth-century Protestants as "the morning star of the Reformation."[31] Writing in 1895, Rashdall concluded that after the Council of Clarence "the leaven of Wyclifism went on silently working beneath the surface of Oxford life," preparing the way for the English Reformers.[32]

VIII

Ten Other Universities

Many universities were established during the Middle Ages, especially during its later period but not all of them survived. Disregarding what Rashdall calls the "paper universities" (universities for which bulls were granted but which never came into existence) but counting all the questionable cases (academic institutions whose status as full universities is open to dispute), as many as 86 universities existed between about 1188 and 1500. As of the latter date, however, only between 63 and 66 universities were still functioning.[1]

Medieval universities varied so much in their location, beginnings, financing, historical development, life span, academic quality, and number of masters and students that they cannot easily be compared. It is more useful instead to look at a representative sample of these universities at a given point in time. We shall therefore take stock of them at about 1300, a date which marks, roughly, the midpoint of the era of medieval universities.

At that time, Paris, Bologna and Oxford were by far the most important universities but at least 10 others merit discussion here.[2] Ranked by their approximate founding dates, they are: Montpellier (beginning of the thirteenth century), Cambridge (1209–1229), Padua (1222), Naples (1224), Toulouse (1229), Angers (1229), Orléans (1306), Prague (1347–1348), Vienna (1365), and Glasgow (1451). These 10 "lesser," i.e., less famous, universities are the subject of this chapter.

Montpellier (beginning of the thirteenth century)

Montpellier's fame initially rested on its medical school: as early as 1137, excellent physicians are said to have been teaching there. Adalbert, later archbishop of Mainz, studied in Montpellier that year after graduating from the arts course at Paris. Medical studies at Montpellier flourished because the lords of the Guillem dynasty, who ruled Montpellier, decreed that any licensed physician could lecture there. There was thus no ceiling on the potential number of medical professors. As teachers multiplied, so did the number of courses offered and the number of students.

It is not feasible here to attempt more than a brief sketch of academic medicine as it was taught and practiced in the Middle Ages.[3] (See also Appendix 6 — "Medieval requirements for becoming a physician, 1270–1274.") Medieval medicine was largely based on classic texts, e.g., the writings of the famous Greek physician Galen (129–c. 200), whose theories dominated Western medical thinking for more than 1300 years. In the Middle Ages, medicine revolved around two basic concepts. The first was *complexio* ("temperament"), i.e., the balance of the elementary qualities of hotness, wetness, coldness, and dryness. This balance was sought not only in the four types of "humours" (fluids) produced by the body itself (black bile, phlegm, blood, and yellow bile) but also in the herbal and other substances used for curative purposes. Diet and bloodletting (by using leeches) were also employed by physicians to restore the balance of humours.

The second concept was medical astrology, i.e., the influence of the heavenly bodies on terrestrial events, especially on health. Some professors of medicine paid little attention to this subject but others drew heavily on astrological materials when diagnosing disease and prescribing treatments.

Legal teaching at Montpellier began in 1160 when the Italian jurist and glossator Placentinus (d. 1192) moved there from the law school at Bologna. After teaching for a time at Montpellier, he then spent two years teaching at Bologna — thereby, as he remembered complacently, "provoking the other masters to envy by emptying their classrooms, and opening up the hidden secrets of the law."[4] He then returned to Montpellier where he enjoyed continued success.

Cardinal Conrad von Urach, the legate of Pope Honorius III, formally organized the medical school of Montpellier into a university in 1220 and gave it statutes and privileges. This papal favor imposed a degree of church control over what was essentially a lay university, but the ecclesiastical burden was not a heavy one. The presiding bishop at Maguelonne simply delegated some of his supervisory authority to a university chancellor chosen from among the professors.[5] Pope Nicholas IV formally confirmed in 1289 that Montpellier had indeed become a *stadium generale* and conferred upon its doctors the *ius ubique docendi* (the right to teach anywhere without further examination).[6] In the charter given to the new university the papal envoy voiced in fulsome terms the high hopes being held for it as a new seat of medical learning:

> Comme depuis longtemps l'exercice de la science médicale, sous le signe glorieux du progrès, a brillé à Montpellier, fleuri et porté une saine abondance de fruits aux diverses parties de la terre, nous avons pensé que tous nous devions veiller à la conservation des études de médecine et pourvoir à leur organisation, ayant mesuré le profit de tous et de chacun de ceux qui étudient dans cette discipline, d'autant plus que l'exercice de la science médicale rend la nature des choses familière, fait de ceux qui la pratiquent des hommes plus sages et se justifie volontiers par le rétablissement de la faiblesse humaine. Certainement, la formule de sage nous convainc que cette science doit être vénérée....[7]
>
> [Because for a long time the practice of medical science, under the glorious sign of progress, has shone in Montpellier, flourishing and conveying an abundance of useful results to different parts of the earth, we have decided that we should all attend to the conservation of medical studies and should help to implement them, having taken account of the advantage to everyone and to those who study this discipline — all the more so because the practice of medical science reveals the nature of familiar things, making the men who practice it wiser, and justifying their work by the existence of human weaknesses. This wise policy has certainly convinced us that this science must be venerated....]

Students at Montpellier were not hesitant about challenging the university authorities. In the early fourteenth century, for example, the law students protested vigorously when the bishop and university lecturers tried to suffocate the growth of the student nations. The reason was that the authorities did not want to encourage greater student participation in the running of the university. A new constitution for the university, drawn up in 1339, was a qualified victory for the students because it gave them a bigger role in university government.[8]

Montpellier students, like their counterparts elsewhere, were often a rowdy lot. Writing in 1877 the French historian Germain gives us this undated account of what happened when the university students started a riot near the law school. Several townsmen were wounded in the brawl. Germain reports that

> A great uproar ensued. The citizens of Montpellier, who had never liked the students over-much determined upon vengeance. The next day, when the bell rang, they lay in wait for the rioters as they came out of school, and hemmed them into a street so narrow that not one of them could escape. In order to distinguish their own countrymen from the foreigners, against whom they had

a special grudge, they obliged each of them to say in their local idiom: "*Dieu vous donne bona nioche*" [literally "God give you good night"]. As strangers were not able to pronounce the last two words of this evening salutation correctly, it was easy to recognize the foreign rioters. Several of them were killed and their bodies cast into neighboring wells.... The name of Rue Bona-nioch continues to mark the scene of the bloody drama.[9]

Even the law students were not above serious reproach. In 1425, we are told, six or seven law students, wearing masks, broke into a house one night and abducted a young woman. The university later protected them from civil prosecution on the grounds of their clerical status.[10]

Cambridge (1209–1229)

Cambridge evolved into a university between about 1209, when students left Oxford to protest the hanging of two of their fellows, and 1229, when the English king Henry III offered asylum to the dispersed students of Paris.[11] Papal recognition of the new university dates from 1233. Initially, Cambridge specialized in the arts, canon law and theology; faculties of civil law and medicine appeared only in the thirteenth century. In 1381 Pope John XXII officially confirmed that Cambridge was a *studium generale.*

Compared with the many records which have survived from the University of Oxford's medieval era, only a small *corpus* of material is available on the University of Cambridge in the thirteenth and fourteenth centuries. This fact led Rashdall to denigrate the early importance of Cambridge. He wrote:

> Up to the end of the fourteenth century — that is to say virtually up to the downfall of scholasticism — Cambridge was a third-rate university.... It was not until Oxford had become impregnated with the Wyclifite heresy that Cambridge came into fashion with cautious parents and attracted the patronage of royal champions of orthodoxy and their ecclesiastical advisers.... It is almost impossible to say anything about medieval Cambridge which has not already been said of Oxford.[12]

Rashdall may have been too harsh. Later scholars have concluded that, largely thanks to its colleges (13 of them were founded at Cambridge between 1284 and 1497), Cambridge played a more important role in medieval English academic life than had previously been thought.[13]

Town-gown brawls were unfortunate facts of life in medieval Cambridge. Cambridge University statutes of 1236–1254 clearly attest to a widespread concern about keeping the public peace.[14] In 1249, for example, several people were killed or wounded and many houses were broken into and wrecked. As the chronicler Matthew Paris describes this incident,

> At this time, too, namely in Lent [1249], a dispute over some minor matter arose at Cambridge between town and gown. From it ensued litigation and fights, housebreaking, wounding and homicide. Noise of this came to the king's ears, along with serious complaints, and both sides suffered not a little from the damage, and the scandal spread abroad.[15]

Town-gown clashes continued. In 1260 rival student groups (assisted by townsmen) burned not only student hostels but also some of the records of the university. In 1304 townsmen attacked several hostels and assaulted masters and students. Major rioting took place in 1322, when students were injured or jailed and a parish priest was killed. Violent town-gown clashes also occurred in 1371 and 1381.[16]

Padua (1222)

Like Bologna, Padua was a "students' university." Rashdall sums it up in one elegant sentence:

> By far the most important of the daughters of Bologna was the great University of Padua, which early proved a formidable rival of the mother university, and eventually surpassed it in everything but the incommunicable prerogative of greater antiquity.[17]

A famous Bologna jurist, Martinus, appears to have taught at Padua before 1169 but a *studium generale* did not develop there until 1222 — a result of a migration of students from Bologna. Four years later we hear of a Latin text being read in the cathedral "in the presence of the professors of civil and canon law, and of all the doctors and scholars dwelling at Padua."[18] Pope Clement VI confirmed the university's status as a *studium generale* in 1346 for all faculties except theology: Urban V approved the latter discipline in 1363.

Padua reached the apex of its glory during the fifteenth and sixteenth centuries, when it became one of the leading universities of Europe. The Venetian government forbade its subjects to study anywhere else than Padua and even required a period of study there as a prerequisite for holding public office. Venice conferred on the rector of Padua the right to wear a robe of purple and gold. When he resigned from office, he would be awarded the title of doctor for life and would be given a golden collar, which symbolized his membership in the order of St. Mark, a highly respected Venetian order.[19]

Naples (1224)

The University of Naples was founded by the emperor of Sicily, Frederick II, in 1224 for three reasons: to compete with the University of Bologna, which owed allegiance to a rival Italian dynasty; to train the jurists and bureaucrats he needed to administer his vast realm; and to burnish his own reputation as a learned and generous ruler. The new university was entirely independent of the church and was the first university in Europe to be founded at a specific time by a specific charter. That is to say, unlike all the other major universities (Bologna, Paris and Oxford) it had no pre-charter era of gradual evolution. Instead, it was from the very beginning an artificial and relatively weak political creation rather than the result of any genuine educational groundswell.

Perhaps for this reason, it frequently needed reforming. Indeed, not until a major reform was carried out with the support of Pope Clement IV in 1266 did the new university finally begin to hit its stride.[20] Even then, it still suffered — and would always suffer — from a grave impediment. Rashdall, never one to mince his words, has this to say:

> The University of Naples was the creation of despotism and was habitually treated as such. There is no parallel in medieval history for such an absolute subjection of a university, in the minutest as well as in the most important matters, to the royal authority. It was placed under the jurisdiction of the royal chancellor till the time of Ferdinand II (1497), when the King's grand chaplain became governor of the university.... A certain measure of freedom was essential to healthy university life: Naples may possibly have been in its later days a not inefficient educational institution, but it has no place in the history of medieval thought.[21]

The University of Naples was not an autonomous corporation of independent scholars but was a hierarchical institution directly controlled by the emperor himself. He approved and appointed the professors; paid them from the royal coffers; oversaw the conferral of degrees; could examine candidates himself and could lecture at academic exercises, if he so wished; and, if he decided to do so, he could even confer degrees without any examination at all. Moreover, when a new graduate received a degree, he had to swear loyalty to the emperor and had to agree to lecture at the university for 16 months.[22]

Toulouse (1229)

The eagerness of medieval authorities not only to support existing universities but also to found new ones shows the political and religious importance they attached to these institutions. The earliest papal university was that of Toulouse, founded by Gregory IX in 1229 under the provisions of the Treaty of Paris. This treaty, which was imposed by the French king Louis IX on Count Raymond VII of Toulouse at the end of the Albigensian Crusades (launched to suppress the Cathar heresy in southwestern France), required the count to establish a university at Toulouse.

The new university was to serve as a garrison of orthodoxy in the heart of the conquered land of heresy.[23] To finance it, Raymond was obliged to pay 4,000 marks to support 14 masters for 10 years. The university pay scale reflects the weight given to different subjects: 50 marks per year for the masters of theology, 30 for canon law, 20 for liberal arts and 10 for grammar.[24] Ironically, however, Toulouse would make its mark as a university of law because of the numerous job openings in southwestern France in that field.

Papal bulls of 1233 and 1245 conferred on graduates of Toulouse the *ius ubique docendi* and all the other privileges and immunities enjoyed by the masters of Paris. In the fourteenth century there were probably between 1,500 and 2,000 students studying at Toulouse.[25] The university would be rich in colleges, many of them well endowed: between 1243 and 1440 no fewer than 14 colleges were founded. Not all students opted for the clerical life. We are told that in about 1406 "les escolliers desdiz collèges, quant il leur plaist, se marient et sont gens lais" ("the scholars of these colleges, when it pleased them, married and became members of the laity.")[26]

Toulouse was not exempt from town-gown problems. According to contemporary reports, in 1332 five brothers from a noble family (the de la Pennes)—all of them senior ecclesiastics—were living together in a house in Toulouse while they studied civil and canon law. Peter de la Penne, the bastard son of their father, lived with them as a squire. After dinner on Easter Day, Peter, together with Aimery Béranger (also a squire of the household) and other students, began dancing with women in the street below the household, singing and shouting and beating out time for their impromptu dance by banging "metallic vessels and iron culinary instruments."

Hearing all this commotion, a *capitoul* (a municipal officer of Toulouse) and his men appeared on the scene and demanded that the riotous students surrender the long daggers they were carrying in defiance of the law prohibiting bearing arms in the city. The five brothers insolently refused to comply. When the *capitoul* tried to arrest one of them, they attacked him. Aimery struck the *capitoul* in the face with a dagger, cutting off his nose, part of his chin and lips, and knocking out or breaking 11 teeth. Physicians testified that if the *capitoul* ever recovered, which he eventually did, he would never again be able to speak intelligibly. Peter, for his part, killed one of the *capitoul*'s men outright.

The next day other *capitouls*, leading a mob of 200 people, seized the brothers and their squires and led them off to prison, pillaging the house in the process. Aimery was dressed like a layman: he wore "divided and striped clothes" and had a long beard. Even though the tonsure was said to have been plainly visible upon his head, the authorities rejected his claim to ecclesiastical immunity as a servant of clerics and instead treated him like a common criminal. Put to the torture, he confessed his crime and was sentenced to death. First his hand was cut off at the scene of the crime. He was then dragged by horses to the place of execution, where he was hanged. His body would remain dangling on the gibbet for three years.

In the meantime, the university had complained to the *parlement* in Paris about this gross violation of the royal privilege exempting scholars' servants from civil law. The *parlement* ruled in its favor. The *capitouls* who had led the mob were imprisoned, excommunicated, sentenced to pay enormous damages, and ordered to build a chapel for the slain man. The body was cut down from the gibbet and was given a solemn funeral, attended by 3,000 students. The city of Toulouse lost all its privileges and eventually had to pay a fine of 15,000 *livres tournois* ("Tours pounds," one of the numerous currencies used in France during the Middle Ages) to regain them. There is no record that Peter himself received any punishment for killing the *capitoul*'s man.[27]

Recalling the point made earlier (in the introductory essay Setting the Stage) about "the palpable uncertainty of life in medieval Europe," we can note here that the citizens of Toulouse suffered a number of grave setbacks during the fifteenth century. These must have affected university students and masters as well because of their sweeping nature. According to the medievalist Jacques Le Goff,

> Les habitants de Toulouse ... subirent, entre 1410 et 1443, six famines sévères, six pestes ou épidémies, huit grands incendies ou inondations, des opérations militaires ou des agressions de bandits pendant vingt ans, et deux importantes révoltes sociales. Des quatre ponts sur la Garonne qui existaient à la fin du XIII siècle il n'en subsista plus qu'un, les faubourgs disparurent, la population chuta d'un bon tiers.[28]
>
> [Between 1410 and 1443, the inhabitants of Toulouse were subjected to six severe famines, six outbreaks or epidemics of the plague, eight big fires or floods, military operations or bandit attacks for twenty years, and two major social revolts. Of the four bridges that spanned the Garonne River at the end of the thirteenth century, only one remained; the suburbs disappeared; and the city's population fell by a good third.]

Angers (1229)

An ancient cathedral school which gradually evolved into a university, Angers — like Orléans — profited from an influx of law students after the 1219 prohibition on teaching civil law in Paris. In 1229 Angers also welcomed many of the displaced students of the University of Paris when they had to find a university beyond the easy reach of the French king. It received in 1364 a charter from Charles V, which confirmed its preexisting status as a university and conferred upon it all the privileges and rights of the University of Orléans.[29]

A listing of the six student nations, as they existed in 1410, gives us good insight into the geographic origins of the students of Angers. These student nations were Anjou, including Tours; Brittany; Maine; Normandy; Aquitaine, which included Bourges, Bordeaux, Narbonne, Toulouse, and Auch; and "France," i.e., other parts of the country.[30]

Orléans (1306)

As mentioned earlier, by a bull of 1219 Pope Honorius III prohibited the teaching of civil law at the University of Paris because it had become so popular that it was threatening the primacy of theology. This meant that French students who wanted to study civil law had to make their way to Orléans instead. Thus by 1235 there was already a good law school in existence at Orléans, which was recognized as a *studium generale* by the mid–thirteenth century. Throughout the Middle Ages Orléans would grow until it became the best and most famous university of civil law.[31] During the era of the Hundred Years' War, for example, most of the members of the *parlement* of Paris had studied civil law there.[32]

In a bull of 1306 Pope Clement V, who had himself studied at Orléans, granted to it all the privileges that had already been accorded to Toulouse. Rashdall finds that the constitution of the new university "exhibits a remarkable compromise between the rival types of Paris [a masters' university] and Bologna [a students' university]."[33] For example, the ordinary affairs of the university were jointly administered by a special college consisting of professors and the 10 proctors of the student nations. These nations represented students from France, Germany, Lorraine, Burgundy, Champagne, Picardy, Normandy, Touraine, Aquitaine, and Scotland. The rector of the university was elected by the nations. The special college could not spend more than 20 *solidi* (a modest amount of money) in a single rectorship without consulting the student nations.[34]

Legal scholars trained at Orléans were quick to criticize the archaic and inconsistent qualities of *la loi coutumier* (the traditional, unwritten law based on local custom), which governed northern France. They had been trained in and were much more comfortable with the law of southern France, known as *le pays de droit écrit*, that is, the land of written, i.e., Roman, law.[35] Thus, in an ordinance of 1312, King Philip IV would praise Orléans for teaching a "fair and rational [written] law," which he described as remedying deficiencies in early royal legislation and as a marked improvement over customary law because it resulted in a more consistent administration of justice throughout the whole kingdom.[36] (Customary law did not exclude written law entirely but used it only where it did not conflict with local usage.[37])

In addition to its fame as a center for legal studies, Orléans was also a center for *dictamen* (rhetorical composition). Students put this skill to practical use in their letters home: "Dear Father, please send money." Moreover, one of the cleverest writers of Goliardic poetry, a man known to history only as "Hugh Primas" (Hugh the Primate, perhaps c. 1090–c. 1160,) is thought to have been a canon and teacher at Orléans. In 1142 he was described by a contemporary in these terms:

> In those days there flourished ... an academic named Hugh — whom his colleagues nick-named "the Primate" — wretched of aspect, misshapen of face. He had been imbued with secular literature from his earliest years, and the renown of his name grew radiant in diverse provinces, because of his quick wit and literary sensibility. Among his colleagues he was most elegant and quick-witted in making verses....[38]

Hugh may be the author of a rhyming two-sentence summary of the Old and New Testaments. It is surely the most concise description of these holy books:

> Quos anguis tristi virus mulcedine pavit.
> Hos sangui Christi mirus dulcedine lavit.
> [They who were so tragically seduced into tasting the poison of the serpent were joyfully washed clean by the saving blood of Christ.][39]

Finally, like most other universities, Orléans had its own share of town-gown riots. A good example dates from 1387. According to contemporary documents, it involved Jean Rion, a citizen of Orléans, and Guillaume Entrant, a bachelor of law at the university. Guillaume had seduced Jean's wife. Although Jean had forgiven him and Guillaume had promised to mend his ways, Guillaume nevertheless continued the affair. Jean therefore hired two thugs to murder him. They waylaid Guillaume when he was riding a horse outside of town, pulled him off his horse, and were prevented from killing him only by the timely arrival of help.

On a later occasion, the thugs were nearly successful. They wounded Guillaume "atrociously and inhumanly in the head and other parts of the body," cut off one of his fingers, left an arm dangling only "by a slender strip of skin," "tyrannically" pulled out an eye, and left him for dead. Somehow Guillaume survived and brought suit against Jean, claiming enormous damages. The court reduced the damages but ordered Jean to pay 300 *livres tournois* in compensation; a fine of 100 *livres tournois*; and, on bended knee and wearing only his shirt, to beg forgiveness from the court, from Guillaume, and from the proctor of the university. This sentence, however, struck the townsmen as being much too lenient and led to a general outbreak of rage against the students.

One was beaten and mutilated so badly that he was expected to die. A mob assembled "to the ringing of bells and the sound of trumpets"; houses were broken open and students pulled out and cast into prison. Although the townsmen threatened to kill all the students, they contented themselves by beating a student's servant and ransacking a house. The students, however, were so frightened that they fled to the outskirts of Orléans. The captain of the city guard rode through the outskirts with a band of his men, bellowing "death to the scholars!" One student was so frightened that he hid in a sewer "for a long time." In the end, the captain and his men had to do penance and pay a fine, part of which was to be used for a painting showing the offenders on their knees before the rector and other scholars.[40]

Prague (1347–1348)

Remarkably, until around the middle of the fourteenth century there was no university in Germany: students who wanted an advanced education had to go elsewhere, e.g., to the universities of France and Italy. The Holy Roman emperor King Charles IV (1316–1378) decided that establishing a university in Prague would help develop the intellectual and economic potential of Bohemia. He was extremely well suited to this project because he was a scholar himself, was fluent in five languages (Latin, Czech, German, French, and Italian), had been educated in France and was very receptive to French ideas.

The new university would be known as Charles University and, not surprisingly, it would be modeled on that of Paris.[41] In 1346 Charles IV sent to the pope a petition for a bull of foundation. The bull was issued by Clement VI the next year and was then followed by an imperial charter for the university itself. The new institution quickly attracted not only German but also foreign students: by 1400 there were about 4,000 students there.[42]

John Hus (a Czech religious thinker and reformer) was elected rector of the university in 1402. His followers became known as Hussites. The university was deeply caught up in the papal schism but the details of its involvement are not of great relevance to us here. What is important is that because the teachings of Huss (which echoed some of those of Wycliffe) were judged to be heretical, he was eventually excommunicated, condemned by the Council of Constance, tried, and burned at the stake in 1415.

Vienna (1365)

The foundation of the University of Vienna dates from a charter granted by Duke Rudolf IV in 1365. Conveniently ignoring the fact that universities never existed in Athens or in Rome, he ordered that a "general and privileged *studium*" be established in Vienna, "according to the ordinances and customs observed first at Athens, then at Rome, and after than at Paris."[43] Pope Urban V granted a bull of foundation in 1365; the constitution of the new university was modeled after that of Paris.

There were four student nations: the Austrian, including Italy; the Rhenish, covering western Germany and the rest of western Europe; the Hungarian, also embracing the Slavonic nationalities; and the Saxon, covering northern and eastern Germany, Scandinavia, and the British Isles.[44] The university reached its apogee during the rule of the Holy Roman emperor Maximilian I (r. 1493–1519), when it had more than 1,000 students. It was an early center of humanistic thought. Two chairs — one for Poetry and Rhetoric, the other for "Mathematical Disciplines" (i.e., the natural sciences) — were endowed in the newly formed *Collegium poetarum et mathematicorum* (College of Poets and Mathematicians), which was founded by Emperor Maximilian I and was incorporated into the university.[45]

Glasgow (1451)

Unlike St. Andrews, which was the first university in Scotland (founded in 1411), Glasgow has a well-documented history of its earliest years, consisting of the *Munimenta Universitais Glasguensis*, a complete collection of university documents from its inception until 1727. The University of Glasgow was founded by a bull of Nicholas V, who had been a student at and was later bishop of Bologna. The bull was issued at the request of William Turnbull, the bishop of Glasgow. Turnbull was well regarded. The king described him as his "well-beloved councillor," he held a doctorate in decrees, and had been custodian of the king's privy seal.

The university began auspiciously in 1451, its birth being marked by a sweeping indulgence (forgiveness of sins), which the bishop had procured for Glasgow. As a contemporary chronicle reports,

> That samyn yer [1451] the privilege of the universite of Glasqw come to Glasqw throw the instance of King James the Secund and throw instigacioun of master William Turnbull ... and was proclamit at the croce of Glasqw on the Trinite Sonday the xx day of June; and on the morne thar was cryit ane gret indulgence.[46]

The three Scottish universities — St. Andrews, Glasgow, and Aberdeen (the last was founded in 1494) — were all based on the Parisian model. Most of the students were arts undergraduates. There were four student nations at Glasgow, embracing students from Clydesdale, Teviotdale, Albany, and Rothesay. But Glasgow was always a small university and its survival was never certain. The lure of foreign universities was still strong: in the sixteenth century many Scots continued to study abroad.[47]

IX

Medieval Universities
and Humanism

In this chapter we shall set our sights high by trying to accomplish four things:

- Describe humanism, which helped change medieval education.
- Understand humanism's relationship with scholasticism, which was the intellectual powerhouse of the medieval universities.
- Examine some of the scholars who were great ambassadors of humanist thought and many of whom played a direct or indirect role in the theory and practice of education.
- Touch briefly on late scholasticism.

Humanism

There is an alluring vagueness about humanism because it cannot be corralled by a single explanation. The definitions offered by a modern dictionary variously refer to devotion to the humanities; literary culture; and the revival of classical letters, individualistic and critical spirit, and emphasis on secular concerns that characterized the Renaissance. For our purposes here, however, humanism can best be understood as follows:

(1) It was the philosophic belief that people are rational beings endowed with dignity, worth and a capacity for truth and goodness.

(2) It was a movement away from the contemplative religious ideal of the earlier Middle Ages and toward a more active involvement in public life and in intellectual, moral, political and even military action.

(3) It was a curriculum for secondary and university education between the fifteenth and seventeenth centuries.

The term "humanism" is relatively recent. It was coined only in the early nineteenth century — in 1808, by the German educator F. J. Niethammer who used it to describe academic studies that were distinct from scientific and engineering programs. The underlying concept, however, had a distinguished life of its own long before 1808. Humanism developed largely *outside* the framework of the universities, between about 1260 and 1400.[1]

Italian humanists generally were not attracted to academic careers. There were some exceptions: one fragmentary study, written in about 1943, lists 12 Italian university lecturers and professors who taught between 1396 and 1584.[2] Humanists were more inclined to seek employment as chancellors (between 1375 and 1466 five of the seven chancellors of Florence were famous humanists[3]); secretaries to powerful men; foreign affairs experts; officials of princes, cities and the church; court historians; tutors for the sons of the rich; self-employed free literati; and, after the establishment of the first printing press in Italy in 1465, as printers' assistants, editors and proof-readers.[4]

Italy was the cradle of humanism. This way of thought arose because some medieval men of letters, historians, moralists and statesmen began to tire of a sterile scholasticism that devoted its energies to creating and resolving innumerable logical paradoxes. They saw no purpose in such tedious intellectual gymnastics and began instead to champion the *aurea sapientia* ("golden wisdom"), which they held was embodied in the work of the philosophers and writers of the classic period.[5] It is impossible to determine precisely when humanism (or, to be more accurate, the early pre–Petrarch humanism of about 1260 to 1400) first became established in the universities; this depends upon how the term is defined.

Defensible dates include 1220 at the University of Valencia, 1315 at the University of Padua, and 1321 at the University of Bologna.[6] In 1369 the Florentine chancellor, Coluccio Salutati, mentioned the *studia humanitatis* ("studies of human things"), confident that this reference to the classics would immediately be understood by his erudite readers. In using this term, he was referring to all the academic disciplines other than theology and the natural sciences. These disciplines included the classics, poetry, grammar, rhetoric, ethics, history, literary studies, and politics and economics.[7]

Because by the thirteenth century (and increasingly thereafter) the law had become a lucrative profession, many of the leading humanists were initially trained as lawyers.[8] In the fifteenth century, the term *umanista* (humanist) was being used to describe a teacher who was a classical scholar and who specialized in teaching the *studia humanitatis*. Two terms came into use: *literae humaniores*, meaning the classic literature of Rome and the imitation of its literary forms in the "new learning" of humanism, and *literae sacrae*, referring the theological traditions of scholasticism.

Humanism reached its high-water mark in Renaissance Italy. By 1500 it was a recognized discipline there, strong in some universities, weak in others. It began as a movement to revive the Greek and Latin classics. In a letter of 1527, for example, the eminent humanist and Venetian noble Pietro Bembo (1480–1547) counseled an academic overseer who had asked him for advice: "You should not be so parsimonious with the professors of Latin and Greek whose letters are called humane. Indeed, they are the foundation of all learning."[9]

Humanism gradually spread into such diverse fields as politics, social relations, architecture, music, and medicine but the works of the orator-statesman Cicero (106–43 BCE) and the poet Virgil (70–19 BCE) were always especially valued.[10] Humanists believed that such classics had a twofold value. Not only did they teach a powerful style of Latin, which aspiring humanists wanted to emulate, but they also contained a great deal of practical advice on how to live a socially engaged, moral and effective life. Such a way of life was the avowed goal of many humanists.[11]

The celebrated Oxford medieval historian R. W. Southern (1912–2001) concluded that what he termed "scientific humanism" had a much longer history than was previously believed. Southern argued that academic developments from about 1050 to the end of the thirteenth century represent "the first great age of a humanism which is scientific rather than literary in character and aim."[12] He held that this humanism did not vanish suddenly, only to reappear with Petrarch 200 years later. It was instead, he claimed, "the first expression of a scientific humanism that went on developing for two hundred years until it was submerged in a sea of doubts and contradictions in the schools of the early fourteenth century."[13]

Southern held that this early humanism shared certain characteristic features: belief in the dignity of human nature; valuing introspection as an instrument of enquiry; cultivating friendly relations, with both fellow human beings and with God; and what he termed "systemic intelligibility," i.e., the conviction that it is possible for human beings to gain some knowledge of nature and of God.[14] A later medievalist, A. B. Cobban, qualified Southern's views somewhat but agreed that the features listed above were relevant to intellectual life in the medieval universities themselves.

Cobban confirmed that "the humanistic movement of the eleventh and twelfth centuries bequeathed a set of values that were firmly implanted in the universities."[15] Chief among these values were the belief in the dignity of man and in his capacity for intellectual and spiritual knowledge; a conviction that the universe is rationally ordered and is therefore accessible to rational human inquiry; and the expectation that man can influence his environment through his intellect, cumulative knowledge and experience.[16]

The progress of humanism in Italy was greatly encouraged by an unforeseen external factor: the influx of Byzantine, i.e., Greek, scholars who fled to Italy after Constantinople (today's Istanbul) fell to the Ottoman Turks in 1453. These scholars, fearing that their treasured Greek texts and commentaries would be destroyed by the Muslims, made them available to Western thinkers.

The rise of humanism in Italy also helped to revive the sagging fortunes of the lesser Italian universities, e.g., Florence, Sienna, Pavia, Ferrara, Pisa, Rome, and Naples. (Only Bologna, Padua, and possibly Perugia had continued to flourish.) During the fifteenth century leading humanists finally began to win university "rhetoric and poetry" professorships. Perhaps it was thanks to the leaven of humanism that the universities became more diversified: progress was made there not only in humanistic studies but also in logic, medicine, mathematics, natural philosophy and law.[17]

Humanism and Scholasticism

As an academic discipline, humanism was quite different from scholasticism but was not invariably antagonistic toward it.[18] Nevertheless, often there was no love lost, especially in the universities of northern Europe, between the partisans of the new wave of humanism and the old-guard advocates of scholasticism. (This conflict did not occur to the same extent in Italy because theology did not play such a major role in universities there.[19]) Northern humanists would argue that, under scholasticism, academic words and phrases had regrettably declined into mere abstractions entirely divorced from their historical and linguistic contexts. According to these humanists, if the Schoolmen refused to study patristics (the lives and backgrounds of the church fathers) and classical literary traditions, their traditional way of thought would be ethically unresponsive to new human interests and needs.

In return, university theologians in northern Europe complained that the humanists were interfering with the university's traditional work. The theologians said that the humanists "put their sickles into other men's crops" by erroneously using historical and philological criticism to interpret the sacred texts. In reply, humanists dismissed the Schoolmen as simply being out of touch with the needs of the real world. Passions ran high in this intellectual give-and-take. Conditions at the University of Leipzig, for example, had deteriorated to the point where in 1502 one humanist had this to say about the dead hand of scholasticism:

> We cannot go on as before, when one lecturer covered eight chapters in Jeremiah in 24 years and there are several doctors and holders of chairs who have given less than fifty lectures in Scripture in ten years or more.[20]

The academic atmosphere even at the conservative University of Cologne dripped with contention and dissatisfaction. As the German poet Konrad Celtes (1459–1508), who led a wandering life as a humanist professor of poetry and eloquence, put it:

> This is the city where I learned
> to proffer fraud and sophistry
> with syllogistic knots, as taught
> by dialectic with contentious tongue.
> [There was at Cologne] No teacher of Latin style,
> no student of smooth rhetoric...
> They laugh at learned poetry;
> the books of Vergil and of Cicero
> are feared by them more than the meat
> of swine is by the stomach of a Jew.[21]

Celtes was instrumental in the diffusion of humanism north of the Alps. The dukes of Bavaria honored him and his program of study by adding a humanist faculty to their university at Ingolstadt. He also won the honor of being the first poet laureate of Germany, a distinction conferred on him by Emperor Frederick III, who was thereby reviving an ancient practice of the Romans.[22]

Strongly held feelings were expressed in insulting terms by humanists and scholastics alike. In 1519 the humanist Willem Nesen issued an appeal to his fellow humanists: "If men of letters know what's good for them, they'll sharpen their pens and overwhelm [the scholastics] with a myriad of books. They don't deserve mercy. They are beasts, not human beings."[23] The German linguist Johann Reuchlin, whom we shall discuss later, certainly agreed. He railed that the scholastics were "more inhuman than brute beasts ... rather like pigs or sows delighting in their own filth and treading on the pearls of others."[24]

In his 1585 book *De la Sagesse* (*On Wisdom*) the French humanist philosopher Pierre Charron (1541–1603) took pains to equate the scholastic method with pedantry and obfuscation.[25] On the other hand, old-line Schoolmen must have recoiled in horror as they watched the new humanists cheerfully ignore the treasured, meticulous "thesis — antithesis — synthesis" paradigm of the dialectical thought, which had become an intellectual cornerstone of the medieval university.

Not all humanists, however, rejected scholasticism outright. Indeed, one or two would even champion it. Nevertheless, after a long-running intellectual tussle with scholasticism, humanism ultimately carried the day. In the late Middle Ages it must have seemed to contemporary observers that scholasticism had little exciting or new to offer. It is thus not surprising that by the middle of the fifteenth century the *studia humanitatis* had crept into the faculties of arts in Italian universities. By 1444 poetry, history, and moral philosophy would be added to the traditional academic disciplines there.[26]

By the fifteenth century a small number of humanists were teaching, chiefly in the Italian universities. Although these universities still showed a strong preference for medicine and law, a number of humanist chairs had already been established.[27] Humanist reforms in the French universities would have to wait until the sixteenth century, but within a few generations the brightest graduates of Italian universities were likely to be humanists. This was the result of a slow but growing academic acceptance of more rational approaches to experimentation, measurement, and philological and historical comparative analysis.[28]

A Sampling of Humanists

These scholars have been selected because they are skilled ambassadors of humanist thought and had a direct or an indirect influence on medieval education. Although many humanists were themselves university graduates, as noted earlier, in their professional callings they were usually not professors. Our chosen humanists are:

FRANCESCO PETRARCH (1304–1374)

Petrarch, an Italian poet, is renown for three reasons. The first, and for our purposes the most important, is that he was "the first humanist": his emphasis on classical thought set in motion the intellectual currents that gradually broadened into the literature and art of the Renaissance. The second reason is that *Canzoniere*, or *Songbook*, Petrarch's famous book of poems, written in the vernacular, i.e., in Italian, not in Latin, would become the greatest model for European love poetry in the Renaissance and beyond. Finally, Petrarch has also been hailed as "the first modern man" because of his sense of alienation and his wanderings. He wrote:

> I am a citizen of no place, everywhere I am a stranger.... When you compare my peregrinations with those of Ulysses, aside from the fame of his enterprise and his name, he wandered neither longer nor further afield that I have.[29]

Petrarch denounced scholasticism as a barbaric holdover from earlier medieval culture. It was, he held, simply an exercise in intellectual gymnastics, not a serious pursuit of knowledge. He argued that the Schoolmen were engaging in endless theological debates for no real purpose. He wrote: "He [the medieval dialectician] would rather fight than win ... he takes the greatest pleasure in arguing; he is not looking for the truth but for a fight."[30] By taking this forceful position, Petrarch rejected the dialecticians' implicit claim that their speculation would eventually lead them and their followers to a better understanding of God.

For these reasons, Petrarch was not slow to heap scorn on the Schoolmen. Here, for example, is an excerpt from *De vera sapientia* (*On True Wisdom*), a biting satire on doctoral ceremonies. It is thought to have been written after 1348 and has traditionally been attributed to Petrarch. This is what we learn from it:

> Un jeune imbécile s'approche du temple pour y recevoir les insignes de docteur. Ses précepteurs lui rendent hommage soit par amour, soit par erreur. Celui-ci rougit, le vulgaire est ébahi, les amis et la famille applaudissent. Sur ordre, il monte sur la cathèdre, regardant désormais tout de haut et murmurant je ne sais quoi d'inintelligible. Alors les plus éminents docteurs le portent aux nues à qui mieux mieux. Les cloches sonnent, les trompettes résonnent, on échange des baisers, des anneaux vont et viennent, on lui impose sure la tête bonnet rond et magistral. Une fois ceci accompli, lui qui était idiot redescend sage. Admirable métamorphose, inconnue même d'Ovide. Ainsi égaie-t-on aujourd'hui les savants.[31]
>
> [A young imbecile approaches the university's cathedral, there to receive his insignia as a professor. His tutors pay homage to him, either through affection or by mistake. He blushes, the common herd is much impressed, his friends and family applaud. On command, he goes up to the bishop's official throne, head up and murmuring something unintelligible. The most eminent professors praise him to the skies, each one outdoing the other. Bells ring, trumpets sound, kisses are exchanged, rings are given and received; a round magisterial cap is placed upon his head. Once all this has been done, the man who had been an idiot leaves as a wise man. An admirable metamorphosis, unknown to the Roman poet Ovid. Thus are scholars produced in large numbers today.]

Complying with his father's wishes, Petrarch studied law at the universities of Montpellier and of Bologna but did not enjoy this subject: in fact, he later complained that he had "wasted" seven years studying law.[32] When his father died in 1326, Petrarch returned to Avignon, where he had been raised, and took minor orders in about 1330. (Minor orders were the lowest and most numerous ranks of the clergy. They included porters, lectors, exorcists, cantors, acolytes and parish clerks. These men were permitted to marry but not to hold benefices.)

Today Petrarch is remembered primarily for his Italian love sonnets, especially for his poems to Laura, his unrequited love. In his own time, however, he was hailed for his works in Latin, for disseminating classical literature and for his famous letters. Beginning in 1351 he began to compile what would become 24 books of letters. These *Epistolae familiares* (*Familiar Letters*) were addressed to long-dead Greek and Roman personalities as if they were still alive. Petrarch hoped in this creative way to recapture the individuality, beauty and stylistic purity he found in classical works. Indeed, he believed that the lessons of the ancient life could help reinvigorate contemporary Christianity and that they could even ease the weighty burdens of disease, hunger and other medieval hardships.[33]

COLUCCIO SALUTATI (1331–1406)

Like Petrarch, Salutati, chancellor of Florence, was not a teacher himself but he was an early advocate of humanism and one of the most important political and cultural leaders of Renaissance Florence. His ideas influenced education indirectly. For example, he put the study of law, which specializes in the complexities of relationships between human beings, above that of medicine, which deals with the health of individuals. He also placed law above all the natural sciences because in his view they dealt only with *things*.

A skilled writer and orator, Salutati came to the defense of secular learning, upholding poetry and the classics as legitimate and, indeed, admirable ways to help Christians understand the Bible better. In 1405 he explained his approach in these words:

> First I shall show how we must understand the term poetry; next I shall make clear that the Holy Writ and divine Scripture is related to poetry ... thirdly I shall attempt, as far as is pertinent, to show that faithful Christians should not be forbidden to read pagan poets.[34]

He added: "I confess that sincere faith can be conceived without letters, but divine Scripture and the expositions of the doctors cannot be understood without them."[35]

Salutati spent much of his salary on books. He had about 800 of them — a large private library at the time. He discovered the hitherto lost letters of Cicero, which enhanced medieval scholars' understanding of Roman statesmen. Perhaps most importantly, he pioneered the model of a new kind of public official — one who was learned in the classics and who reflected in his personal life the Ciceronian ideals of eloquence, wisdom, duty and a commitment to the common good.[36]

LEONARDO BRUNI (C. 1370–1444)

Bruni was Salutati's disciple and succeeded him as chancellor of Florence. A prominent humanist in his own right and a strong advocate of a humanistic education, Bruni believed that those who ignored moral philosophy and devoted themselves to physical science were neglecting the truly important matters of life and were focusing instead on lesser matters that were basically foreign to them.

Bruni valued the *studia humanitatis* because it produced highly accomplished men who were willing to accept the burden of civic duties. His concept of education stressed the importance of practical experience and put heavy emphasis on historical studies. His own 12-volume *Historia florentini populi* (*History of the Florentine People*), a Latin history of Florence which celebrates the greatness of the city and its people, was extremely influential.

Bruni was the first historian to divide history into three successive stages, which he termed Antiquity, Middle Age, and Modern. Petrarch had described a "Dark Age" as extending from the fall of Rome to his own time. Bruni believed that since humanity had already reached the end of the Dark Age and was now about to enter the modern age, the intervening period must be the Middle Age. This secular interpretation of human history was widely imitated by humanist historians for two centuries after its appearance in 1442.[37]

Bruni also produced translations of Plato and Aristotle. These broke sharply with medieval tradition by giving readers a better sense of the original *meaning* of the Greek prose, rather than merely translating it word-for-word into Latin, as had previously been the practice. He did not shy away from controversy. In 1416, for example, he produced a new translation of Aristotle's *Ethics*, which was designed to replace an earlier translation by the revered scholar Robert Grosseteste. In a classic controversy between a humanistic translator and a scholastic theologian, Bruni denounced Grosseteste on the grounds that he had left a number of Greek words untranslated. Grosseteste, he complained, spoke "half Greek, half Latin, deficient in both languages, competent in neither."[38]

Guarino Veronese (c. 1370–1460) and
Vittorino da Feltre (c. 1373–1446)

Both these humanists worked hard to expand secondary school education in the Middle Ages. Using persuasion, example and reason rather than the traditionally harsh discipline of medieval schoolmasters, they led students, step-by-step, from elementary Latin up to the point where they were fully prepared for professional studies in a university.[39] Because these men founded the first humanistic school in Venice in about 1414 and influenced each other very closely, they can best be considered together. They were fellow students at the University of Padua in about 1400 and tutored each other there: Vittorino taught Guarino Latin, Guarino taught Vittorino Greek.

A summary of the topics in covered Guarino's *Regule grammaticales* (*Rules of Grammar*) shows how deeply medieval students were immersed in Latin grammar. This work deals with parts of speech; nouns; verbs, including concordance; and verbal syntax. This last subject is quite detailed, being subdivided into personals (active, passive, neutral, and common), impersonals, phonetics, interrogatives, appellative nouns, supines, gerunds, participles, comparatives, superlatives, relatives heteroclyte nouns, derivative verbs, patronymics, distributives, partitives, and figures.[40] In 1426 Guarino, a gifted linguist, also discovered a classic work on medicine — the *De medicina* of Celsus (42 BCE–37 CE) — which was then widely circulated and was later quoted by Leonardo da Vinci.

Vittorino, for his part, became a professor at the University of Padua in the early 1420s. According to his biographer, the insolence and licentiousness of the students displeased him so much that he resigned after only five months.[41] In 1423 he accepted the invitation of Gianfrancesco Gonzaga, marquis of Mantua, to become tutor to the ruling family and set up a school in Mantua. There Vittorino would spend the remaining 22 years of his life. His school was one of the first to apply the humanistic program, together with its implications in other arts and sciences, to the education of the young. In a sharp break with medieval tradition, it advocated close, friendly contacts between teacher and pupil and adapted the pace of teaching to the needs of the child.

The curriculum focused on Latin literature, Latin composition, and Greek literature. Great importance was attached to the study of Roman history as an educational treasure-house of great men and great deeds. Rhetoric was a central topic as well — not as an end in itself but as a way to channel moral virtue into political action. Other studies at Mantua included music, drawing, astronomy, and mathematics. Remarkably, in an age when the physical education of students was totally neglected (on the grounds that physical activity would heighten passions and would distract students from their academic pursuits), the meadows around the school at Mantua were turned into playing fields.

Vittorino summed up his community-oriented theory of humanistic education in these words:

> Not everybody is called to be a physician, a philosopher, to live in the public eye, nor has everyone outstanding gifts of natural capacity, but all of us are created for the life of social duty, all are responsible for the personal influence that goes forth from us.[42]

LORENZO VALLA (C. 1406–1457)

An Italian humanist, rhetorician, and educator, Valla studied under Leonardo Bruni and other accomplished teachers in Rome, from whom he learned Latin and Greek. He attended the University of Padua and in 1429 taught rhetoric there but had to leave after publishing an open letter poking fun at scholastic jurisprudence. Having taken holy orders, Valla became something of a wandering scholar, teaching for short periods at several Italian universities. He was also a prolific writer, attacking scholasticism and monastic asceticism and analyzing Latin grammar and the rules of Latin style.

As a result of these latter efforts, humanistic Latin would become refined, elegant and closer to its Roman roots. Yet the more it differed from the familiar church-based Latin of the Middle Ages, the harder it was for non-scholars to write Latin correctly. Ironically, Valla's search for linguistic purity in Latin would encourage others to write in the vernacular instead. At the same time, his own mastery of classical Latin resulted in a major historical discovery.

This involved a document known as the Donation of Constantine. The faithful naively believed that through this document the Roman emperor Constantine I, in thanks for having been miraculously cured of leprosy by Pope Sylvester I, had given the western portion of the Roman Empire to the church. The Donation of Constantine was often used to support papal claims to temporal power. In an essay of 1440, however, Valla proved that this document was a forgery. It could not possibly have been written at that time because its Latin clearly belonged to a later era — specifically, to a period four centuries after Constantine's death.

For understandable reasons, the church prevented Valla's essay from being published; indeed, it would not be published until 1517, when Protestant influence was increasing. The famous Dutch humanist and theologian Desiderius Erasmus, who will be discussed later, paid this tribute to Valla:

> Valla, a man who with so much energy, zeal and labor, refuted the stupidities of the barbarians, saved half-buried letters from extinction, restored Italy to her ancient splendor of eloquence, and even forced the learned to express themselves henceforth with more circumspection.[43]

GIOVANNI PICO DELLA MIRANDOLA (1463–1494)

This scholar was a philosopher and humanist whose avowed goal was to reconcile philosophy and religion; unlike most other humanists, he was quite sympathetic to scholasticism. The son of a minor Italian prince, Pico was a precocious child with an amazing memory. He learned Latin and possibly Greek at an early age. At the urging of his mother, in 1477 he enrolled at the University of Bologna to study canon law. When his mother died two years later, he decided to take up philosophy instead and went to the universities of Ferrara and Padua. He studied Hebrew and Arabic thought in Padua from 1480 to 1482 with Elia del Medigo, a Jewish Averroist, and learned to read Aramaic manuscripts with him as well.

His studies convinced Pico that it was possible and, indeed, highly desirable, to reconcile the contradictions in the various systems of thought he had encountered. He tried to do so by popularizing "syncretism," a philosophy that claimed all systems of thought contain some truth, which should be studied and defended. No single system, however, has a monopoly on truth. As a result, said Pico, scholars should try to expose the errors in each one.[44]

By 1485 Pico was studying at the University of Paris, the most important center for scholastic philosophy and theology. The next year he published *Oration on the Dignity of Man*, his most famous work and one which came close to being a manifesto of the Italian Renaissance.[45] In this book he used syncretism to draw ideas from many different sources, arguing that what gives dignity to mankind is the ability and the freedom to choose whether to be good or bad.

In 1486 Pico, then only 23 years old, issued a dramatic challenge to all of Europe's scholars. He drew up a list of 900 propositions, using ideas taken from Greek, Arabic, Hebrew and Roman thought, and invited scholars to travel to Rome at his expense, where he would publicly defend his views. Alas, this great debate never occurred: Pope Innocent VIII suspended it and named a commission to study the propositions. The upshot was that seven of them were declared to be unorthodox and six more were held to be dangerous.

Infuriated by this papal rebuff, Pico published a spirited defense of his beliefs. This act, however, only outraged the pope, who condemned all 900 propositions and reportedly muttered, "That young man wants someone to burn him!"[46] In 1487 the pope said of Pico's propositions:

> Elles sont pour partie hérétiques, et pour partie fleurent l'hérésie: d'aucunes sont scandaleuses et offensantes pour des oreilles pieuses; la plupart ne font que reproduire les erreurs des philosophes païens ... d'autres sont susceptibles d'exciter l'impertinence des juifs; nombre d'entre elles, enfin, sous prétexte de philosophie naturelle veulent favoriser des arts ennemis de la foi catholique et du genre humain.[47]
>
> [These propositions are in part heretical, in part the flower of heresy: several are scandalous and offensive to pious ears; most do nothing but reproduce the errors of pagan philosophers [e.g., Aristotle] ... others capable of inflaming the impertinence of the Jews; a number of them, finally, under the pretext of natural philosophy, wish to favor arts that are enemies to the Catholic faith and to the human race.]

Pico fled to France, seeking refuge at the Sorbonne, which supported some of his propositions. In 1488 he was arrested near Lyon and imprisoned at Vincennes, where he was permitted to receive visitors and was well treated. The University of Paris had not condemned his propositions and worked to get him out of jail. The pope eventually permitted him to be released. He moved to Florence and then traveled and wrote extensively.

Political instability in Italy gave increasing power to the Dominican friar Girolamo Savonarola (1452–1498), a charismatic, reactionary reformer who was deeply opposed to humanism. Pico fell under Savonarola's spell, gave away his own fortune, destroyed his own poetry and planned to become a monk. In 1494 Pico died under circumstances that are still unclear. It was rumored that he was poisoned by his own secretary, Cristoforo di Casalmaggiore, because the secretary believed that Pico had become too influenced by Savonarola. Whatever the reason for Pico's death, it was Savonarola who delivered the funeral oration. In 1494 the king of France, Charles VIII, who had invaded Italy, made a triumphal march through Pavia, Florence, and Rome. This event was reflected in the description of the funeral, which was written by Marsilio Ficino, Pico's teacher, who wrote:

> Notre cher Pico nous a quittés le jour même où Charles VIII entrait dans Florence, et les pleurs des lettrés compensaient l'allégresse du people. Sans la lumière apportée par le roi de France, peut-être Florence n'eût-elle jamais vu jour plus sombre que celui où s'éteignit la lumière de la Mirandole.[48]
>
> [Our dear Pico left us the same day that Charles VIII was entering Florence, and the tears of men of letters compensated for the joy of the people. Without the light brought by the king of France, Florence might perhaps

have never seen a more somber day than that which extinguished Mirandola's light.]

WILLIAM GROCYN (C. 1446–1519)

Grocyn was an English scholar and a friend of Erasmus. In 1465 he was elected to a scholarship at New College and became a fellow there two years later. By 1481 he was a reader in divinity at Oxford's Magdalen College. That year, in the presence of King Richard III, he held a disputation with John Taylor, professor of divinity. The king was so impressed by Grocyn's debating skills that he awarded him a generous present — a deer plus 5 marks, a tidy sum of money at the time.

Grocyn taught Greek at Oxford before visiting Florence, Rome and Padua from about 1488 to 1491. Later, as a lecturer at Exeter College at Oxford (Exeter is a college founded by Walter de Stapeldon, Bishop of Exeter, in 1314), he helped introduce English students to the new Greek learning. Grocyn was very generous to his friends — so generous, in fact, that he was often in debt himself and even had to pledge his silver serving platters and dishes (these constituted a prestigious and easily negotiable store of wealth in the Middle Ages) as security.

Grocyn had developed a close relationship with Erasmus and supported him financially when Erasmus was living in London. In return, Erasmus praised Grocyn with these warm words:

> Vir severissimae castissimae vitae, ecclesiasticarum constitutionum observantis-
> simus pene usque ad superstitionem, scholasticae theologicae ad unguem doc-
> tus ac natura etiam acerrimi judicii, demum in omni disciplinarum genere
> exacte versatus.[49]
> [A man of the most austere and chaste life, most strict in the observance of
> ecclesiastical rules, almost to the point of superstition, closely learned in
> scholastic theology, and by nature of the keenest judgment: in sum, closely
> acquainted with every kind of discipline.][50]

JOHN COLET (1476–1519)

Colet was an English churchman, an educational pioneer, the chief Christian humanist in England, and dean of St. Paul's Cathedral in London. He earned his MA from Magdalen College, Oxford, in 1490 and then went to Paris and Italy, studying canon law, civil law and patristics. Returning to England in 1496, he took holy orders there and settled in Oxford, where he lectured on the epistles of Saint Paul. In so doing, he replaced the traditional scholastic method of interpretation with his own reform-minded approach, shifting the emphasis from the intellectual to the devotional.

Some time before 1505, Colet took the doctor of divinity degree. His most famous sermon, preached at the London cathedral in 1512, combined a strong sense of human freedom and individuality (both products of the new humanism) with traditional ecclesiastical conservatism. At this time, there was widespread agreement about the need to reform the church: the burning question was how this could best be accomplished. Colet had a simple solution.

He argued that if the high officials of the church began *to reform themselves*, this would have a trickle-down effect and would soon improve the lower clergy and the laity as well. No new laws or onerous regulations would be needed. His sermon had a dramatic impact on the public because it used specific examples of the luxury, covetousness, sloth and simony of the bishops and senior clergy of England. As a result, Colet's own bishop, FitzJames of London, tried to have him convicted of heresy. This charge, however, was dismissed as frivolous.[51]

A scholar who disliked the dictatorship of exact definitions in theology, Colet had a rooted dislike of Thomas Aquinas and other Schoolmen who had, in his view, created an intellectual imperialism in which Christian doctrines were expressed with a dogmatic and tyrannous legal precision. Colet looked back instead to the earlier Christian thinkers and the Greek theologians who were not enmeshed in legalistic ideas. In his own writings, he emphasized the worth of the individual soul, attacked the abuses and idolatry he saw in the church of his day, and rejected the intricacies of scholastic thought.

Colet believed that the real goal of studying the Bible was to discover in it the personal message that the original writers, e.g., St. Paul, had wanted to convey to the reader. To make this discovery, argued Colet, it was essential that the reader first understand the political, economic and social milieu in which the early Christians lived and worked. This conviction led Colet to study the conditions of the Roman man-on-the-street during the first century CE. By being the first to introduce this new historical method of studying Scripture, Colet drew crowds of students and many learned men to his lectures at Oxford. They relished his novel method of teaching because it was so different from the traditional medieval method, i.e., studying Scripture simply by stringing quotations together, with little attempt at explanations.[52]

Today Colet is best remembered for his educational reforms. He allocated part of his great private fortune to endow St. Paul's School, a new institution where boys could learn Latin and Greek. Facilities for the school were built near St. Paul's churchyard in London. They consisted of a schoolhouse, a large schoolroom and houses for two masters. A celebrated grammarian, William Lilye, was appointed as the first headmaster. A chaplain lectured on divinity. With the help of his friend Erasmus, Colet produced a well-regarded and well-used Latin grammar book for use in the school. By 1758 this book had evolved into the *Eton Latin Grammar.*

Colet also wrote a series of rules for the guidance of his teachers and their students and a final set of statutes for the school. He refused to permit any ecclesiastical control over his school, on the grounds that transferring power from the clergy back to the laity was the only sure way to correct the evils that he saw investing both church and society. He held that to reform the church itself, the faithful must first revert to the thoughts and practices of early Christian society.[53]

JOHANN REUCHLIN (1455–1522)

A German humanist and a scholar of Greek and Hebrew, Reuchlin was the central figure in Germany for the study of these languages. After learning Latin at a local monastery school, he attended the University of Freiburg but did not graduate. Instead, thanks to his knowledge of Latin, he was chosen to accompany Prince Frederick to the University of Paris. There Reuchlin began to learn Greek, attached himself to the French scholar Jean Heynlin, and in 1474 followed Heynlin to the new University of Basel (Switzerland). Reuchlin discovered that he was a born teacher and took his master's degree in 1477. To support himself, however, he felt that he needed another arrow in his professional quiver. He therefore studied law at Orléans in 1478 and then at Poitiers, where he became licentiate in 1481 and sparred with the "obscurantists," i.e., the Schoolmen opposed to his humanistic methods and ideas.

He taught Greek at the University of Tübingen (Germany) before joining Count Eberhard of Württemberg in 1482 as an interpreter for the count's forthcoming trip to Italy. In Florence Reuchlin met many Italian scholars and so pleased the count that his employment became permanent. When he returned with the count to Stuttgart, he was given important posts in Eberhard's court. In 1496, however, Eberhard died and Reuchlin, to escape persecution by enemies, sought refuge in Heidelberg, which was then an important literary center. He translated the Greek authors and had a circle of private pupils. Philip, Count Palatine of the Rhine, hired him to direct the studies of his sons and in 1498 sent him to Rome to collect Hebrew books.

When Reuchlin returned to Heidelberg he found that a change of government made it possible for him to return to Stuttgart. In about 1500 he was given a high judicial office. This allowed him time to pursue his studies of Hebrew. In 1506 Reuchlin published his famous *De rudimentis hebraicis*, a Hebrew grammar and lexicon, which was based on the grammatical and exegetical tradition of the medieval rabbi David Kimhi. His expertise in Jewish studies was soon put to good use.

The emperor Maximilian appointed a commission to study a radical proposal, put forward by Johann Pfefferkorn, a Jew who had converted to Christianity, that all Hebrew books in the empire should be confiscated. The commission, which consisted mainly of theology professors from the University of Cologne, endorsed the proposal but Reuchlin dissented. He was subsequently arraigned before an inquisitorial court and was accused of favoring the Jewish religion. Reuchlin was acquitted in the first round of the trial but the prosecutor then appealed the case to Rome (the highest ecclesiastic court), where Reuchlin was found guilty and was forced to pay a fine. German humanists, however, hailed him as a hero and a martyr to their cause.[54]

THOMAS LINACRE (C. 1460–1524)

Linacre was the English humanist and physician after whom Oxford's Linacre College is named. He was instrumental, along with William Grocyn, in bringing humanism to Oxford. Educated at the cathedral school of Canterbury, Linacre was an excellent scholar. He entered Oxford in about 1480 and was elected a fellow of All Souls College four years later. (Academically, All Souls is still the most prestigious Oxford college. It was founded in 1438 by Archbishop Chichele of Canterbury as a memorial to those who died in the Hundred Years' War.) Linacre accompanied his patron, the prior of Canterbury, William Celling, to Bologna, where he studied under the Italian humanists and learned Greek. He took the degree of doctor of medicine (with great distinction) at Padua. When he returned to Oxford as a professor of philosophy, imbued with the learning and spirit of Italian humanism, he joined the circle of English scholars so praised by Erasmus.

When Henry VIII came to power, Linacre was appointed as his personal physician and also practiced medicine in London, where some of the great statesmen and prelates were his patients. He was a chief founder of the Royal College of Physicians and its first president. He willed both his house and his library to it. Linacre was an usually gifted translator — a true master of Greek. Erasmus even joked that in Linacre's translations of Aristotle (which unfortunately have not survived), Aristotle displayed a grace which he only rarely attained in Greek.[55]

JOHN FISHER (1469–1535)

Fisher, an English humanist, cardinal, and martyr, was (together with Erasmus) responsible for bringing humanism to the University of Cambridge. He had a singularly meteoric rise there. Fisher entered Cambridge in 1483; took his BA degree in 1487 and his MA 1491; became proctor of the university in 1494; master of Michaelhouse college in 1497; received his doctorate in theology in 1501 and that same year was elected vice-chancellor of the university. In 1502 he became the first holder of the prestigious Lady Margaret Professorship of Divinity, was named chancellor of the university in 1504, and was elected to that post for life in 1514.[56]

Fisher was an excellent teacher and played a key role in the evolution of Cambridge from a medieval university into a modern seat of learning. His strategy was to assemble funds, attract leading scholars from Europe, and encourage the study of Latin, Greek and Hebrew authors. Fisher also induced Erasmus to visit Cambridge. On the political front, however, Fisher's great personal integrity led to his downfall.

He strenuously resisted Henry VIII's claim to be head of the Church of England and refused to endorse the king's divorce of Catharine of Aragon and his subsequent marriage to Anne Boleyn. This stubbornness cost Fisher his life: he was beheaded in 1535, together with Thomas More. His head was stuck up on a pole on London Bridge but, ironically, its ruddy, lifelike appearance attracted so much public and anti-royal attention that within two weeks it was taken down and thrown into the Thames.

THOMAS MORE (1478–1535)

A celebrated English lawyer, author, statesman and martyr, More was the leading humanist scholar of his time. As a youth he served as a page to Archbishop Morton, who predicted that when he grew up More would be a "marvelous man."[57] The archbishop was right: much later, in 1520, a contemporary said of More, who was then 42 years old,

> More is a man of angel's wit and singular learning. I know not his fellow. For where is the man of that gentleness, lowliness and affability? And, as time requireth, a man of marvelous mirth and pastimes, and sometimes of as sad gravity. *A man for all seasons.*[58]

More studied at Oxford under Thomas Linacre and William Grocyn. One of his first works was a translation of a Latin biography of Giovanni

Pico della Mirandola, which would be printed by Wynkyn de Worde in 1510. Returning to London in about 1494, More was admitted to Lincoln's Inn in 1496 and became a barrister in 1501. (Lincoln's Inn is still one of England's four Inns of Court. For five centuries these unincorporated bodies of lawyers have had the power to call to the bar students who have met the requirements for the degree of Barrister-at-Law.) Later, among many other achievements, More served as high steward for both the universities of Oxford and Cambridge.

More's most famous and most memorable work is *Utopia* (1516), in which a fictional traveler, one Raphael Hythloday, describes the politics of an imaginary island nation known as Utopia. In our own time, the title of this book is still well known to many readers but its contents probably are not. For this reason, a brief summary may be useful here, even if it cannot convey how well written and how witty *Utopia* really is.

According to the narrator Raphael, in contrast to the violent, contentious life of European countries, Utopia is governed extremely well.[59] It is, in fact, a perfect country, being disciplined and highly regulated. There are 54 cities on the island, all as identical as possible; none may have more than 6,000 families. Magistrates are elected each year by 30 leading families. Gold is of no value; everything is free and flashy behavior and clothes are strongly discouraged. Only during their first days in Utopia do ignorant ambassadors from barbarian countries ever wear rich clothing and jewelry. Alcohol is not used. Slavery exists but in a humane form. No free person is idle but none is overworked.

Precocious youths can become scholars and will thereby be excused from manual labor but Raphael makes it clear that "if any of these fall short of those hopes that they seemed at first to give, they are obliged to return to work."[60] Students are educated to such a high standard that they exceed European logicians. The reason, Raphael explains, is that the students of Utopia

> have never yet fallen upon the barbarous niceties that our youth are forced to learn in those trifling logical schools that are among us; they are so far from minding chimeras, and fantastical images made in the mind, that none of them could comprehend what we meant when we talked to them of man in the abstract, as common to all men in particular (so that though we spoke of him as a thing that we could point at with our fingers, yet none of them could perceive him), and yet distinct from everyone, as if he were some monstrous Colossus or giant.[61]

Citizens of Utopia spend most of their leisure hours reading the many enlightening works that exist in their native language. These books are on a par with European learning. Farm families divide their time between city and country, passing two years at each location. Citizens can travel easily, thanks to a passport issued by the ruling prince. Women may not marry before the age of 18, nor men before 22. Premarital sex is prohibited, as are polygamy and adultery. There are no lawyers: citizens must defend themselves in court.

Although well trained for military service, the Utopians, hating war and being rich, hire mercenaries to fight their wars. There are different religions in Utopia. People are free to practice whichever religion they believe, but everyone must believe in one divine being and no one may believe that a person's soul dies with his or her body. Raphael hopes that European governments will be able to learn from the Utopians — a view that More clearly shares but does not believe will ever come to pass.

On the political and religious front, More is remembered for his adamant refusal to accept King Henry VIII's claim to be head of the Church of England. The result was that he was convicted of treason and was beheaded alongside Bishop John Fisher in 1535. More's final words were: "The king's good servant, but God's first."

DESIDERIUS ERASMUS (1466–1536)

We come now to that famous poet and man of letters Erasmus of Rotterdam, a truly remarkable Dutch humanist who has already been mentioned repeatedly in this book. Limitations of space make it impossible to discuss the productive life of this independent scholar in the detail it merits, but a brief summary is needed here.[62]

The illegitimate son of a physician's daughter, Erasmus first attended a school in Deventer (Netherlands), run by the Brothers of the Common Life, a religious lay community that in the fifteenth century produced some of the country's best teachers. When his parents died, his guardians insisted that he enter a monastery and become an Augustinian canon at Steyn (Netherlands). There he spent six or seven years. Erasmus came away from Steyn with an acute and permanent dislike of the monastic experience — but also with a genuine love for classical literature and classical thought that would last the rest of his life.

Henry of Bergen, bishop of Cambrai (France), appointed Erasmus as his private secretary because of Erasmus' skill in Latin and his reputation as a young but promising man of letters. In 1495 the bishop encouraged him to continue his studies in Paris. There Erasmus attended the Collège de Montaigu, an academically and religiously conservative institution. It was not part of the University of Paris, which was still the chief seat of scholasticism but was gradually being exposed to humanism. Erasmus took a profound dislike to the Schoolmen, with their cliques, intolerance, and hostility toward new ways of thinking.[63] He therefore devoted himself to biblical courses rather than to scholastic theology, supporting himself in the process by tutoring the sons of prominent European families. This teaching furthered his own career because he thereby met their fathers, who constituted, to use a classic English phrase, "the great and the good."

One of his aristocratic pupils was Lord Mountjoy, who invited Erasmus to visit England as his guest. Erasmus did so in 1499 and lived chiefly at Oxford, where (through the influence of John Colet) his dislike of the Schoolmen increased even further. He found that an intellectual battle was then raging in England: the Schoolmen were opposing the fruits of the Italian Renaissance, namely, the rediscovery of the classical learning of the Greeks and Romans. He had little good to say about legal studies in England. "The study of English law," he wrote, "is as far removed as can be from true learning, but in England those who succeed in it are highly thought of."[64]

Erasmus returned to Paris in 1500. The first edition of his *Adages*, a compilation of more than 3,000 proverbs by classical authors, was published in Paris in 1500. It confirmed his reputation as the leading scholar of northern Europe. Erasmus later moved to Louvain (a famous center for learning in what is now Belgium), where he declined a professorship. In 1505–1506 he revisited England and then went to Italy, where at Padua he tutored Alexander (the archbishop of St. Andrew's and an illegitimate son of James IV of Scotland) before making a visit to Rome. He found much that was corrupt in the papacy.

When Henry VIII came to power in England, conditions there seemed to Erasmus to be quite promising. So when in 1509 Lord Mountjoy encouraged him to make England his home, Erasmus did so. There he taught divinity at the University of Cambridge and in 1509 published *The Praise of Folly*, a hard-hitting satire on church and lay corruption, arrogance and incompetence. This work was addressed to his good friend Thomas More. Indeed, the Latin title of Erasmus' book, *Moriae Encomium*, is a play on More's name; it also means "the praise of More." Although Erasmus himself would have denied it vehemently, later reformers found that *The Praise of Folly* had helped prepare the way for the Protestant Reformation. This book has enjoyed enormous success from the author's lifetime down to our own day. In 1983, for example, the editor of the London office of the Yale University Press hailed it as one of the most intense and lively presentations of the literary, social and theological aims of humanism in northern Europe.[65]

To appreciate the witty quality of *The Praise of Folly*, let us see how Erasmus pokes fun at some of the most dignified medieval professions of his time. He writes:

Rhetoricians: "[They] think themselves in a manner gods if, like horse leeches, they can but appear to be double-tongued [a horse leech is a large blood-sucking leech that attacks the lips and mouths of horses], and believe they have done a mighty act if in their Latin orations they can but shuffle in some ends of Greek like mosaic work.... And if they want hard words, they run over some worm-eaten manuscript and pick out half a dozen of the most old and obsolete to confound their reader, believing, no doubt, that they that understand their meaning will like it the better, and they that do not will admire it the more by how much less they understand it.[66]

Grammarians: "... they think themselves the most excellent of all men, so greatly do they please themselves in frightening a company of fearful boys, with a thundering voice and big looks, tormenting them with ferules, rods, and whips; and, laying about them without fear or wit, imitate the ass in the lion's skin."[67]

Scholarly writers: "[They] hunt after immortality of fame by setting out [i.e., writing] books.... For they that write learnedly to the understanding of a few scholars ... seem to be rather to be pitied than happy, as persons that are ever tormenting themselves; adding, changing, putting in, blotting out, revising, reprinting, showing it to friends, and nine years in correcting, yet never fully satisfied; at so great a rate do they purchase this vain reward, to wit, praise, and that too of so few, with so many watchings, so much sweat, so much vexation and loss of sleep, the most precious of all things."[68]

Philosophers: "[They are] so much reverenced in their furred gowns and starched beards that they look upon themselves as the only wise men and all others as shadows. And yet how pleasantly do they dote while they frame in their minds innumerable worlds; measure out the sun, the moon, the stars, nay, heaven itself, as it were, with a pair of compasses; lay down the causes of lightning, winds, eclipses, and other like inexplicable matters; and all this too without the least doubting, as if they were Nature's secretaries, or dropped down among us from the council of the gods."[69]

Senior clerics: "... they look with haughtiness on all others as poor creeping things and could almost find in their hearts to pity them; while hedged in with so many magisterial definitions, conclusions, corollaries, propositions explicit and implicit, they abound with so many starting-holes [i.e., ways to escape] that Vulcan's net cannot hold them so fast, but they'll slip through with their distinctions, with which they so easily cut all knots asunder that a hatchet could not have done it better, so plentiful are they in their new-found words and prodigious terms."[70]

Monks: "And next come those that commonly call themselves the religious and monks, most false in both titles, when a great part of them are farthest from religion, and no men swarm thicker in all places then themselves ... they reckon it as one of the main points of piety if they are so illiterate that they can't so much as read. And when they run over their offices, which they carry about them, rather by tale than understanding, they believe the gods more than ordinarily pleased with their braying ... there is scarce an inn, wagon, or ship into which they intrude not, to the no small damage of the commonwealth of beggars."[71]

Rulers and courtiers: "[Rulers] leave all this care [i.e., the proper conduct of affairs of state] to the gods and are only taken up with themselves, not admitting anyone to their ear but such as know how to speak pleasant things and not trouble them with business. They believe they have discharged all the duty of a prince if they hunt every day, keep a stable of fine horses, sell dignities and commanderies, and invent new ways of draining the citizens' purses and bringing it into their own exchequer....

[Courtiers] are mere sots.... They sleep till noon and have their mercenary Levite [cleric] come to their bedside where he chops over matins [quickly runs through morning prayers] before they are half up. Then to breakfast, which is scarce done but dinner stays for them. From thence they go to dice, tables, cards, or entertain themselves with jesters, fools, gambols, and horse tricks."[72]

After 1514 Erasmus lived in Basel, England, and Louvain. The first edition of *Colloquia*, widely regarded as a masterpiece, appeared in 1519. By strongly attacking the abuses of the church, it helped prepare medieval men's minds for the subsequent works of the great reformer Martin Luther (1483–1546).[73] Erasmus also published the first Greek text of the New Testament (1516) and nine volumes on St. Jerome (1519). The goal of all these works was to put forward a more rational understanding of Christian doctrine and to free men's minds from the conceptual straightjacket of scholastic theology.

As Erasmus famously explained his campaign in a prefatory essay to the Greek New Testament,

I could wish that every woman might read the Gospel and the Epistles of St. Paul. Would that these were translated into each and every language so that they might be read and understood not only by Scots and Irishmen, but also by Turks and Saracens.... Would that the farmer might sing snatches of Scripture at his plough and that the weaver might hum phrases of Scripture to the tune of his shuttle, that the traveler might lighten with stories from Scripture the weariness of his journey.[74]

Erasmus always criticized scholasticism for its complex and ultimately meaningless arguments, pointing instead to the simplicity of the early church and the unpretentiousness of the church fathers as role models to be emulated. The proper test of theology, he held, was whether it was actually put into practice in a Christian lifestyle. Erasmus assures us that

He is truly a theologian who teaches not with syllogisms and contorted arguments, but with compassion in his eyes and his whole countenance, who teaches indeed by the examples of his own life that riches are to be despised, that the Christian man must not put his faith in the defenses of this world, but depend entirely upon heaven.[75]

The Lutheran revolt put Erasmus in an exceptionally difficult position. Schoolmen blamed him for upsetting the old intellectual and religious order. Lutherans, on the other hand, criticized him for refusing to press his opinions to their logical, i.e., pro–Lutheran, conclusions and for failing to side publicly with Luther. Caught in this crossfire, Erasmus left Louvain and, after spending six years in Freiburg, spent most of the remainder of his life in Basel. He edited the works of classical and patristic writers and continued to wage verbal wars. Attacked by theological conservatives and progressives alike, he even took on new adversaries, e.g., those humanists who, in his view, were making style more important than substance. Thanks to his continuing brilliance and achievements, his final years in Basel added to his already great fame.

Late Scholasticism

In fairness to scholasticism, it must be said that it did make an effort to respond to the challenges posed by humanism. The last outstanding representative of scholasticism was the Spanish Jesuit philosopher Francisco Suárez (1548–1617), who eventually settled at the University of Coimbra in Portugal and who taught a modified version of scholasticism there. It turned out to be a big step toward humanism because it focused on the needs of human beings, rather than simply on the demands of Aristotelian logic.

As a young man, Suárez was hardly a star student. He failed the entrance examination at the University of Salamanca (founded c. 1227) on his first two attempts and nearly abandoned his hopes for an academic career. He finally passed on his third try and then it was clear sailing for him. He would go on to teach philosophy and to write extensively on learned subjects: his works in Latin run to 26 volumes. Suárez was regarded by his contemporaries as one of the greatest living philosophers and theologians. When he visited the University of Barcelona, all the doctors of the university turned out to greet him, wearing the colorful insignia of their respective faculties. His *De Legibus* (*On Laws*) of 1612 was an early work on international law. It argued in favor of using reason to devise both laws and governments that were consonant with human nature. It held that laws must help people cooperate, so that they can work together to pursue their secular and spiritual goals.

Suárez argued that "natural" associations, such as the family, and spiritual associations, such as the church, had an inherent legitimacy. The state has to be ready and willing to use force if necessary to preserve law and order. The overriding goal of the government must be to help the public; if the government fails to do so and becomes tyrannical, it must be resisted and replaced. While states are permitted to wage war legitimately to defend their own lands or to protect innocent victims, war must be conducted in such a way as to minimize collateral damage to noncombatants. Later philosophers — notably Hugo Grotius (1583–1645), who is often called the father of international law — would draw on the teachings of Suárez.[76]

X

The Impacts of the
Universities on Medieval Life

The first sentence in the introductory essay of this book, Setting the Stage, is worth repeating here: the university is indigenous to Western Europe and is probably the greatest and most enduring achievement of the Middle Ages. Although it profited from earlier Greek, Roman, Byzantine and Arabic learning, it was really something new under the sun. Today the university still is — in countries free from political or religious authoritarianism — a uniquely flexible, resilient, voluntary community of students and professors who are accorded certain rights and responsibilities so that "gladly wold they lern and gladly teeche."

The medieval university's privileges, which are echoed in most universities today, included:

- A good deal of autonomy, e.g., the ability to draw up and enforce its own regulations; to recruit, reward and punish its own members; and to offer public and private advice on the major intellectual, religious, political, economic and social issues of the day.
- The freedom and, indeed, the encouragement to research, to teach, and to write about a great range of subjects, not only for their practical applications (e.g., law and medicine) but also, more idealistically and therefore much more rarely, for *amor sciendi* — the love of knowledge for its own sake.
- The exclusive right to award publicly recognized and socially valued degrees from the faculties of liberal arts, theology, law, and medicine — for example, the bachelor's degree, the master's degree, and the doctorate.

Centers of advanced learning had existed elsewhere in the world before the university itself came into being in Western Europe. One can note the philosophical schools of Athens, dating from the fourth century BCE; the law school of Beirut, which flourished between the early third and mid–sixth centuries; the imperial academy of Constantinople, founded in 425; and Al-Azhar, Cairo's center of Islamic jurisprudence, established in about 970. Other examples, e.g., of Chinese, Indian and Jewish centers of learning, could probably be found by specialists in these fields. Yet as the French medievalist Jacques Verger puts it categorically,

> No one today would dispute the fact that universities, in the sense which the term is now used, were a creation of the [European] Middle Ages, appearing for the first time between the twelfth and thirteenth centuries. It is no doubt true that other civilizations ... were familiar with forms of higher education which a number of historians, for the sake of convenience, have sometimes described as universities. Yet a closer look makes it plain that the institutional reality was altogether different and ... there is no real link such as would justify us in associating them with medieval universities in the West.[1]

As stated in chapter I, the university arose, uniquely, in medieval Europe at a special time and for special reasons — the need to expand the scope of higher education to meet the growing demands of an increasingly literate, prosperous, urbanizing society, and the need of students to organize themselves to prevent exploitation by townsmen. In this last chapter we will try to summarize the impacts of the universities on medieval life at five different but mutually reinforcing levels: *personal, intellectual, political and legal, economic,* and *cultural.* A brief epilogue will discuss the universities of the Renaissance and Reformation.

Impacts on the Personal Level

In the relatively static societies of medieval Europe, there were not many avenues for upward social mobility. The universities gave ambitious men a solid foothold on the career and social ladder. University students who graduated with what the British now call "first class degrees" were ideally positioned for rapid advancement in the church, law, medicine, royal government, city administration, and education. The French medievalist Jacques Verger gives us some examples:

> Il est également manifeste que l'université était une voie d'ascension sociale, surtout pour ceux qui parvenaient à obtenir une licence ou un doctorat d'une faculté supérieure. Dès le XIIIᵉ siècle, le royaume d'Angleterre venant sans

doute en tête, une bonne partie du haut clergé—évêques et dignitaires capitu-laires, cardinaux, abbés ou supérieurs d'ordres religieux—était constituée de gradués en théologie or en droit. On en trouvait aussi dans l'entourage des princes—on pense aux fameux "légistes" des rois de France—sans parler de tous ceux dont on peut suivre les belles carrières de médecins, de juges ou de podestats.[2]

[It is equally clear that the university was a path of social advancement, especially for those who were able to earn a teaching license or a doctorate from a higher faculty. Since the thirteenth century, with the kingdom of England clearly taking the lead, a large part of the higher clergy—bishops and chapter house dignitaries, cardinals, abbots or heads of religious orders—con-sisted of university graduates in theology or in law. Similar university-trained officials could also be found in the entourage of princes—here one thinks of the famous legal specialists of the kings of France. Many other university grad-uates took up respected careers as doctors, judges or city magistrates.]

Some aspects of university life were collective but the university expe-rience as a whole can be seen as a crucible of Western individualism. A stu-dent succeeded or failed academically almost entirely as a result of his own efforts, not because of his social standing. Medieval students—and, of course, their parents, who had to pay the bills—obviously believed that a univer-sity education was a wise long-term investment. This is clearly shown by its growing popularity during and after the Middle Ages.

As the number of viable universities increased from the original 3 in about 1200 to perhaps as many as 66 in 1500, the number of students increased as well. The only reliable estimate we have on total student num-bers is that between 1348 and 1505 there were some 200,000 German uni-versity students.[3] No other firm figures are available but it is estimated that during the medieval era as a whole a total of about 750,000 students attended the universities.[4] The appeal of the universities was such that even the stu-dents who did not graduate must have enjoyed the wine, women and song of undergraduate life and must have recommended this liberating experi-ence to their friends at home.

The university offered not only intellectual training but also practical skills for upwardly mobile students. For example, Thomas Sampson, an Oxford teacher, ran what amounted to a management school in Oxford between about 1360 and 1409. By using cram courses, he taught students a good range of useful administrative skills, e.g., how courts should be held, how to deal with the coroner's office, and how a clerk should handle his lord's money. Students also studied hypothetical letters drafted by Sampson him-self.

The most self-serving of these purports was from a father whose son was studying at Oxford for a bachelor of arts degree. According to the letter, the father just heard that a certain earl would like to take the student into his service. The father therefore instructs his son to stop studying for his degree, to enroll with Sampson for one year to learn letter writing, composition and accountancy, and to pay Sampson 100 shillings "to be sure that he is well taught." Another hypothetical letter, written of course by Sampson, boasts that "Thomas Sampson is incessant in teaching his pupils."[5]

Impacts on the Intellectual Level

The universities surfed the great wave of the intellectual renaissance of the twelfth century, which, as noted earlier, actually extended from about 1050 to 1250. It reintroduced Europeans to Greek learning and Roman law; encouraged the universities and their graduates to play pivotal roles in law, theology, philosophy, science, literature and scholarly debate; and strengthened reliance on classic authorities, commentaries and rational proofs. Even more important, academic credentials would become a major requirement for jobs in many fields. Based on personal effort rather than on birth and property, these credentials would play a growing role in the gradual modernization of medieval society.[6]

Conscientious university professors shouldered heavy responsibilities. In a teachers' manual of 1255 the Italian law professor Martino da Fano explained that if he wanted to do his job properly a master had to meet the following stiff criteria:

> Il doit enseigner les choses nécessaires; répondre rapidement et de façon satisfaisante aux questions que lui posent les étudiants; supporter volontiers la contradiction; donner des bases solides à ses assertions en se fondant l'Écriture sainte.
>
> Voici quelles seront les questions que Dieu posera au maître, quand celui-ci se présentera devant lui:
>
> > – "A quelle fin as-tu étudié?"
> > – "Comment as-tu 'lu' (enseigné)?"
> > – "Comment as-tu prêché?"
> > – "Comment as-tu 'disputé'?"
> > – "As-tu été zélé?"[7]

[He must teach the things that are necessary; reply quickly and accurately to questions posed to him by the students; put up, willingly, with being contradicted; give solid reasons to his assertions, basing them on the Bible.

Here are the questions God will pose to the professor, when the professor stands before him:

- "Toward what goal did you study?"
- "How did you 'read' (teach)"?
- "How did you preach?"
- "How did you 'dispute'? [conduct academic disputations]
- "Were you eager about teaching?"]

Despite the efforts of the conscientious masters, humanists and their successors often denounced the universities as ivory towers that devoted all their energies to academic hairsplitting, thus ignoring the more pressing day-to-day needs of medieval society. It was the humanists who so memorably criticized the scholastic philosophers for arguing about how many angels can dance on the point of a needle. (Although this problem had indeed once been raised, it was done purely as a deliberately humorous exercise for undergraduate students of scholastic thought, not as a serious intellectual challenge.[8])

We can now see that such criticisms of the universities were misplaced. The medievalist A. B. Cobban was certainly right when he concluded that

A popular view in the past has been that the universities turned out hordes of dialecticians who were without any immediate professional or social value: in other words, graduates who would require a reorientation in outlook and a basic retraining to fit them for the world of secular or ecclesiastical employment. But it is not really plausible that Western medieval society would have continued to give of its limited surplus wealth for so long to support social parasites living a fantasy existence in ivory towers.[9]

Medieval society was willing to pay for the long, costly education of its university students only because these young men were in great demand and were needed to keep church and state running smoothly. As Cobban explains,

Medieval university education, at all but the most rarefied levels, was considered to be socially useful, providing a range of intellectual skills germane to community functioning.... In a legally-oriented society of competing rights and privileges, conferred by a hierarchy of authorities and jealously guarded, there was endless scope for the utilization of the dialectical and disputational expertise of the graduate in law.... The same type of dialectical subtlety was required in the diplomatic service.... There were also good opportunities for the harnessing of dialectic and rhetoric to the service of propaganda ... the theological and philosophical *studia* were more absorbed in the direction in which society was or *ought to be* progressing. This combination of the empirical and the abstract ... bore a direct relevance for the ordering and creative forces in society.[10]

Impacts on the Political and Legal Level

Through the jobs held by their graduates, especially the lawyers, medieval universities increasingly put the day-to-day administration of affairs into the hands of educated men. Although royalty still held a monopoly on power, kings and princes were forced to rely, more and more, on the carefully honed skills of university-trained lawyers and other technocrats. Indeed, Rashdall argues that

> From a broad political and social point of view one of the most important results of the universities was the creation, or at least the enormously increased power and importance, of the lawyer-class. Great as are the evils which society still owes to its lawyers, the lawyer-class has always been a civilising agency. Their power represents at least the triumph of reason and education over caprice and brute force.[11]

However, in England during the late fourteenth century theologians at Oxford and Cambridge were quick to complain about the "money-hungry lawyers" who were taking their places at the universities. Such lawyers, the theologians claimed, were corrupting both the church and medieval society as a whole. This shift from theology to law is clearly evident among the English bishops: the majority had their highest degree in law, not theology. The tide toward law in England soon gathered force, to the extent that by the fifteenth century, as one medievalist has put it, both church and university had become "immoderately legalistic."[12]

The shift was evident, too, on a much smaller, personal, level: the short life of an ill-fated student named Walter Paston. His story is relevant here not only for substantive reasons but also because it gives us one of the few opportunities to hear the words of a medieval student himself.

The Pastons were a prominent English family living in eastern Norfolk during the fifteenth century. The Paston Letters, now preserved mainly in the British Library in London, constitute the largest surviving collection of English correspondence from this period. They reflect the family's trials and tribulations during a long series of lawsuits over ownership of a number of manors in Norfolk and Suffolk, particularly the estates of Sir John Fastolf around Caister Castle. More important for our purposes here, they also provide unique, candid insights into aristocratic life in this part of England in the late Middle Ages.[13]

The Paston family had initially wanted young Walter to enter the church after he earned his BA degree at Oxford, but his mother Margaret urged him not to present himself for ordination before he was old enough to be sure of his vocation. As she put it with her usual clarity and good sense, "I will love hym better to be a good secular man than to be a lewit [lewd] priest."[14] By the time of Walter's graduation the family had decided that he should be trained as a lawyer at one of the Inns of Court in London, rather than becoming a priest.[15] By March 1479 Edmund Alyard, Walter's tutor at Oxford, could reassure Margaret about her boy's career: he was to go into law, after first earning his Oxford BA.

When Walter graduated in the summer of 1479 and the customary "determining feast" was held at Oxford (this was a party to celebrate the awarding of the BA degree), he wrote to his mother:

And yf ye wyl know what day I was mead Baschyler, I was maad on Fryday was sevynyth, and mad my fest on the Munday after. I was promysyd venyson ageyn my fest of my Lady Harcort, and of a noder man to, but I was desevyd of both; but my gestes hewld them plesyd with such mete as they had, blyssyd be God. Hoo have yeo in Hys keeping. Wretyn at Oxon, on the Wedenys day next after Seynt Peter.[16]

[And if you want to know when I received my BA degree, it was a week ago last Friday; my feast was held on the following Monday. Two people — Lady Harcort and a gentleman — had promised to provide venison for the feast but they let me down. Nevertheless, my guests said they were happy with such food as they had — thanks be to God, Who has you in His care. Written at Oxford on the next Wednesday after St. Peter's Day.]

Sadly, only weeks after his graduation Walter fell seriously ill, probably due to a recurrent epidemic of the plague. He was brought from Oxford to be cared for at home in Norwich, where he made out his will and died soon after.[17] He had very little to leave to others: a number of academic gowns (willed to Oxford friends) and some sheep and lands (left to his own family). No books are mentioned in Walter's will. Perhaps they had been sold to pay for the feast, usually an expensive undertaking, or perhaps he never had any of his own. As an undergraduate, he would not have been permitted to use the glorious but still-unfinished Duke Humfrey's Library at Oxford. On the other hand, he must have had access to the more modest libraries, where scholarly works, chained up to prevent theft, could be read free of charge. The cost of Walter's illness and funeral was about 30 shillings.[18]

On the political and legal front, one thing was sure:

Les grandes universitaires, et spécialement les plus élevés d'entre eux (maîtrise en théologie, doctorat en droit), jouissaient à la fin de Moyen Age d'un grand prestige.... Le docteur était *vir eximiae scientiae.* Son nom s'inscrivait sur la liste des "autorités," anciennes et modernes, dont les avis définissaient l'"opinion commune," qui était une des sources du droit.[19]

[The senior men at the universities, especially the most exalted among them (those holding masters of arts degrees in theology or doctorates in law) enjoyed an enormous prestige.... The academic doctor was hailed as "a man of the highest knowledge and learning." His name was inscribed on the list of ancient and modern "authorities" whose opinions constituted the "collective opinion," which was one of the sources of the law.]

As the dominant university of Western Europe, the University of Paris played a major role in many highly charged political and legal controversies. Some of the clearest examples are:

- The Western Schism of 1378–1417, when it acted as an adviser to the French king and also provided a sizeable proportion of the personnel of the French government.[20]
- The first trial of Joan of Arc (1431), when it was instrumental in bringing her to the stake.
- The long-running "dual monarchy" crisis of the Hundred Years' War (not finally resolved until 1446), which arose because the English, who controlled over 40 percent of the territory of France and the majority of its population, claimed that their presence amounted to a dual Anglo-French monarchy. Most of the French south of the Loire (except for Gascony) never recognized the English claim as being legally valid. The University of Paris took a pacifist position in this dispute and tried to play the rival parties off against each other to protect its own rights and privileges.[21]

Impacts on the Economic Level

The universities had strong, favorable impacts on the commercial life of their host cities, which were their sole source of food, lodging and other necessities. We can get a good idea of what this involved by looking at the contents of John of Garland's Latin vocabulary. As mentioned earlier, to help his students master Latin, John prepared a descriptive vocabulary of the people, professions and objects the students would see during the course of a stroll through the streets of Paris. He listed only a handful of them: according to a *Livre des métiers* (*Book of Trades*) of 1262 there were about 100 different trades in the city.[22]

The presence of a university meant more business for the merchants we meet in John's vocabulary. Although most students were not rich, they did have enough money to patronize, at least occasionally, some of John's book sellers, stationers, poultry dealers, money changers, goldsmiths, saddle and glove makers, furriers, cobblers, apothecaries, wine salesmen, fruit and vegetable sellers, bread and pastry makers, butchers, purveyors of roasted pigeons and geese, and hawkers of uncooked pâtés of beef, pork and mutton — seasoned with garlic and rich sauces.[23]

Impacts on the Cultural Level

The universities supported the status quo in the Middle Ages. They upheld social and religious orthodoxy. The popes endorsed them because they could provide a rationally intelligible defense of Christianity. This helped to clarify Christian doctrines, e.g., by laying out the correct party line, and thus strengthened the popes' hands in their campaigns to suppress heresy. The universities also helped shore up the temporal powers of the papacy against rival claims by regional feudal lords. Finally, the universities provided for the popes a reliable supply of highly intelligent, disciplined, ambitious men who were well qualified to staff the senior offices of the church.[24] Once appointed to such offices they usually worked hard, did a good job, and reflected credit on their superiors.

The University of Paris was well aware of the central role it played in medieval culture. The chancellor of the university, Jean Gerson, even claimed in 1405 that through its four faculties the university "represented" the sum of accessible human knowledge, both in theoretical and in practical terms. He added that by recruiting its members from all over Western Europe it also served as a microcosm of human society. It was, he said, the best of all possible interpreters of the public good and its advice should therefore be heeded by the society at large.[25]

Epilogue: The Universities of the Renaissance and Reformation

Modern scholars agree that, as the medievalist Jacques Verger put it, "Les universités de la fin du Moyen Âge ont longtemps eu mauvaise presse." ["Universities at the end of the Middle Ages have for a long time had a bad press."][26] Paul Grendler, an expert on the Renaissance, gives us what he calls the "stereotypical judgment on Renaissance universities." It holds as follows:

> Renaissance universities were conservative homes of outmoded knowledge. Professors droned on about Aristotle when they should have been teaching Copernicus and Galileo. Innovative research and religious revolution went on outside the lecture halls. Students came to the university only to get the all-important arts or law degree that would give them entry into the expanding bureaucracies of government, the important area of life. Once in the university, they spent their time brawling and laying siege to the virtue of the women of the town.[27]

A third scholar, the medievalist Léo Moulin, holds that medieval universities ended up being controlled by civil and religious powers — to such an extent that they became pawns or even active participants in nonacademic quarrels and rivalries. The shameful role played by the University of Paris in the case of Joan of Arc is perhaps the best example here. University teaching itself was unreceptive to the new and more liberal currents of Renaissance thought. Indeed, it soon ossified and became the butt of jokes and the target of criticism by more enlightened commentators.[28] Yet all this, true as much of it is, should be seen as only one side of the story.

The most penetrating question we can ask is this: if medieval universities were indeed in such bad shape near and after the end of the Middle Ages, why were many new ones were being formed? It is striking that some 49 new universities were founded between 1400 and 1625. They were located as follows[29]:

Spain	8
France	9
Netherlands and Belgium	3
Switzerland	2
Italy	7
Germany	14
Scotland	4
Scandinavia	2

(England did not found any new universities during the Renaissance but both Oxford and Cambridge added several new colleges then.)

The answer to our question must be that the universities, despite whatever shortcomings they may have had, continued to play vital roles in postmedieval life. If potential founders had not seen the need for more universities, they would certainly have directed their money and energy elsewhere. In fact, however, European universities enjoyed one of their most productive periods during the Renaissance and Reformation.[30] They successfully educated Europe's scholarly, civic, and church elites and trained a large number of Latin schoolteachers.

Administratively, the Italian universities of that time were unstructured, a fact that seems to have encouraged scholars to undertake more research on their own. More fundamentally, this trend reflected the new importance that the Renaissance was giving to innovation: Italian scholars were trying to break new ground in law, medicine, philosophy, mathematics, and the humanities and were often succeeding. The other side of the coin was that the German universities, for their part, were rigorously structured. This may have given them the confidence and solidity needed to introduce far-reaching changes into religion and society. The best example here is the University of Wittenberg, where Martin Luther taught and where he became the dominant figure.

In summary, it is a reasonable guess that Italian university professors shifted the direction of scientific scholarship through their own innovative research, while German universities and professors profoundly affected Europe by ushering in the Reformation.[31] Nevertheless, times were changing during the latter half of the seventeenth century. Universities now had to deal with profound religious divisions, e.g., the splitting of Europe into Catholic and Protestant spheres; international and civil wars; plagues; professorial absenteeism; unruly students; intellectual conservativism; and competition from the new Catholic and Protestant schools of Europe, which seriously eroded the universities' former competitive advantage. The end result was that the universities ultimately lost the preeminent place in higher education that they had held before and during the Renaissance.[32]

Appendix 1: A University Student's Possessions

Lightly edited, this is an inventory made on 26 August 1345 following the death of a student at the College of Saint-Nicholas d'Annecy in Avignon. It lists all his possessions.[1]

- 13 livres de droit civil et canonique; textes des deux *Corpus juris* et commentaires.
- Des *Répétitions* reliées ensemble, sur papier, couvertes de parchemin ... écrites d'écritures diverses.
- Un vêtement long, vert, pour l'été, fourré d'agneau noir.
- Un autre, court, pour aller á cheval, de drap noir, fourré de fourrure noire.
- Un autre vêtement simple, de gros drap.
- Une veste de futaine, avec une bourse de soie.
- Un vieux capuchon de drap noir.
- Une paire de chaussures noires, déjà portée.
- Une autre paire de chaussures neuves, noires, et une pointe de capuchon ...
- Un vieux capuchon noir, de faible valeur.
- Un coffre de sapin, neuf ... où on a trouvé ce qui suit: un acte relatif au collège Saint-Nicolas; six vieux draps, bien déchirés, pratiquement sans valeur; dans une bourse de velours noir, deux écus d'or, un salut d'or, trois florins d'or, quatre ducats d'or; en gros du pape et du roi, 19 florins; une épée avec une paire d'éperons; une ceinture d'argent ... à la mode nouvelle; un béret d'écarlate, presque neuf.
- Un autre coffre de sapin, vieux, de faible valeur, dans lequel on a trouvé deux pièces de tissu bleu foncé.

- Une pièce de toile de sept cannes, bonne mesure, qui appartiendrait au collège.
- Cinq bonnes chemises et une de faible valeur.
- Un petit livre de médicine, en papier.
- Un banc, avec sa roue, où il étudiait.
- Une couverture noire, de serge.
- Un matelas, avec un coussin de plumes et deux couvertures, une blanche et une rapiécée; des draps de diverses couleurs, possédés en commun par le défunt et un autre étudiant.
- Une robe de drap bleu foncé, doublée de toile rouge, et le capuchon correspondant, vert ...

Translated, this list reads:

- 13 books on civil and canon law, plus texts of the 2 volumes of the *Corpus juris*, and commentaries on them.
- *Repetitions*, bound together and covered with diverse writings.
- A long green garment, trimmed with black wool, for summer wear.
- Another garment, short, made of black woolen cloth, trimmed with black fur, for horseback riding.
- Another simple garment, made of heavy woolen cloth.
- A jacket made of strong cotton and linen fabric, with a silk money purse.
- An old coat made of black heavy woolen cloth.
- A pair of worn black shoes.
- Another pair of shoes, new, black, and the hood of a jacket.
- An old black jacket of little value.
- A new chest made of fir and containing a regulation relating to the College of Saint-Nicholas; six sheets, thoroughly torn, of no real value; a velvet purse containing various gold coins and 19 florins; a sword and a pair of spurs; a money belt ... made in the new style; a scarlet beret, almost new.
- Another fir chest, old and of little value, containing two pieces of dark blue cloth.
- A long piece of cloth, belonging to the college.
- Five good shirts and one shirt of little value.
- A small paper book on medicine.
- A moveable bench for studying.
- A black cloth blanket.
- A mattress, with a feather-filled pillow; two blankets, one white and the other patched; and sheets of diverse colors, jointly owned by the deceased student and another student;
- A dark blue robe of heavy cloth, lined with red cloth, with an attached green hood.

Appendix 2: Three Excerpts from Peter Abelard's Historia Calamitatum (The Story of My Misfortunes)[1]

1. In Chapter III of his Historia Calamitatum, *Peter Abelard recounts what happened when he went to Laon to learn from Anselm, a famous French theologian whose interlinear gloss on the Bible was one of the great intellectual authorities of the Middle Ages. Abelard writes:*

[Anselm] had a miraculous flow of words, but they were contemptible in meaning and quite void of reason.... I went to his lectures less and less often, a thing which some among his eminent followers took sorely to heart, because they interpreted it as a mark of contempt for so illustrious a teacher. Therefore they secretly sought to influence him against me, and by their vile insinuations made me hated of him.

It chanced, moreover, that one day, after the exposition of certain texts, we scholars were jesting among ourselves, and one of them, seeking to draw me out, asked me what I thought of the lectures on the Books of Scripture. I, who had as yet studied [only other matters], replied that ... it appeared quite extraordinary to me that educated persons should not be able to understand the sacred books, simply by studying them themselves, together with the glosses thereon, and without the aid of any teacher.

Most of those who were present mocked at me, and asked whether I myself could do as I had said, or whether I would dare to undertake it. I answered that if they wished, I was ready to try it. Forthwith they cried out and jeered all the more. "Well and good," said they: "We agree to the test. Pick out and give us an exposition of some doubtful passage in the Scriptures, so that we can put this boast of yours to the proof." And they all chose that most obscure prophecy of Ezekiel.

I accepted the challenge, and invited them to attend a lecture on the very next day.... In truth at this first lecture of mine only a few were present, for it seemed quite absurd to all of them that I, hitherto so inexperienced in discussing the Scriptures, should attempt the thing so hastily. However, this lecture gave such satisfaction to all those who heard it that they spread its praises abroad with notable enthusiasm, and thus compelled me to continue my interpretation of the sacred text.

When word of this was bruited about, those who had stayed away from the first lecture came eagerly, some to the second and more to the third, and all of them were eager to write down the glosses which I had begun on the first day, so as to have them from the very beginning.[2]

2. In Chapter VI, Abelard tells about his passionate affair with his student Heloise. He writes:

Now there dwelt in that same city of Paris a certain young girl named Heloise, the niece of a canon who was called Fulbert.... Of no mean beauty, she stood out above all by reason of her abundant knowledge of letters. Now this virtue is rare among women, and for that very reason it doubly graced the maiden, and made her the most worth of renown in the entire kingdom ...

We were united first in the dwelling that sheltered our love [i.e., Fulbert's house], and then in the hearts that burned with it. Under the pretext of study we spent our hours in the happiness of love, and learning held out to us the secret opportunities that our passion craved. Our speech was more of love than of the books that lay before us; our kisses far outnumbered our reasoned words. Our hands sought less the book than each other's bosoms — love drew our eyes together far more than the lesson drew them to the pages of our text.... No degree in love's progress was left untried by our passion, and if love itself could not imagine any wonder as yet unknown, we discovered it. And our inexperience of such delights made us all the more ardent in our pursuit of them, so that our thirst for one another was still unquenched.[3]

3. In Chapter VII, Abelard explains that Fulbert and his kinsmen came to believe (incorrectly) that Abelard was trying to get rid of Heloise by forcing her to become a nun. He explains how his enemies castrated him. He writes:

Violently incensed, they laid a plot against me, and one night while I all unsuspecting was asleep in a secret room in my lodgings, they broke in with the help of one of my servants whom they had bribed. There they had vengeance on me with a most cruel and most shameful punishment, such as astounded the whole world; for they cut off those parts of my body with which I had done that which was the cause of their sorrow. This done, straightway they fled, but two of them were captured and suffered the loss of their eyes and their genital organs. One of these two was the aforesaid servant, who even when he was still in my service, had been led by his avarice to betray me.[4]

Appendix 3:
John of Garland on
"How Students Should Behave"

This is some of Garland's advice to students. It has been broken into paragraphs for easier reading[1]:

"Be not a fornicator, O student, a robber, a murderer, a deceitful merchant, a champion at dice...

Do not constantly urge your horse with the spur, which should be used only on rare occasions. Give your horse reins when he mounts an incline; fearing a serious accident, avoid crossing swollen rivers, or the Rhine. If a bridge is not safe, you should dismount and let the horse pick his way over the smooth parts. Mount gently on the left stirrup. Select beautiful equestrian trappings suitable to your clerical station. Ride erect unless you are bent by age. If you are of the elect you should have a rich saddle cloth. The cross should be exalted, the voice be raised in prayer, Christ should be worshiped, the foot should be taken out of the stirrup. The horseman will descend from his horse and say his prayers; no matter how far he will then travel, he will ride in safety...

Have nothing to do with the prostitute, but love your wife; all wives should be honored but especially those who are distinguished by virtue. A person who is well should not recline at table in the fashion of the ancients. When you walk after dinner keep on frequented streets, avoid insecure speeches. Unless you wish to be considered a fool learn to keep your mouth shut in season..."

Appendix 4:
The Pecia System

These comments, which have been lightly edited, were provided by Dr. Andrew E. Larsen. He has generously given me permission to use them here.

Medieval manuscripts were composed of quires, each of which was formed of several sheets of parchment, vellum, or paper laid on top of each other, folded down the middle and (normally) sewn together. Four sheets stacked on top of each other would produce eight pages, with the first and last page being the same sheet. A codex (this is what we now call a book; in this case, it was a manuscript book) would be composed of multiple quires stacked on top of each other and then bound together. Many (but not all) modern books are still composed of quires: if you look at the spine from the top or the bottom you can see the individual quires.

Before the invention of the printing press by the German goldsmith Johannes Gutenberg in 1445, all books were hand copied, including the textbooks used by students at universities: The first book printed at Oxford dates from 1478. Since this labor-intensive process of hand copying made books very expensive, most university towns had booksellers who did not actually sell books but rather *rented them out* for copying. Some universities maintained an official bookseller whose exemplars (books) had been inspected for quality. A wealthy student might simply buy a book but a poorer one would have to rent out an exemplar and copy it by hand himself, thus saving a lot of money but spending a lot of time. To maximize the number of students who could use an exemplar, it was often stored as a stack of unbound quires; the student could then rent one quire at a time.

Poor students could also earn money by copying a manuscript for a richer but lazier student.

Some manuscripts still show signs of having been *pecia*: their quires bear *pecia* marks, usually a "p" followed by a number, showing which quire they formed before being bound together. The standard *pecia* was two two-columned double leaves in folio, measuring about 12¼ inches by 8¼ inches.

This system was not universal, however. Some exemplars were rented out as whole volumes. University lectures traditionally consisted of the teacher actually reading out a portion of a text, such as Aristotle's *Metaphysics*, and then commenting on it. Indeed, the word "lecture" means "a reading." Smart students who wrote quickly could transcribe the text as it was being read, thus producing their own copy in the classroom, free of charge.

Appendix 5: Two Letters of 21 November 1430 from the University of Paris

The first is to Bishop Pierre Cauchon, the second is to the English king Henry VI.[1]

Letter to Bishop Cauchon

To the reverend father in Christ the lord bishop and count of Beauvais.

We are amazed, reverend father, by the great delay in the case of the woman commonly called the Maid, which does great harm to the faith and ecclesiastical jurisdiction, especially since she is reportedly already in the hands of our lord and king. Christian princes have always shown favor to the interests of the Church and the true faith, such that, if some zealot opposed the dogmas of the catholic faith, they would immediately deliver him to ecclesiastical judges for correction and punishment. Perhaps had you shown keener diligence in pursuing the matter, this woman's case would already be proceeding to an ecclesiastical trial. Since you hold an illustrious bishopric in God's holy Church, you have no small concern to suppress scandals against the Christian religion, especially when they fall into your jurisdiction for judgment. Therefore, to protect the authority of the Church from the great injury of further procrastination, may it please you to strive with fatherly zeal and utmost diligence to see that this woman is quickly delivered to your power and that of the inquisitor of heresy. Should this happen, please try in due time to bring her here to Paris, where there are a great many wise and learned men, so that her case can be diligently examined and expertly judged to the edification of the Christian people and to the honor of God. May he grant you guidance in all things, reverend father, by his special care.

Written in Paris, in our general assembly solemnly celebrated on the feast of Saint Mathurin, November 21, in the year of the Lord 1430. Yours, the rector and the University of Paris.

Signed: Hébert [rector of the University of Paris]

Letter to King Henry VI

To the most excellent prince, the King of France and England, our most dread and sovereign lord and father.

We have recently heard that the woman called the Maid has been delivered into your power. We rejoice greatly in this, confident that by your good offices the woman will be brought to justice to make amends for the great evils and scandals she has notoriously brought upon this kingdom, to the great prejudice of divine honor, our holy faith, and all your good people ...

We urgently pray you, by the honor of our Savior Jesus Christ, to order that this woman be handed over to the justice of the Church in short order — that is, to the reverend father in God our honored lord the bishop and count of Beauvais, and to the inquisitor for France, who are especially concerned with her misdeeds against our faith. Then a reasonable discussion can take place about the charges against her and the appropriate remedy, to preserve the holy truth of our faith and to banish all error and all false and scandalous opinion from the souls of your good, loyal, and Christian subjects ...

Written at Paris in our general assembly solemnly celebrated on the feast of Saint Mathurin, November 21, 1430. Your most humble and devoted daughter, the University of Paris.

Signed: Hébert

Appendix 6:
Medieval Requirements for Becoming a Physician

This excerpt is taken from the Chartularium Universitatis Parisiensis, *which, as noted earlier, contains the regulations of the University of Paris between 1200 and 1452 and the papal bulls affecting it. Translated by the University of Pennsylvania's Department of History between about 1897 and 1907 and lightly edited, it reads as follows[1]:*

This is the form for licensing bachelors of medicine. First, the master under whom the bachelor is [studying] ought to testify to the chancellor, in the presence of the masters called together for this purpose, concerning the suitability of licensing the bachelor. He ought to prove his time of study by at least two examinations; and the time which he ought to have studied is five and one-half years, if he has ruled [studied] in arts or has been a licentiate; or six, if he has not.

The course of study is as follows: he ought to have read the *Medica* [of Galen] twice in the regular courses and once in an extraordinary course, with the exception of Theophilus's [a seventh-century Byzantine physician] *On Urines*, which it is sufficient to have heard once in either a regular or an extraordinary course; the *Viaticum* twice in regular courses; the other books of Isaac [a Jewish physician] once in a regular course, twice in extraordinary courses, except the *Particular Diets*, which it is sufficient to have heard once in an extraordinary or regular course; the book of *Antidotes* of Nicholas [of Salerno] once. The *Verses of Aegidius* [by Corbeil, who taught at Paris] is not required. Also, he ought to have read the books on Theory and Practice [this may refer to a medical textbook by Ali ben Abbas, which was divided into Theory and Practice.]

And he ought to swear this. Moreover, if any one is convicted of perjury or lying he, although licensed, may be degraded.

Chronology

789	King Charles of the Franks ordains that monasteries and cathedrals are to teach boys how to read.
c. 1050–c. 1250	The "renaissance of the twelfth century" is a watershed in Western European thought.
1079–1142	Life of Peter Abelard, one of the greatest and most interesting intellectuals of the twelfth century.
c. 1120–1180	John of Salisbury, one of the most influential scholars of his age, recounts how the French philosopher and administrator Bernard of Chartres ran the cathedral school at Chartres.
Last quarter of 11th century	Pepo, the first law professor at Bologna, teaches Roman law there.
End of 11th century–first half of 12th century	Irnerius teaches law at Bologna, drawing students from across the Alps.
c. 1095–1160	Peter Lombard, bishop of Paris, writes one of the most important textbooks of the Middle Ages: the *Four Books of the Sentences* (c. 1150).
By 1119	A loose conglomeration of monastery schools and the cathedral school of Notre-Dame now exists in Paris.

1126–1198	The Muslim philosopher Averroës, known in the Islamic world as Ibn Rushd, translates and comments on the writings of Aristotle. During the thirteenth century his work will strongly influence scholars at the University of Paris.
c. 1140	Gratian compiles *The Concord of Discordant Canons*, a famous work on canon law.
1155	Holy Roman Emperor Frederick I Barbarossa issues the *Authentica Habita*, an edict designed to protect university students at Bologna and elsewhere in his kingdom.
c. 1167	Bulgarus emerges as the leading figure of the "Four Doctors" — the most famous twelfth-century jurists of the University of Bologna's law school.
c. 1175–1253	Robert Grosseteste becomes the leading figure in the growth of scientific studies at Oxford.
1176–1177	Pope Alexander III encourages the teaching of law at Bologna.
1179	Pope Alexander III orders that every cathedral should have a master to teach Latin grammar.
c. 1200	The first three universities of the world, i.e., Bologna, Paris, and Oxford, gradually come into being. Bologna is, by a small margin, the oldest one.
1200	First recorded town-gown brawl in Paris.
c. 1200–1259	The Benedictine monk Matthew Paris chronicles European affairs.
Early 13th century	Gradual evolution of the University of Montpellier.
1205–1210	Jacques de Vitry (then a student, later a cardinal) writes about the seamy, sinful side of Parisian life.
1209	A town-gown incident at Oxford prompts masters to go on strike and leave Oxford, followed by their pupils. They settle in Cambridge and found a new university there.
1209–1229	Cambridge gradually evolves into a university, a development sparked by the 1209 town-gown riot in Oxford.
1214	Oxford receives its first papal statutes, granting scholars immunity from secular arrest.

1214–1216	Tancred, Master of Decrees at the University of Bologna, writes a famous textbook on ecclesiastical procedural law known as the *Ordo iudicarius*.
c. 1214–c. 1292	Roger Bacon, one of the most famous men of his time, is a major advocate of Aristotle and of experimental science.
1215	The English cardinal Robert of Courson, formerly a master at the University of Paris, draws up the first permanent statutes for the young university.
c. 1217–1274	Bonaventure of Bagnoregio, minister general of the Franciscan order, steers the Franciscans along a moderate but highly intellectual course that makes them the most prominent order in the church until the coming of the Jesuits.
1219	Pope Honorius III prohibits the teaching of civil law at the University of Paris. As a result, French civil law students must attend the University of Orléans.
1222	The University of Padua begins as a result of a migration of students from Bologna.
1224	The emperor of Sicily Frederick II founds the University of Naples.
c. 1225–1274	Thomas Aquinas, one of the greatest theologians of the Middle Ages, sets himself the task of reconciling Aristotle's thought with the tenets of Christianity.
1228–1229	A tavern brawl at the University of Paris ends with the university outmaneuvering the monarchy itself.
1229	The earliest papal university, the University of Toulouse, is founded by Gregory IX under the provisions of the Treaty of Paris.
1230s	The success and highhandedness of the monastic schools at the University of Paris infuriates secular masters.
1231	Pope Gregory IX's bull *Parens scientiarum* serves as the charter of the University of Paris.
c. 1240–between 1281 and 1284	Siger of Brabant, a professor of philosophy at the University of Paris, finds the works of Aristotle (as interpreted by the Spanish Muslim commentator Averroës) so inspiring that his own teachings begin to run directly contrary to Christian doctrines.

1252	The University of Bologna's statutes are formally issued, stabilizing it as an educational and scholarly institution.
1263	John Balliol founds a hostel in Oxford for 16 impoverished students. In time this will become Oxford's Balliol College.
c. 1263	Accursis, known as the "idol of the glossators," produces the *Glossa ordinaria*. It makes available to others the great wealth of Roman law scholarship.
1265/1266–1308	John Duns Scotus, one of the most influential philosopher-theologians of the Middle Ages, leaves his intellectual mark on a wide range of subjects.
c. 1270–1348	Giovanni d'Andrea, one of the last great figures of the classical age of canon law, writes *A treatise on war, reprisals and the duel*, which will later become influential in the history of international law.
1277	Bishop Tempier makes public a list of 219 heretical, theological and philosophical theses. These are thought to reflect Averroës' translations of Aristotle.
c. 1285–1348	William of Ockham popularizes a pragmatic method of thought known as Ockham's Razor.
1292	Pope Nicholas IV confirms that the University of Paris is a full university in the modern sense of the word.
1304–1374	Francesco Petrarch, the first humanist, denounces the scholastic method.
1306	In a bull issued this year Pope Clement V, who had studied at Orléans, grants it all the privileges which had already been accorded to the University of Toulouse.
1321	The last important town-gown collision at the University of Bologna during the Middle Ages centers on the execution of a student who tried to abduct a notary's daughter.
1323	Jean de Jandun's *Treatise in Praise of Paris* gives a glowing account of life at the University of Paris.
1329	The legal case of John le Fourbeur, a University of Paris student arrested for rape, pits the claim of papal authority against the claim of a higher good.

1330–1376	Edward of Woodstock, Prince of Wales (better known as the Black Prince), is one of the most famous examples of warrior nobility.
c. 1330–1384	John Wycliffe arranges for the first complete translation of the Bible into English and vigorously urges the church to give up all its worldly goods.
1331–1406	Coluccio Salutati, chancellor of Florence, is a pioneer of humanism.
c. 1334–c. 1405	Jean Froissart is one of the finest of all medieval chroniclers.
1341	Robert of Eglesfield founds Queen's College at Oxford. Each Christmas the Boar's Head ceremony is still celebrated there — to commemorate a student who saved himself from a wild boar by stuffing his manuscript book on Aristotle down the boar's throat.
1347	Pope Clement VI issues a bull for the foundation of the University of Prague; Charles IV follows it up with an imperial charter for the university itself.
1348–1349	An outbreak of the Black Death (bubonic plague) kills between one-third and one-half of Europe's population.
c. 1350	Oldradus da Ponte is the first medieval jurist to produce large numbers of *concilia* (analyses of the law relevant to specific cases) and *quaestiones* (questions) in the same vein.
1355	St. Scholastica's Day riot: the most famous case of town-gown friction at Oxford.
1363–1429	Jean Gerson, an exceptionally able chancellor of the University of Paris, helps resolve the Great Schism of the West.
1365	Duke Rudolf IV issues a charter founding the University of Vienna.
c. 1370–1444	Leonardo Bruni, another chancellor of Florence, strongly advocates humanistic education.
c. 1370–1460	Guarino Veronese is one of the founders of humanistic education in Italy.

c. 1373–1446   Vittorino da Feltre is one of the first to apply the humanistic program to the education of the young.

1378–1417   Christianity is split in two by the Great Western Schism.
The University of Paris will play a major role in helping to
resolve this dispute.

1379   William of Wykeham founds Oxford's New College, where
the tutorial system begins. This system is still used at
Oxford and Cambridge today.

1386–1387   Chaucer begins *The Canterbury Tales*.

1380   The University of Paris brings suit against the senior royal
official of Paris, Hugues Aubriot, for manhandling the
rector of the university.

1392–1394   The Ménagier of Paris (the Householder of Paris) drafts a
tender set of instructions for his young wife.

c. 1400   Eustache Deschamps, a French poet, leaves us a sample
"Dear Father, please send money" letter from an impoverished university student.

c. 1400–1420   A young Polish woman disguises herself as a man and
enters the University of Krakow.

c. 1406–1457   Lorenzo Valla, an Italian humanist, rhetorician and educator, proves that a historic document known as the Dona-
tion of Constantine is a forgery.

1424–1483   The Divinity School, one of Europe's finest architectural
monuments, is built at the University of Oxford.

1431   Joan of Arc, a simple peasant girl who led the French army
to victory at Orléans, is burned at the stake as a relapsed
heretic. The University of Paris plays a key role in her first
trial.

1431–after 1463 The poet François Villon is the most famous *criminal graduate* of the University of Paris.

c. 1446–1519   The humanist William Grocyn teaches at Oxford and helps
introduce students to Greek learning.

1446   Charles VII orders that all legal disputes related to the University of Paris must be settled by the *parlement* of Paris,

not by the university itself. This is an early step in the assertion of royal control over French universities.

1451	A bull of Nicholas V, issued at the request of the bishop of Glasgow, founds the University of Glasgow.
1455–1456	At her second (posthumous) trial, Joan of Arc is fully acquitted.
1455–1522	The German humanist Johann Reuchlin is the central figure in Germany for the study of Greek and Hebrew.
c. 1460–1524	Oxford's Linacre College is named after Thomas Linacre, an English humanist and physician.
1463–1494	The humanist Giovanni Pica della Mirandola tries to reconcile philosophy and religion by his philosophy of syncretism. It holds that all systems of thought contain some truth but that none has a monopoly on truth.
1466–1536	Desiderius Erasmus's humanist and satiric work, *The Praise of Folly*, published in 1511, helps prepare the way for the Protestant Reformation.
1469–1535	An English humanist, cardinal and martyr, Fisher has a meteoric rise at the University of Cambridge.
1476–1519	John Colet, the chief Christian humanist in England, founds St. Paul's School to teach boys Latin and Greek.
1478–1535	Thomas More — lawyer, author, statesman and martyr — is the leading humanist scholar of his time.
1489	Duke Humfrey's Library, one of Europe's finest scholarly monuments, opens at the University of Oxford.
1499	Louis XII rescinds the right of the University of Paris to go on strike, thus depriving it of its most powerful weapon and solidifying royal control over it.
Late 15th century	The Heidelberg *Manuale Scholarium* (*Scholar's Manual*) imposes fines on students who speak the vernacular, rather than Latin, outside the classroom.
1500	By the end of the Middle Ages, political society in its modern form, symbolized by the nation-state, has made

its initial appearance in Western Europe: the long era of the university's relative independence is now over.

1612   The last outstanding representative of scholasticism, the Spanish Jesuit philosopher Francisco Suárez, writes *De Legibus* (*On Laws*), an early work on international law.

Glossary

Artes liberales The seven liberal arts that formed the basis for most university studies: grammar, rhetoric, dialectic, music, astronomy, geometry, and arithmetic.

Baccalarius artium Bachelor's degree (BA)

Benefice A church position or endowment providing income for a cleric

Capitoul A municipal officer of Toulouse

Cursory lectures Elementary lectures given by bachelors of arts in the afternoon as part of their training as apprentice masters

Determine To receive the BA degree

Dictamen The art of drafting accurate, well phrased letters

Disputations Oral debates, usually held once a week, following the rules of Aristotelian logic

Extraordinary lectures Lectures given by masters in the afternoon to cover less essential law texts

Feudalism A construct dating from the mid-eighteenth century that has now fallen out of scholarly favor but has not been replaced by any other widely accepted "ism." The best approximation today would be something like "power and social relationships in the Middle Ages."

Goliardi Footloose "students without masters"

Humanism As used here, (1) a philosophic belief that people are rational beings with dignity, (2) a movement away from the contemplative religious ideal of the earlier Middle Ages toward a more active involvement in public life, and (3) a curriculum for secondary and advanced education.

Ius commune The "general law" taught in medieval universities

Licentia docendi License to teach in a given university faculty

Magister artium Master of arts (MA)

197

Ordinary lectures Lectures delivered in the morning by a master

Pecia **system** Before the invention of printing, manuscript books were unbound and loaned out for copying in fascicles (parts of a book) known as *pecia* ("pieces").

Peregrinatio academica The "academic pilgrimage," which was undertaken by students who had to travel long distances to their universities

Puncta Law books were divided into a number of parts known as *puncta*.

Quadrivium The more advanced liberal arts: music, astronomy, geometry, and arithmetic

Respond to the question To play an active role in a logical disputation

Scholaris simplex "Simple student," i.e., the typical university undergraduate

Schoolmen University masters who taught and wrote using the scholastic method (see scholasticism)

Scholasticism A system of thought, often based on Aristotelian logic, used extensively in medieval university education

Studium generale (*studium* for short) An educational institution that is a full university in the modern sense of the word

Three philosophies To obtain the MA degree, students had to master heavy doses of the three philosophies: natural, moral, and metaphysical

Trivium The first three liberal arts: grammar, rhetoric, and dialectic

Universitas A collective organization of university students

Chapter Notes

Preface

1. Prefatory Note by Theodor E. Momm-sen in Haskins, *Rise of the Universities*, p. viii.
2. Verger, "Teachers," p. 161.
3. Rüegg, "Themes," p. 3.
4. This financial record forms the basis for Courtenay's book, *Parisian Scholars*.
5. Riché and Verger, *Nains*, p. 249. The English translation is my own.
6. Private e-mail communication of 14 April 2007 from Eric Urbanc.
7. Rashdall, *Universities of Europe*, vol. I, p. 19.

Setting the Stage

1. Moulin, *La vie des étudiants*," p. 9. Moulin does not state where in Rashdall's works these statements appear. The English translation is my own.
2. Bloch, *Feudal Society*, vol. 1, p. 112.
3. Bellomo, *Common Legal Past*, p. 149.
4. Janin, *Medieval Justice*, p. 5.
5. Palmer, *Whilton Dispute*, pp. 5, 8.
6. Quoted in Evans, *Life in Medieval France*, p. 16. The translation is his as well.
7. Bartlett, *Medieval Panorama*, p. 101.
8. Some of what follows is drawn from Koenigsberger, *Medieval Europe*, p. 343.
9. Cobban, *English University Life*, pp. 183, 189.
10. Painter, *History of the Middle Ages*, p. 104.
11. Bloch, *Feudal Society*, vol. 2, p. 411.
12. Medieval Sourcebook, "Crisis, Recovery, Feudalism?" p. 1.
13. Quoted by Hewitt, *The Black Prince's Expedition*, p. 175.
14. Medieval Sourcebook, "Jean Froissart," p. 3.
15. Keen, *English Society*, p. 297.
16. Jean-Claude Schmitt, "Dieu," pp. 271, 276.
17. Paris, *Chronicles*, p. 182.
18. Ladurie, *Montaillou*, pp. xiv-xvii.
19. This account is drawn from Ladurie, *Montaillou*, p. 362.
20. This account is drawn from Power, *Medieval People*, pp. 115–44. Power's own source was *Le Ménagier de Paris, Traité de Morale et d'Economie Domestique, composé vers 1393 par un Bourgeois Parisien*, published in Paris in 1846 in two volumes.
21. Quoted in Power, *Medieval People*, p. 127. A few words have been changed for the sake of clarity.
22. Janin, *Medieval Justice*, p. 11.
23. Trevelyan, *History of England*, p. 137.
24. Nardi, "Relations with authority," p. 85.
25. Both the French and English texts are from Evans, *Life in Medieval France*, pp. 132–33. I have lightly edited them in the interests of clarity.
26. Cobban, *Medieval Universities*, p. 125.
27. Rashdall, *Universities of Europe*, vol. III, p. 407.

28 Quoted by Moulin, *La vie des étudiants*, p. 38.

29. After Moulin, *La vie des étudiants*, p. 38.

30. Quoted in Koeningsberger, *Medieval Europe*, p. 281.

31. "Plague Readings," pp. 7–8.

32. Quoted by Barber, *Two Cities*, p. 5.

33. Haskins, *Rise of the Universities*, pp. 4–5.

34. Nederman, *John of Salisbury*, p. 43.

35. Quoted by Piltz, *World of Medieval Learning*, pp. 92–93.

36. Adapted from a quotation by Haskins, *Renaissance of the Twelfth Century*, pp. 354–55.

37. Barber, *Two Cities*, p. 402.

38. Stump, "Dialectic," p. 127.

39. *Historia Calamitatum*, quoted by Evans, *Life in Medieval France*, p. 106.

40. Verger, "Patterns," p. 37.

41. Verger, "Université," p. 1170.

42. Abelard, *Historia Calamitatum*, p. 8.

43. Quoted by Pernoud, *Héloïse et Abélard*, p. 67. The English translation is my own.

44. Rashdall, *Universities of Europe*, vol. I, p. 57. Italics added.

45. Quoted by Haskins, *Renaissance of the Twelfth Century*, p. 168.

Chapter I

1. Verger, "Université," p. 1166. The English translation is my own.

2. Quoted by Haskins, *Renaissance of the Twelfth Century*, p. 73.

3. Quoted by Harlow, "Sweden Loans the Devil to Prague," p. 2.

4. Extract from the *Admonitio generalis*, Chapter 72, in *Monumenta Germaniae Historica, Leges, Capitularia regum Francorum I*, Hanover, 1883, p. 60, quoted by Riché and Verger, *Nains*, p. 32.

5. Quoted in Haskins, *Renaissance of the Twelfth Century*, p. 135.

6. Rüegg, "Themes," pp. 22–23.

7. Rashdall, *Universities of Europe*, vol. III, p. 342.

8. Quoted by Tuchman, *Distant Mirror*, p. 27.

9. Rashdall, *Universities of Europe*, vol. III, p. 342.

10. Schwinges, "Student education, student life," p. 227.

11. This account is drawn from Rashdall, vol. III, pp. 378–81.

12. Quoted in Seybolt, *Manuale Scholarium*, pp. 24–25. This quote has been lightly edited for ease of reading.

13. Cobban, *English University Life*, p. 149 ff.

14. Quoted in Baldwin, *Scholastic Culture*, p. 59.

15. Quoted by Riché and Verger, *Nains*, pp. 138–39. The English translation is my own.

16. Cobban, *Medieval Universities*, p. 12.

17. Verger, "Teachers," p. 163.

18. Asztalos, "The faculty of theology," pp. 436–437.

19. Schwinges, "Student education, student life," p. 201.

20. Private communication of 16 April 2007 from Andrew E. Larsen. He said that this account comes from an article by Michael Shank entitled "A Female University Student in Late Medieval Krakow," which appeared in *Signs* 12 (1987) and was reproduced in *Sisters and Workers in the Middle Ages*, ed. Judith M Bennett, (Chicago: University of Chicago, 1989). No pages numbers were given.

21. Schwinges, "Student education, student life," p. 223.

22. Moulin, *La vie des étudiants*, p. 32.

23. Schwinges, "Student education, student life," p. 214.

24. Haskins, *Rise of Universities*, p. 39.

25. Rashdall, *Universities of Europe*, vol. I, p. 509.

26. Rashdall, *Universities of Europe*, vol. I, pp. 479–80.

27. These examples are taken from Evans, *Life in Medieval France*, pp. 133–134.

28. Haskins, *Rise of Universities*, p. 18.

29. Rashdall, *Universities of Europe*, vol. III, pp. 176–78.

30. Verger, "Patterns," p. 62.

31. Schwinges, "Student education, student life," pp. 214–15.

32. Schwinges, "Student education, student life," p. 219.

33. Quoted by Schwinges, "Admission," p. 173.

34. Cobban, *English University Life*, p. 7, and Schwinges, "Admission," pp. 177–78.

35. Adapted from MetraNet, "Guadeamus Igitur—A Translation," p. 1.

36. Moulin, *La vie des étudiants*, p. 103.

37. Quoted by Pernoud, *Lumière du Moyen Age*, p. 125.

38. Quoted by Haskins, *Rise of Universities*, p. 84. I have lightly edited this quote to make it clearer.

39. Adapted from Waddell, *Wandering Scholars*, pp. 210–13.

40. Adapted from Sommerville, "Twelfth Century Renaissance," pp. 1–2.

41. Adapted from Time-Life, "What Life Was Like," p. 105.

42. Cobban, *English University Life*, pp. 160–61.

43. Southern, *Scholastic Humanism*, p. 12.

44. Piltz, *World of Medieval Learning*, p. 261. Italics added.

45. The following list is drawn from Piltz, *World of Medieval Learning*, pp. 254–55.

46. Verger, "Patterns," p. 44.

47. Sommerville, "Intellectual trends," p. 5.

48. Private communication of 31 July 2007 from Dr. Erika Rummel.

49. Piltz, *World of Medieval Learning*, p. 261.

50. Rashdall, *Universities of Europe*, vol. III, p. 447.

51. Quoted by Rashdall, *Universities of Europe*, vol. II, p. 119.

52. Rashdall, *Universities of Europe*, vol. II, p. 126.

53. Siraisi, "The faculty of medicine," pp. 361–63.

54. Adapted from Bartlett, *Medieval Panorama*, pp. 210–11.

55. Huntsman, "Grammar," p. 59.

56. Quoted by Huntsman, "Grammar," p. 60.

57. Quoted by Huntsman, "Grammar," p. 72.

58. Quoted by Piltz, "World of Medieval Learning," p. 19.

59. Cobban, *Medieval Universities*, p. 5.

60. Quoted by Sommerville, "Intellectual trends," p. 2.

61. Camargo, "Rhetoric," pp. 96–97.

62. This discussion of the *ars dictandis* is drawn from Cobban, *Medieval Universities*, pp. 221–24, and Grendler, *Universities of the Italian Renaissance*, p. 201.

63. Cobban, *Medieval Universities*, pp. 221–22.

64. Quoted by Haskins, *Renaissance of the Twelfth Century*, p. 144.

65. North, "The *quadrivium*," p. 343.

66. Quoted by Karp, "Music," p. 174.

67. Karp, "Music," p. 177.

68. Kren, "Astronomy," p. 234.

69. Shelby, "Geometry," p. 212.

70. Quoted by Piltz, "World of Medieval Learning," pp. 220–21.

71. Masi, "Arithmetic," pp. 148, 156.

72. Moulin, *La vie des étudiants*, pp. 34–35.

73. Rashdall, *Universities of Europe*, vol. I, p. 218.

74. Verger, "Teachers," p. 157.

75. Evans, *Life in Medieval France*, p. 133.

76. The following account is drawn from Piltz, "World of Medieval Learning," pp. 114–15.

77. Evans, *Life in Medieval France*, p. 133.

78. Jean de Jandun, *De laudibus Parisius*, in *Paris et ses historiens aux XIV et XV siècles*, Le Roux de Lincy and L. M. Tisserand (eds.), Paris, 1867, pp. 34–45, cited by Riché and Verger, *Nains*, pp. 260–61. The English translation is my own.

79. Brundage, *Medieval Canon Law*, p. 53.

80. Quoted by Brundage, *Medieval Canon Law*, p. 52.

81. Piltz, *World of Medieval Learning*, p. 224.

82. Rashdall, *Universities of Europe*, vol. III, pp. 397–99, and Leff, "The Trivium," 325–28.

83. Leff, "The *trivium*," p. 325.

84. Rashdall, *Universities of Europe*, vol. III, p. 153.

85. Stanford Encyclopedia of Philosophy, "The Medieval Problem of Universals," p. 1.

86. Rashdall, *Universities of Europe*, vol. I, p. 40.

87. Stanford Encyclopedia of Philosophy, "The Medieval Problem of Universals," p. 5.

88. Quoted by Ross, "Porphyry," p. 1.

89. Rashdall, *Universities of Europe*, vol. III, pp. 397–99.

90. Leff, "The *trivium* and the three philosophies," p. 326.

91. Adapted by Dr. Ursula Carlson from Seybolt, *Manuale Scholarium*, pp. 113–14.

92. Rashdall, *Universities of Europe*, vol. III, pp. 154–60.

93. Southern, *Scholastic Humanism*, p. 103.

94. Internet Encyclopedia of Philosophy, "Peter Lombard," pp. 1–3.

95. Haskins, *Rise of Universities*, p. 38.

96. Gieysztor, "Management and resources," p. 128, and British Library, "Pecia System," p. 1.

97. Chaucer, *Canterbury Tales*, pp. 107–8.

98. Adapted from "The Miller's Prologue and Tale," lines 3199–3207, 3219–20.

Chapter II

1. Haskins, *Renaissance of the Twelfth Century*, p. 391.

2. Winroth, *Making of Gratian's Decretum*, p. 196.

3. After Moulin, *La vie des étudiants*, p. 230.

4. Nardi, "Relations with authority," p. 80.

5. Nardi, "Relations with authority," p. 80.

6. García, "Faculties of Law," p. 388.

7. Catholic Encyclopedia, "The University of Bologna," p. 1.

8. Rashdall, *Universities of Europe*, vol. I, p. 18.

9. Rashdall, *Universities of Europe*, vol. I, p. 17.

10. Barber, *Two Cities*, p. 409.

11. Cobban, *Medieval Universities*, pp. 51–52.

12. Quoted by Riché and Verger, *Nains*, p. 116. The English translation is my own; italics have been added.

13. De Ridder-Symoens, "Mobility," p. 300.

14. De Ridder-Symoens, "Mobility," p. 300.

15. Quoted by de Ridder-Symoens, "Mobility," p. 301.

16. Riché and Verger, *Nains*, p. 193.

17. Powicke and Emden, in Rashdall, *Universities of Europe*, vol. I, p. 232.

18. Brundage, *Medieval Canon Law*, pp. 46–47.

19. Brundage, *Medieval Canon Law*, p. 55, and Bellomo, *Common Legal Past*, p. 71.

20. Nardi, "Relations with authority," p. 94.

21. Quoted by Brundage, *Medieval Canon Law*, p. 155.

22. Quoted by Piltz, *World of Medieval Learning*, pp. 67–68.

23. García, "The faculties of law," p. 398.

24. Quoted by Brundage, *Medieval Canon Law*, p. 52.

25. Quoted by Haskins, *Renaissance of the Twelfth Century*, pp. 203–4.

26. Quoted by Cobban, *Medieval Universities*, p. 66.

27. García, "The faculties of law," p. 400.

28. Cobban, *Medieval Universities*, p. 73.

29. Rashdall, *Universities of Europe*, vol. I, pp. 172–73.

30. Quoted by Encyclopedia Britannica Online, p. 2.

Chapter III

1. Haskins, *Rise of Universities*, p. 7, and Winroth, *Making of Gratian's Decretum*, p. 158.

2. This paragraph, including the quote, is drawn from Janin, *Medieval Justice*, p. 31.

3. Verger, "Patterns," p. 48.

4. Cobban, *Medieval Universities*, p. 50.

5. Bellomo, *Common Legal Past of Europe*, p. 160.

6. For an excellent Web site on Gratian, see Anders Winroth's "Domus Gratiani," pp. 1–6.

7. Winroth, *Making of Gratian's Decretum*, p. 7.

8. Brundage, *Medieval Canon Law*, p. 190.

9. Brundage, *Medieval Canon Law*, p. 212.

10. Bellomo, *Common Legal Past of Europe*, pp. 162–63.

11. Southern, *Scholastic Humanism*, p. 305.

12. Quoted by Haskins, *Renaissance of the Twelfth Century*, p. 97.

13. Haskins, *Renaissance of the Twelfth Century*, p. 97.

14. Brundage, *Medieval Canon Law*, pp. 49, 224.

15. Adapted from Winroth, *Making of Gratian's Decretum*, pp. 7–8.

16. Adapted from Winroth, *Making of Gratian's Decretum*, p. 8.

17. D'Avray, "Scholastic Humanism," pp. 3–4.

18. Brundage, *Medieval Canon Law*, pp. 59–60.

19. Brundage, *Medieval Canon Law*, pp. 59–60.

20. Quoted by Piltz, "World of Medieval Learning," pp. 68–69.

21. Adapted from a quotation by Piltz, "World of Medieval Learning," p. 69.

22. Piltz, "World of Medieval Learning," p. 69.

23. Brundage, *Medieval Canon Law*, p. 226.

24. García, "The faculties of law," p. 391.

25. Some of these comments are drawn from "Johannes Andreae," p. 1.

26. Bellomo, *Common Legal Past*, p. 177.

27. This paragraph is drawn from Brundage, "Medieval Canon Law," pp. 221–22.

28. Cited by Janin, *Medieval Justice*, p. 38.

29. The quotations and comments come from Janin, *Medieval Justice*, pp. 39–40, and Brundage, *Medieval Canon Law*, p. 60.

Chapter IV

1. Quoted by Riché and Verger, *Nains*, p. 174. The English translation is my own.
2. Jordan, *Europe in the High Middle Ages*, p. 226.
3. Schwinges, "Admission," p. 183.
4. Adapted from Schwinges, "Student education, student life," pp. 196–200.
5. Rashdall, *Universities of Europe*, vol. III, p. 408.
6. Verger, "L'étudiant maître de l'université," p. 40.
7. Gieysztor, "Management and resources," p. 129.
8. Rashdall, *Universities of Europe*, vol. I, p. 472.
9. Cobban, *Medieval Universities*, p. 79.
10. Cobban, *English University Life*, p. 185.
11. The account is drawn from Rashdall, *Universities of Europe*, vol. I, pp. 294–98.
12. For these and other ordeals, see Janin, *Medieval Justice*, pp. 13–19.
13. *Chartularium Universitatis Parisiensis*, edited by Denifle and Châtelain, Paris, Delalain, vol. 1, no.1, quoted by Riché and Verger, *Nains*, p. 189.
14. Cobban, *Medieval Universities*, pp. 79–80.
15. Most of the points in this paragraph are drawn from Nardi, "Relations with authority," p. 82.
16. Quoted by Evans, *Life in Medieval France*, p. 128.
17. Quoted and translated by Evans, *Life in Medieval France*, p. 128.
18. Verger, *Les universités françaises au Moyen Age*, p. 31. The English translation is my own.
19. Evans, *Life in Medieval France*, p. 131.
20. Quoted by Evans, *Life in Medieval France*, p. 131.
21. Quoted by Bellomo, *Common Legal Past*, p. 115.
22. Quoted in Medieval Sourcebook, "Jacques de Vitry," p. 1.
23. Nardi, "Relations with authority," p. 83.
24. This section is adapted from Medieval Sourcebook, "Robert de Courçon," pp. 1–3.
25. Verger, "Patterns," pp. 51–52.
26. Rashdall, *Universities in Europe*, vol. I, p. 334.
27. Rashdall, *Universities in Europe*, vol. I, pp. 334–43.
28. Barber, *Two Cities*, p. 409.

29. Piltz, "World of Medieval Learning," p. 135.
30. Rashdall, *Universities of Europe*, vol. I, p. 338.
31. *Chartularium Universitatis Parisiensis*, *op. cit.*, vol. I, no. 79 (Charles Vulliez trans.), quoted by Riché and Verger, *Nains*, p. 190. The English translation is my own.
32. Quoted by Rüegg, "Themes," p. 15.
33. Cobban, *Medieval Universities*, pp. 84–86.
34. Verger, *Les universités françaises*, p. 68.
35. Holmes, *Oxford Illustrated History of Medieval Europe*, p. 353.
36. Riché and Verger, *Nains*, p. 222. The English translation is my own.
37. This account is drawn from Cobban, *Medieval Universities*, pp. 90–94.
38. Quoted by Jordan, *Europe in the High Middle Ages*, pp. 216–17.
39. Evans, *Fifty Key Medieval Thinkers*, p. 100.
40. Leff, "The *trivium* and the three philosophies," p. 322.
41. Asztalos, "The faculty of theology," p. 424.
42. Asztalos, "The faculty of theology," p. 424.
43. The following account draws heavily from the Stanford Encyclopedia of Philosophy, "Condemnation of 1277," pp. 1–7.
44. Quoted by Riché and Verger, *Nains*, p. 226.
45. Verger, "Patterns," p. 35.
46. Cobban, *Medieval Universities*, pp. 23–27.
47. Cobban, *Medieval Universities*, p. 31.
48. This account is taken from Courtenay, *Parisian Scholars*, pp. 49–56.
49. *Chartulaium Universitatis Parisiensis*, *op. cit.*, vol. 3, 1894, no. 1454, quoted by Riché and Verger, *Nains*, p. 279. The English translation is my own.
50. Moraw, "Careers of graduates," p. 253.
51. "The Great Schism: from Froissart's *Chronicles*," pp. 1–3.
52. Medieval Sourcebook, "The Great Schism: University of Paris and the Schism," p. 1.
53. Evans, *Fifty Key Medieval Thinkers*, p. 168.
54. Quoted by Rummel, *Humanist-Scholastic Debate*, p. 37.
55. Jean Gerson, *Œuvres complètes*, edited by Monsignor Glorieux, vol. II (1), *L'œuvre française. Sermons et discours*, Paris, 1968, pp. 1144–45, quoted by Verger, "*Les professeurs*

des universités françaises," p. 187. The English translation is my own.

56. Verger, "Teachers," p. 164.

57. Jean Gerson, Œuvres complètes, edited by Monsignor Glorieux, vol. II (1), L'œuvre française. Sermons et discours, Paris, 1968, pp. 1144–1145, quoted by Verger, "Les professeurs des universités françaises," p. 187. The English translation is my own.

58. Swanson, Universities, Academics and the Great Schism, pp. 13–14.

59. Stanford Encyclopedia of Philosophy, "Medieval Political Philosophy: The Conciliar Movement," p. 15.

60. Quoted and translated by Burl, Danse Macabre, p. 30.

61. Unless otherwise noted, this account of Villon's life comes from Janin, Medieval Justice, pp. 144–46.

62. This account is drawn from Burl, Danse Macabre, pp. 69–71.

63. "Ballade des Pendus: François Villon," p. 1.

64. "François Villon: Poems," p. 1.

65. Burl, Danse Macabre, p. vii.

66. Cobban, Medieval Universities, pp. 94–95.

67. Rashdall, Universities of Europe, vol. I, pp. 426–27.

68. Quoted by Cobban, Medieval Universities, p. 95.

69. Courtenay, Parisian Scholars, p. 20.

70. Rashdall, Universities of Europe, vol. I, p. 430.

71. Nardi, "Relations with authority," p. 104.

Chapter V

1. Barber, Two Cities, p. 410.

2. Evans, Fifty Key Medieval Thinkers, p. 129.

3. Baldwin, Scholastic Culture, pp. 95–96.

4. Quoted by Conway, St. Thomas Aquinas, pp. 2–3.

5. Quoted by Piltz, World of Medieval Learning, pp. 187–88.

6. The comments that follow are adapted from the text in Summa Theologica, pp. 3–5.

7. This account is drawn from the Stanford Encyclopedia of Philosophy, "Saint Bonaventure," pp. 1–19, and from the Catholic Encyclopedia, "St. Bonaventure," pp. 1–9.

8. Quoted by Stanford Encyclopedia of Philosophy, "Saint Bonaventure," p. 2.

9. Quoted by Stanford Encyclopedia of Philosophy, "Saint Bonaventure," p. 3.

10. Evans, Fifty Key Medieval Thinkers, pp. 134–35.

11. Quoted in Baldwin, Scholastic Culture, p. 69.

12. Shaw, Saint Joan, pp. 3–4.

13. Hobbins, "The Trial of Joan of Arc," p. 3.

14. Quoted by Pernoud, Joan of Arc, p. 87.

15. Some of the information on the role of the University of Paris during Joan's trials is drawn from a private communication of 2 June 2007 from the Historical Association of Joan of Arc Studies.

16. Verger, Les universités françaises, p. 205.

17. Pernoud, Joan of Arc, pp. 207–17.

18. Medieval Sourcebook, "The Trial of Joan of Arc," p. 1.

19. Quoted by Pernoud, Joan of Arc, p. 136.

20. Quoted by Williamson, "Joan of Arc," p. 13.

21. Quoted by Williamson, "Joan of Arc," p. 13.

22. Quoted by Williamson, "Joan of Arc," p. 13.

23. Quoted by Favier, La Guerre de Cent Ans, p. 528.

24. Janin, Medieval Justice, pp. 169–70.

Chapter VI

1. Rashdall, Universities of Europe, vol. III, p. 15.

2. See Cobban, Medieval Universities, pp. 97–98.

3. The points in this paragraph are drawn from Rüegg, "Themes," p. 13.

4. Nardi, "Relations with authority," p. 92.

5. Cobban, Medieval Universities, p. 109.

6. After Cobban, English University Life, pp. 191–92.

7. Cobban, English University Life, p. 5.

8. Quoted by Rashdall, Universities of Europe, vol. III, p. 55.

9. Balliol College History, p. 1.

10. These comments are drawn from Janin, Medieval Justice, pp. 111–12.

11. Pitkin City Guides, "Oxford," p. 10, and Rashdall, Universities of Europe, vol. III, pp. 208–9.

12. Quoted in Pitkin City Guides, *Oxford*, frontispiece.

13. "Of showing due propriety," pp. 1–2.

14. Cobban, *Medieval Universities*, p. 107.

15. This account is drawn from Penner, "New College," p. 1, and from a private communication of 28 May 2007 from Dr. Paul Brand.

16. Rashdall, *Universities of Europe*, vol. III, p. 217.

17. Private communication of 7 May 2007 from Dr. Paul Brand.

18. Brand, *Making of the Common Law*, p. 57.

19. Quoted by Keen, *English Society*, p. 234.

20. This discussion draws on Tyack, *Bodleian Library*, pp. 3, 27–35.

21. Rashdall, *Universities of Europe*, vol. III, p. 167.

Chapter VII

1. Rashdall, *Universities of Europe*, vol. III, pp. 240–41.

2. MacTutor, "Robert Grosseteste," p. 1.

3. The Electronic Grosseteste, p. 1.

4. Cobban, *Medieval Universities*, pp. 107–8.

5. MacTutor History of Mathematics, p. 2.

6. Evans, *Fifty Key Medieval Thinkers*, pp. 119–20.

7. Rashdall, *Universities of Europe*, vol. III, pp. 245–46.

8. Quoted by MacTutor History of Mathematics, p. 3.

9. Quoted by Medieval Sourcebook, "Roger Bacon," p. 1.

10. MacTutor History of Mathematics, "Roger Bacon," p. 3.

11. Medieval Sourcebook, "Roger Bacon," pp. 3–4.

12. Quoted by Piltz, "World of Medieval Learning," p. 186.

13. Stanford Encyclopedia of Philosophy, "Roger Bacon," p. 22.

14. Unless otherwise noted, this section is drawn from the Stanford Encyclopedia of Philosophy, "John Duns Scotus," pp. 1–13.

15. Quoted in "English Scholars," p. 1.

16. Stanford Encyclopedia of Philosophy, "John Duns Scotus," pp. 4–5.

17. Stanford Encyclopedia of Philosophy, "Medieval Theories of Haecceity," p. 1.

18. Stanford Encyclopedia of Philosophy, "Medieval Theories of Haecceity," pp. 2–3.

19. Quoted by Rashdall, *Universities of Europe*, vol. III, p. 259.

20. Some of my comments are drawn from the Stanford Encyclopedia of Philosophy's article, "William of Ockham."

21. Stanford Encyclopedia of Philosophy, "William of Ockham," p. 14.

22. Some of these comments and examples are drawn from Wikipedia, "Occam's Razor," pp. 1–18, and Internet Encyclopedia of Philosophy, "William of Ockham," p. 4.

23. Internet Encyclopedia of Philosophy, "William of Ockham," p. 4.

24. After Ozment, *Age of Reform*, pp. 62–63.

25. Stanford Encyclopedia of Philosophy, "John Wyclif," p. 13.

26. Stanford Encyclopedia of Philosophy, "John Wyclif," p. 13.

27. Quoted by Rashdall, *Universities of Europe*, vol. III, p. 127.

28. Medieval Sourcebook, "Pope Gregory XI: The Condemnation of Wycliffe," pp. 1–2.

29. Medieval Sourcebook, "Pope Gregory XI," p. 4.

30. Stanford Encyclopedia of Philosophy, "John Wyclif," p. 2.

31. Quoted by Bartlett, *Medieval Panorama*, p. 309.

32. Rashdall, *Universities of Europe*, vol. I, p. 271.

Chapter VIII

1. Verger, "Patterns," pp. 57, 62–65.

2. Riché and Verger, *Nains*, p. 229.

3. This discussion follows Siraisi, "The faculty of medicine," pp. 382–85.

4. Quoted by Haskins, *Renaissance of the Twelfth Century*, p. 210.

5. Riché and Verger, *Nains*, p. 196.

6. Cobban, *Medieval Universities*, p. 29.

7. *Cartulaire de l'université de Montpellier*, Montpellier, Ricard, 1890, vol. I, no. 2, quoted by Riché and Verger, *Nains*, p. 195. The English translation is my own.

8. Cobban, *Medieval Universities*, pp. 180–81.

9. Quoted by Compayré, *Abelard*, p. 275; lightly edited.

10. Compayré, *Abelard*, p. 275.

11. Rashdall, *Universities of Europe*, vol. III, p. 278.

12. Rashdall, *Universities of Europe*, vol. III, pp. 284–285, 292.
13. Cobban, *Medieval Universities*, pp. 110, 115.
14. Schwinnges, "Student education," p. 225.
15. Paris, *Chronicles*, p. 101.
16. These town-gown clashes are drawn from Cobban, *English University Life*, pp. 194–197.
17. Rashdall, *Universities of Europe*, vol. II, p. 10.
18. Quoted by Rashdall, *Universities of Europe*, vol. II, p. 11.
19. Rashdall, *Universities of Europe*, vol. II, p. 21.
20. Rashdall, *Universities of Europe*, vol. II, pp. 22, 24.
21. Rashdall, *Universities of Europe*, vol. II, pp. 25–26.
22. Pryds, "*Studia* as royal offices," pp. 88–89.
23. Rashdall, *Universities of Europe*, vol. II, p. 162.
24. Barber, *Two Cities*, pp. 409–10.
25. Rashdall, *Universities of Europe*, vol. II, p. 171.
26. Quoted by Rashdall, *Universities of Europe*, vol. II, p. 173.
27. Rashdall, *Universities of Europe*, vol. III, pp. 433–35.
28. Le Goff, "Ville," p. 1196. The English translation is my own.
29. Rashdall, *Universities of Europe*, vol. II, pp. 151, 154.
30. Rashdall, *Universities of Europe*, vol. II, p. 158.
31. Rashdall, *Universities of Europe*, vol. II, p. 143.
32. Riché and Verger, *Nains*, p. 276.
33. Rashdall, *Universities of Europe*, vol. II, p. 149.
34. Rashdall, *Universities of Europe*, vol. II, p. 150.
35. Haskins, *Renaissance of the Twelfth Century*, p. 210.
36. Courtenay, *Universities and Schooling*, pp. 110–11.
37. Maine, *Ancient Law*, p. 69.
38. Quoted by Wikipedia, "Hugh Primas," p. 1.
39. Quoted and translated by Piltz, "World of Medieval Learning," p. 28.
40. Rashdall, *Universities of Europe*, vol. III, pp. 432–33.
41. Rashdall, *Universities of Europe*, vol. II, pp. 213–14.
42. Rashdall, *Universities of Europe*, vol. II, p. 217.
43. Quoted by Rashdall, *Universities of Europe*, vol. II, p. 236.
44. Rashdall, *Universities of Europe*, vol. II, pp. 241–42.
45. University of Vienna, "Renaissance-Humanism," p 1.
46. Quoted by Rashdall, *Universities of Europe*, vol. II, p. 312.
47. Schwinges, "Admission," p. 190.

Chapter IX

1. Private communication of 23 July 2007 from Dr. Robert Black.
2. Zilsel, "Methods of Humanism," p. 4.
3. Zilsel, "Methods of Humanism," p. 3.
4. Zilsel, "Methods of Humanism," pp. 2–5.
5. Abbagnano, "Renaissance Humanism," p. 1.
6. Rüegg, "The rise of humanism," pp. 454–53.
7. Abbagnano, "Renaissance Humanism," p. 2.
8. Brundage, *Medieval Canon Law*, p. 68.
9. Quoted by Grendler, *Universities of the Italian Renaissance*, p. 199.
10. Library of Congress, "Humanism," p. 8.
11. Library of Congress, "Humanism," p. 1.
12. Southern, *Scholastic Humanism*, p. 21.
13. Southern, *Scholastic Humanism*, p. 21.
14. Southern, *Scholastic Humanism*, pp. 22–35.
15. Cobban, *Medieval Universities*, p. 13.
16. Cobban, *Medieval Universities*, pp. 13–14.
17. Grendler, *Universities of the Italian Renaissance*, pp. 509–10.
18. Private communication of 23 July 2007 from Dr. Robert Black.
19. Grendler, *Universities of the Italian Renaissance*, p. 247.
20. Quoted by Rummel, *Humanist-Scholastic Debate*, p. 64.
21. Quoted by Rummel, *Humanist-Scholastic Debate*, p. 66.
22. University of Chicago Library, "Renaissance Humanism," pp. 3–4.
23. Quoted by Rummel, *Humanist-Scholastic Debate*, p. 5.

24. Quoted by Rummel, *Humanist-Scholastic Debate*, p. 5.
25. Southern, *Scholastic Humanism*, p. 18.
26. Rüegg, "The rise of humanism," pp. 455–56.
27. Private communication of 23 July 2007 from Dr. Robert Black.
28. Verger, "Patterns," p. 44.
29. Quoted by Morris, "Petrarch," p. 1.
30. Quoted by Rummel, *Humanist-Scholastic Debate*, p. 31.
31. Petrarch, *De vera sapientia*, in Patrick Gilli, *La Noblesse du droit: débats et controverses sur la culture juridique et le rôle des juristes dans l'Italie médiévale, XII–XV siècles*, Paris, H. Champion, 2003, pp. 175–76, quoted by Riché and Verger, *Nains*, p. 274. The English translation is my own.
32. Grendler, *Universities of the Italian Renaissance*, p. 436.
33. Quoted by University of Chicago Library, "Renaissance Humanism," p. 1.
34. Quoted by Rummel, *Humanist-Scholastic Debate*, p. 42.
35. Quoted by Rummel, *Humanist-Scholastic Debate*, p. 44.
36. "Humanism," p. 1.
37. Harvard University Press, "History of the Florentine People," p. 1.
38. Quoted by Rummel, *Humanist-Scholastic Debate*, p. 56.
39. Black, *Humanism and Education*," p. 16.
40. Black, *Humanism and Education*, pp. 125–26.
41. Grendler, *Universities of the Italian Renaissance*, p. 25.
42. Quoted by Grudin, "Humanism," p. 3.
43. Quoted by Coleman, "Lorenzo Valla," p. 2.
44. "Giovanni Pico della Mirandola," p. 1.
45. Hooker, "Pico della Mirandola," p. 1.
46. Quoted in "Giovanni Pico della Mirandola," p. 1.
47. Quoted in "Biographie," p. 3. The English translation is my own.
48. Quoted in "Biographie," p. 4. The English translation is my own.
49. The Latin is from *Declarationes ad censuras facultatis theoiogiae Parisianae* (1522), quoted by Wikipedia, "Grocyn," p. 1.
50. Translated from the Latin by Dr. Paul Brand.
51. Cambridge History, "John Colet," pp. 1–2.
52. Cambridge History, "John Colet," pp. 2–3.
53. Cambridge History, "John Colet," p. 4.
54. Private communication of 31 July 2007 from Dr. Erika Rummel.
55. NNDB, "Thomas Linacre," p. 3.
56. Cambridge History of English and American Literature, "John Fisher," p. 1.
57. Quoted in "The Life of Sir Thomas More," p. 1.
58. Quoted by O'Connell, "A Man for all Seasons," p. 1. Italics added.
59. This description is largely drawn from "Utopia Book Notes Summary," pp. 1–2.
60. Modern History Sourcebook, "Utopia," p. 21.
61. Modern History Sourcebook, "Utopia," p. 28.
62. This section is variously drawn from the History Guide, "Desiderius Erasmus," pp. 1–3; Douglas, "Desiderius Erasmus, pp. 1–5; and Internet Encyclopedia of Philosophy, "Humanism," pp. 2–3.
63. Douglas, "Erasmus," p. 1.
64. Quoted by Courtney, *Schools and Scholars*, p. 366.
65. Yale University Press — London. *The Praise of Folly*, p. 1.
66. Modern History Sourcebook, "Erasmus," p. 4.
67. Modern History Sourcebook, "Erasmus," p. 31.
68. Modern History Sourcebook, "Erasmus," pp. 32–33.
69. Modern History Sourcebook, "Erasmus," p. 34.
70. Modern History Sourcebook, "Erasmus," p. 35.
71. Modern History Sourcebook, "Erasmus," p. 38.
72. Modern History Sourcebook, "Erasmus," pp. 41–42.
73. History Guide, "Erasmus," p. 1.
74. Quoted by Douglas, "Erasmus," p. 3.
75. Quoted by Douglas, "Erasmus," p. 3.
76. Sommerville, "Intellectual trends," p. 5.

Chapter X

1. Verger, "Patterns," p. 35.
2. Verger, "Naissance," p. 218. The English translation is my own.
3. Moraw, "Careers of graduates," p. 270.

4. Schwinges, "Admission," p. 188.
5. This account follows Keen, *English Society*, p. 232.
6. Moraw, "Careers of graduates," p. 255.
7. Quoted by Moulin, *La vie des étudiants*, p. 169. The English translation is my own.
8. Koenigsberger, *Medieval Europe*, p. 367.
9. Cobban, *Medieval Universities*, p. 219.
10. Cobban, *Medieval Universities*, pp. 219–20. Italics added.
11. Rashdall, *Universities of Europe*, vol. III, p. 457.
12. Courtenay, *Schools and Scholars*, p. 366.
13. See Janin, *Medieval Justice*, pp. 123–24.
14. Quoted by Rait, *Life in the Medieval University*, p. 153.
15. Private communication of 25 September 2007 from Dr. Helen Castor.
16. Quoted by Rait, *Life in the Medieval University*, p. 152. The version in modern English is my own.
17. Castor, *Blood and Roses*, p. 276.
18. Rait, *Life in the Medieval University*, p. 155.
19. Verger, "Les professeurs des universités," p. 175. The English translation is my own.
20. Swanson, *Universities, Academics and the Great Schism*, p. 58.
21. Nardi, "Relations with authority," p. 104.
22. Private communication of 24 March 2006 from Ria van Eil.
23. Haskins, *Rise of Universities*, pp. 67–68.
24. Rüegg, "Themes," pp. 15–16.
25. Verger, "Teachers," p. 164.
26. Riché and Verger, *Nains*, p. 240. The English translation is my own.
27. Grendler, "Universities of the Renaissance and Reformation," p. 1.
28. After Moulin, *La via des étudiants*," p. 286.

29. After Grendler, "Universities of the Renaissance and Reformation," p. 2.
30. Grendler, "Universities of the Renaissance and Reformation," p. 18.
31. Grendler, "Universities of the Renaissance and Reformation," pp. 9, 11.
32. Grendler, "Universities of the Renaissance and Reformation," pp. 19, 23.

Appendix 1

1. M. Fournier, *Les Status et Privilèges des universités françaises,* vol. II, Paris, 1891, no. 1316, pp. 411–12, quoted by Riché and Verger, *Nains*, pp. 254–55. The English translation is mine.

Appendix 2

1. Adapted from Medieval Sourcebook, "Peter Abelard: *Historia Calamitatum.*"
2. Medieval Sourcebook, "Peter Abelard: *Historia Calamitatum,*" pp. 5–6.
3. Medieval Sourcebook, "Peter Abelard: *Historia Calamitatum,*" pp. 7–8.
4. Medieval Sourcebook, "Peter Abelard: *Historia Calamitatum,*" pp. 12–13.

Appendix 3

1. Quoted by Paetow, *Morale Scholarium*, pp. 174–75.

Appendix 5

1. Hobbins, "The Trial of Joan of Arc," pp. 38–39.

Appendix 6

1. "University of Paris, Courses in Theology and Medicine," p. 2.

Bibliography

Abbagnano, Nicola. "Renaissance Humanism." http: etext.virginia.edu/cgi-local/DHI/dhi.cgi?id=dv4-19. Accessed 12 July 2007.

Asztalos, Monika. "The faculty of theology," in Hilde de Ridder-Symoens, *A History of the University in Europe*. Cambridge: Cambridge University Press, 2003, pp. 409–41.

Backhouse, Janet. *Medieval Rural Life in the Luttrell Psalter*. London: British Library, 2000.

Baldwin, John W. *The Scholastic Culture of the Middle Ages, 1000–1300*. Lexington: Heath, 1971.

"Ballade des Pendus: François Villon." http://www.historique.net/philologie/pendus/. Accessed 7 August 2007.

Balliol College. "Balliol College History." http://www.balliol.ox.ac.uk/history/history/. Accessed 24 April 2007.

Barber, Malcolm. *The Two Cities: Medieval Europe, 1050–1320*. 2nd ed. London: Routledge, 2005.

Bartlett, Robert, ed. *Medieval Panorama*. London: Thames & Hudson, 2001.

Bellomo, Manlio. *The Common Legal Past of Europe, 1000–1800*. Translated by Lydia G. Cochrane. Washington, D.C.: Catholic University Press, 1995.

"Bibliographie Giovanni Pico della Mirandola." http//www.lyber-eclat.net/lyber/mirandola/picbio/html. Accessed 25 July 2007.

Black, Robert. *Humanism and Education in Medieval and Renaissance Italy: Tradition and Innovation in Latin Schools from the Twelfth to the Fifteenth Century*. Cambridge: Cambridge University Press, 2007.

Bloch, Marc. *Feudal Society*. Vol. 1. "The Growth of Ties of Dependence." Translated by L. A. Manyon. Chicago: University of Chicago Press, 1961.

_____. *Feudal Society*. Vol. 2. "Social Classes and Political Organization." Translated by L. A. Manyon. London: Routledge, 1995.

Brand, Paul. *The Making of the Common Law*. London: Hambledon, 1992

British Library. Glossary for the British Library Catalogue of Illuminated Manuscripts: "Pecia System." http://www.bl.uk/catalogues/illuminatedmanuscripts/GlossP.asp. Accessed 20 April 2007.

Brundage, James A. *Medieval Canon Law*. Harlow: Longman, 1996.

Burl, Aubrey. *Danse Macabre: François Villon — Poetry & Murder in Medieval France*. Stroud: Sutton, 2000.

Camargo, Martin. "Rhetoric," in David L. Wagner (ed.) *The Seven Liberal Arts in the Middle Ages.* Bloomington: Indiana University Press, 1983, pp. 96–124.

Cambridge History of English and American Literature. "Englishmen and the Classical Renascence: John Colet." http://www.bartleby.com/213/0107.html. Accessed 13 July 2007.

Castor, Helen. *Blood and Roses: The Paston Family in the Fifteenth Century.* London: Faber and Faber, 2004.

Catholic Encyclopedia. "St. Bonaventure." http://www.newadvent.org/cathen/02648c.htm. Accessed 23 April 2007.

_____. "The University of Bologna." http://www.newadvent.org/cathen/02641b.htm. Accessed 9 December 2007.

Chaucer, Geoffrey. *The Canterbury Tales.* London: Penguin, 1996.

Cobban, Alan B. *English University Life in the Middle Ages.* London: University College London Press, 1999.

_____. *The Medieval Universities: Their Development and Organization.* London: Methuen, 1975.

Coleman, Christopher B. "Lorenzo Valla: *Discourse on the Forgery of the Alleged Donation of Constantine.*" http://history.hanover.edu/texts/vallaintro.html. Accessed 2 August 2007.

Compayré, Gabriel. *Abelard and Early History of Universities.* Honolulu: University Press of the Pacific, 2002.

Conway, Placid. *St. Thomas Aquinas.* http://www2.nd.edu/Departments/Maritain/etext/conwayo2.htm. Accessed 22 April 2007.

Courtenay, William J. *Parisian Scholars in the Early Fourteenth Century: A Social Portrait.* Cambridge: Cambridge University Press, 2006.

_____. *Schools and Scholars in Fourteenth-Century England.* Princeton: Princeton University Press, 1987.

_____ and Jürgen Miethke. *Universities and Schooling in Medieval Society.* Leiden: Brill, 2000.

D'Avray, David. "Scholastic Humanism and the Unification of Europe. Volume I. Foundations." http://www.history.ac/uk/reviews/paper/southern.html. Accessed 18 June 2007.

De Wulf, Maurice. "History of Medieval Philosophy." http://maritain.nd/jmc.extext/homp231.htm. Accessed 21 April 2007.

Douglas, J. D. "Desiderius Erasmus: The Ambivalent Reformer." http://www.williamtyndale.com/0erasmusreformation.htm. Accessed 15 July 2007.

Duby, Georges. *France in the Middle Ages, 987–1460.* Translated by Juliet Vale. Oxford: Blackwell, 1988.

Electronic Grosseteste. "Who was Robert Grosseteste?" http://www.grosseteste.com/bio/htm. Accessed 4 May 2007.

Encyclopædia Britannica Online. "Humanism." http://www.britannica.com/eb/article-1178. Accessed 31 January 2007.

"English Scholars of Paris and Franciscans of Oxford: No. 19. Duns Scotus." http://www.bartleby.com/211/1019.htm. Accessed 9 May 2007.

Evans, G. R. *Fifty Key Medieval Thinkers.* London: Routledge, 2002.

Evans, Joan. *Life in Medieval France.* London: Phaidon, 1957.

Favier, Jean. *La Guerre de Cent Ans.* Paris: Fayard, 1996.

"François Villon." http://www.bohemiabooks.com.au/eblinks/spirboho/fringe/villon/villon.htm. Accessed 9 November 2001.

"François Villon: Poems." http://www.tonykline.co.uk/PITBR/French/Villon.htm. Accessed 7 August 2007.

García y García, Antonio. "The Faculties of Law," in Hilde De Ridder-Symoens, *A History of the University in Europe*. Cambridge: Cambridge University Press, 2003, pp. 388–408.

Gieysztor, Aleksander. "Management and resources," in Hilde de Ridder-Symoens, *A History of the University of Europe*. Cambridge: Cambridge University Press, 2003, pp. 108–43.

"Giovanni Pico della Mirandola (1463–1494)." http://www.whitworth.edu/Core/Classics/CO250/Italy/Data/d_pico.htm. Accessed 25 July 2007.

Goetz, Hans-Werner. *Life in the Middle Ages from the Seventh to the Thirteenth Century*. Translated by Steven Rowan. Notre-Dame: University of Notre-Dame Press, 1993.

Grendler, Paul F. *The Universities of the Italian Renaissance*. Baltimore: John Hopkins University Press, 2002.

_____. "The universities of the Renaissance and Reformation." http://www.thefreelibrary.com/The+universities+of+the+Renaissance+and+Reformation. Accessed 22 September 2007.

Grudin, Robert. "Humanism." http://www.compilerpress.atfreeweb.com/Anno%20Grudin%20Humanism%20EB.htm. Accessed 12 July 2007.

Harlow, Dan. "Sweden Loans the Devil to Prague." http://www.danharlow.com/blog/2007/09/21/sweden-loans-the-devil-to-prague/ Accessed 12 December 2007.

Harvard University Press. "History of the Florentine People, Volume I, Books I-IV." www.hup.harvard.edu/catalog/BRUHI1.html. Accessed 12 July 2007.

Haskins, Charles Homer. *The Renaissance of the Twelfth Century*. Cambridge: Harvard University Press, 1955.

_____. *The Rise of Universities*. Ithaca: Cornell University Press, 1965.

Hewitt, H. J. *The Black Prince's Expedition of 1355–57*. Manchester: University of Manchester Press, 1958.

Historical Association for Joan of Arc Studies. http://www.joan-of-arc-studies.org/. Private communication of 2 June 2007.

History Guide. "Desiderius Erasmus, 1466–1536." http:www.historyguide.org/intellect/erasmus.html. Accessed 20 June 2007.

Hobbins, Daniel. "The Trial of Joan of Arc." www.hup.harvard.edu/pdf/HOBTRI_excerpt.pdf. Accessed 25 May 2007.

Holmes, George, ed. *The Oxford Illustrated History of Medieval Europe*, Oxford: Oxford University Press, 2001.

Hooker, Richard. "Pico della Mirandola." Hppt://www.wsu.edu/~dee/REN/PICO.HTM. Accessed 25 July 2007.

"Hugues Aubriot, prévôt de Paris sous Charles V." http://grande-boucherie.chez-alice.fr/Aubriot.htm. Accessed 7 May 2007.

"Humanism." www.wsu.edu/~dee/REN/HUMANISM.HTM. Accessed 11 July 2007.

"Humanism and the Early Italian Renaissance." oak.conncoll.edu/Textbook4Sale/Humanism.doc. Accessed 5 July 2007.

Huntsman, Jeffery H. "Grammar," in *The Seven Liberal Arts in the Middle Ages*, edited by David L. Wagner. Bloomington: Indiana University Press, 1988, pp. 58–95.

Internet Encyclopedia of Philosophy. "Humanism." http://www.iep.utm.edu/h/humanism.htm. Accessed 14 July 2007.

_____. "Peter Lombard (1095)-1160)." http://www.utm.edu/research/iep/l/lombard.htm. Accessed 24 February 2007.

_____. "William of Ockham (c.1280-c.1349)." http://www.iep.utm.edu/o/ockham.htm. Accessed 12 May 2007.

Janin, Hunt. *Medieval Justice: Cases and Laws in France, England and Germany, 500–1500*. Jefferson: McFarland, 2004.

_____. *The Pursuit of Learning in the Islamic World, 610–2003*. Jefferson: McFarland, 2005.

"Johannes Andreae." http://faculty.cua.edu/pennington/1298-h-j.htm. Accessed 16 May 2007.

Jordan, William Chester. *Europe in the High Middle Ages*. London: Penguin, 2002.

Karp, Theodore C. "Music," in *The Seven Liberal Arts in the Middle Ages*, edited by David L. Wagner. Bloomington: Indiana University Press, 1983, pp. 169–95.

Keen, Maurice. *English Society in the Later Middle Ages, 1348–1500*. London: Penguin, 1990.

Koenigsberger, H. G. *Medieval Europe, 400–1500*. Harlow: Longman, 1998.

Kren, Claudia. "Astronomy," in *The Seven Liberal Arts in the Middle Ages*, edited by David L. Wagner. Bloomington: Indiana University Press, 1983, pp. 218–247.

Ladurie, Emmanuel Le Roy. *Montaillou: Cathars and Catholics in a French village, 1294–1324*. Translated by Barbara Bray. London: Penguin, 1990.

Larsen, Andrew E. "Pecia system." Private communication of 20 April 2007.

Laws, Robert Anthony. *Dance of the Hanging Men: The Story of François Villon, killer, thief and poet*. West Bridgford: Pauper's Press, 1993.

Leff, Gordon. "The *Trivium* and the Three Philosophies," in Hilde de Ridder-Symoens, *A History of the University in Europe*. Cambridge: Cambridge University Press, 2003, pp. 307–336.

_____ and Jean-Claude Schmitt. *Dictionnaire raisonné de l'Occident médiéval*. Paris: Fayard, 1999.

Le Goff, Jacques. "Ville," in *Dictionnaire raisonné de l'Occident médiéval*. Paris : Fayard, 199, pp. 1183–1200.

Library of Congress. "Humanism (Rome Reborn: The Vatican Library & Renaissance Culture). http://www.loc.gov/exhibits/vatican/humanism.html. Accessed 5 July 2007.

"The Life of Sir Thomas More (1478–1535)." http://www.luminarium.org/renlit/more-bio.htm. Accessed 1 August 2007.

MacTutor History of Mathematics. "Robert Grosseteste." http://www-history.mcs.st-and-ac.uk/~history/Printonly/Grosseteste.html. Accessed 3 May 2007.

_____. "Roger Bacon." http://www-groups.dcs.st- and.ac.uk-history/Printonly/Bacon.html. Accessed 6 May 2007.

Maine, Henry Sumner. *Ancient Law*. Oxford: Oxford University Press, 1931.

Masi, Michael. "Arithmetic," in *The Seven Liberal Arts in the Middle Ages*, edited by David L. Wagner. Bloomington: Indiana University Press, 1983.

Medieval Society. Leiden: Brill, 2000, pp. 83–99.

Medieval Sourcebook. "Crisis, Recovery, Feudalism?" hppt://www.fordham.edu/halsall/sbook1i.html. Accessed 29 January 2007.

_____. "The Great Schism: from Froissart's *Chronicles*." http://www.uvawise.edu/history/wciv1/civ1/ref/froischi.htm. Accessed 17 May 2007.

_____. "The Great Schism: University of Paris and the Schism, 1393." http://www.fordham.edu/halsall/source/grtschism2.html. Accessed 18 May 2007.

_____. "Jacques de Vitry: Life of the Students at Paris." http://www.fordham.edu/halsall/source/vitry1.html. Accessed 5 June 2006.

_____. "Jean Frossart: On the Hundred Years War (1337–1453)." http://www.fordham.edu/halsall/source/froissart1.html. Accessed 28 January 2007.

_____. "Peter Abelard: *Historia Calamitatum* (*The Story of My Misfortunes*)." http://www.fordham.edu.halsall/basis/abelard-histcal.html. Accessed 11 June 2006.

_____. "Pope Gregory XI: The Condemnation of Wycliffe 1382 and Wycliffe's Reply, 1384." http://www.fordham/edu/halsall/source/1382wycliffe.html. Accessed 26 October 2006.

_____. "Robert de Courçon: Statutes for the University of Paris, 1215." http://www.fordham.edu/halsall/source/courcon1.html. Accessed 9 April 2007.

_____. "Roger Bacon: Despair over Thirteenth Century Learning." http://www.fordham.edu/halsall/source/bacon.html. Accessed 6 May 2007.

_____. "The Trial of Joan of Arc." http://www.fordham.edu/halsall/basis/joanofarctrial.html. Accessed 23 May 2007.

MetraNet. "Gaudeamus Igitur—A Translation." http://www.londonmet.ac.uk/admin/graduation-and-conferments/awards-ceremonies/on-the-... Accessed 5 June 2007.

Miethke, Jürgen. "Practical Intentions of Scholasticism: The Example of Political Theory," in William J. Courtenay and Jürgen Miethke (eds.). *Universities and Schooling in Medieval Society*. Brill: Leiden, 2000, pp. 211–228.

"The Miller's Prologue and Tale—An Interlinear Translation." http://www.courses.fas.harvard.edu/~chaucer/teachslf/milt-par.htm. Accessed 26 May 2007.

Modern History Sourcebook. "Desiderius Erasmus: The Praise of Folly (*Moriae Encomium*), 1509." http:www.fordham.edu/halsall/mod/1509erasmus-folly.html. Accessed 10 July 2007.

_____. "Sir Thomas More: *Utopia*, 1516." http://www.fordham.edu/halsall/mod/thomasmore-utopia.html. Accessed 1 August 2007.

Moraw, Peter. "Careers of graduates," in Hilde de Ridder-Symoens, *A History of the University in Europe*. Cambridge: Cambridge University Press, 2003, pp. 244–279.

Morris, Roderick Conway. "Petrarch, the first humanist." International Herald Tribune, 29 May 2004. http:www.iht/com/articles/2004/05/29/conway_ed3_O.php. Accessed 28 July 2007.

Moulin, Léo. *La vie des étudiants au Moyen Age*. Paris: Albin Michel, 1991.

Nardi, Paolo. "Relations with authority," in Hilde de Ridder-Symoens, *A History of the University in Europe*. Cambridge: Cambridge University Press, 2003, pp. 77–107.

Nederman, Cary J. *John of Salisbury*. Medieval and Renaissance Studies Vol. 228. Tempe: Arizona Center for Medieval and Renaissance Studies, 2005.

NNDB. "Thomas Linacre." http://www.nndb.com/people/623/000104311/. Accessed 14 July 2007.

North, John. "The *Quadrivium*," in Hilde de Ridder-Symoens, *A History of the University in Europe*. Cambridge: Cambridge University Press, 2003, pp. 337–359.

"Occam's razor." http://en.wikipedia/org/w/index.php?title=Occam%27s_razor&printable=yes. Accessed 12 May 2007.

O'Connell, Marvin. "A Man for all Seasons: an Historian's Demur." http://www.catholiceducation.org/articles/politics/pg0078.html. Accessed 2 August 2007.

"Of showing due propriety in the custody of books." http://www.djmacadam.com/duepropriety.html. Accessed 16 May 2007.

Ozment, Steven. *The Age of Reform, 1250–1550*. New Haven: Yale University Press, 1980.

Paetow, Louis John. "*Morale Scholarium* of John of Salisbury," in Louis John Paetow, *Two Medieval Satires on the University of Paris*. Berkeley: University of California Press, 1927, pp. 65–261.

Painter, Sidney. *A History of the Middle Ages, 284–1500*. London: Macmillan, 1975.

Palmer, Robert C. *The Whilton Dispute, 1264–1380: A Social-Legal Study of Dispute Settlement in Medieval England*. Princeton: Princeton University Press, 1984.

Paris, Matthew. *The Illustrated Chronicles of Matthew Paris: Observations of Thirteenth-Century Life*. Translated and edited by Nigel Williams. Cambridge: Alan Sutton, 1993.

Pedersen, Olaf. *The First Universities: Stadium Generale and the Origins of University Education in Europe*. Translated by Richard North. Cambridge: Cambridge University Press, 1997.

Penner, David S. "The Heritage of University Planning: The Medieval Colleges: New College." http://www.andrews.edu/~penner/notebook/colleges/nc_found.html. Accessed 19 May 2007.

Pernoud, Régine. *Héloïse et Abelard*. Paris: Albin Michel, 1970.

_____. *Lumière du Moyen Age*. Paris: France Loisirs, 1981.

_____ and Marie-Véronique Clin. *Joan of Arc: Her Story*. Translated by Jeremy duQuesnay Adams. London: Phoenix, 2000.

Piltz, Anders. *The World of Medieval Learning*. Translated by David Jones. Oxford: Basil Blackwell, 1981.

Pitkin City Guides, "Oxford." Pitkin Unichrome Ltd, 2000.

"Plague Readings." http://www.u.arizona.edu/~afutrell/w%20civ%/2002/plaguereadings.html. Accessed 31 January 2007.

Power, Eileen. *Medieval People*. London: Folio Society, 1999.

Pryds, Darleen. "*Studia* as royal offices: Mediterranean universities of medieval Europe," in William J. Courtenay and Jürgen Miethke, *Universities and Schooling in Medieval Society*. Leiden: Brill, 2000, pp. 83–99.

Rait, Robert S. *Life in the Medieval University*. Cambridge: University of Cambridge Press, 1912.

Rashdall, Hastings. *The Universities of Europe in the Middle Ages*, edited by F. M. Powicke and A. B. Emden. 3 vols. Oxford: Oxford University Press, 1977.

Reilly, John J. "The Life of Thomas More." http://www.johnreilly.into/tomo.htm. Accessed 1 August 2007.

Riché, Pierre, and Jacques Verger. *Des nains sur des épaules de géants*. Paris: Tallandier, 2006.

Ridder-Symoens, Hilde de. "Mobility," in Hilde de Ridder-Symoens, *A History of the University in Europe*, pp. 280–304.

Ross, George MacDonald. "Porphyry: Introduction to Aristotle's *Categories*." http:www.philosophy.leeds.ac.uk/GMR/hmp/texts/ancient/porphyry/isagoge.html. Accessed 21 June 2006.

Rüegg, Walter. "Epilogue: The Rise of Humanism," in Hilde de Ridder-Symoens, *A History of the University in Europe*. Vol. I. *Universities in the Middle Ages*. Cambridge: Cambridge University Press, 2003, pp. 442–468.

_____. "Foreword," in Hilde de Ridder-Symoens, *A History of the University in Europe*. Vol. I. *Universities in the Middle Ages*. Cambridge: Cambridge University Press, 2003, p. xix.

_____. "Themes," in Hilde de Ridder-Symoens, *A History of the University in Europe*. Vol. I. *Universities in the Middle Ages*. Cambridge: Cambridge University Press, 2003, pp. 3–34.

Rummel, Erika. *The Humanist-Scholastic Debate in the Renaissance and Reformation*. Cambridge: Harvard University Press, 1995.

Schmitt, Jean-Claude. "Dieu," in Jacques Le Goff and Jean-Claude Schmitt, *Dictionnaire raisonné de l'Occident médiéval*. Paris: Fayard, 1999, pp. 273–289.

Schwinges, Rainer Christoph. "Admission," in Hilde de Ridder-Symoens, *A History of the University in Europe*. Cambridge: Cambridge University Press, 2003, pp. 171–194.

_____. "Student Education, Student Life," in Hilde de Ridder-Symoens, *A History of the University in Europe*. Cambridge: Cambridge University Press, 2003, pp. 195–243.

Seybolt, Robert Francis. *The Manuale Scholarium: An Original Account of Life in the Medieval University*. Cambridge: Harvard University Press, 1921.

Shaw, George Bernard. *Saint Joan*. London: Constable, 1930.

Shelby, Lon R. "Geometry," in *The Seven Liberal Arts in the Middle Ages*, edited by David L. Wagner. Bloomington: Indiana University Press, 1983, pp. 196–217.

Siraisi, Nancy. "The faculty of medicine," in Hilde de Ridder-Symoens, *A History of the University in Europe*. Cambridge: Cambridge University Press, 2003, pp. 361–387.

Sommervile, J. P. "Intellectual trends in the 17th century." http://hist.wisc.edu/commerville/351/351-17.htm. Accessed 31 January 2007.

_____. "The Twelfth Century Renaissance." http://history.wisc.edu/sommerville/123/123%20112%20renaissance.htm. Accessed 18 February 2007.

Southern, R. W. *Scholastic Humanism and the Unification of Europe*. Vol. 1: "Foundations." Oxford: Blackwell, 2002.

Stanford Encyclopedia of Philosophy. "Condemnation of 1277." http://plato.stanford.edu/entries/condemnation/. Accessed 26 April 2007.

_____. "John Duns Scotus." http://plato.stanford.edu/entries/duns-scotus/. Accessed 10 May 2007.

_____. "John Wyclif." http://plato.stanford.edu/entries/wyclif/. Accessed 13 May 2007.

_____. "Medieval Political Philosophy: The Conciliar Movement." http://plato.stanford.edu/entries/medieval-political/. Accessed 20 May 2007.

_____. "Medieval Theories of Haecceity." http://plato.stanford.edu/entries/medieval-haecceity. Accessed 9 May 2007.

_____. "Roger Bacon." http://plato.stanford.edu/entries/roger-bacon/ Accessed 6 May 2007.

_____. "Saint Bonaventure." http:plato.stanford.edu/entries/bonaventure/. Accessed 3 January 2007.

_____. "The Medieval Problem of Universals." http://plato.stanford.edu/entries/universals-medieval/. Accessed 28 February 2007.

_____. "William of Ockham." http://plate.stanford.edu/entries/ockham/. Accessed 12 May 2007.

Stump, Eleonore. "Dialectic," in *The Seven Liberal Arts in the Middle Ages*, edited by David L. Wagner Bloomington: Indiana University Press, 1983.

Summa Theologica. "Question 2. The existence of God." http://www.newadvent.org/summa/1002.htm. Accessed 20 April 2007.

Swanson, R. N. *Universities, Academics and the Great Schism*. Cambridge: Cambridge University Press, 1979.

Time-Life Books. *What Life Was Like in the Age of Chivalry: Medieval Europe, AD 800–1500*. Alexandria: Time-Life, 1997.

Trevelyan, G. M. *A Shortened History of England*. Harmondsworth: Penguin, 1959.

Tuchman, Barbara. *A Distant Mirror: The Calamitous 14th Century*. New York: Ballantine, 1978.

Tyack, Geoffrey. *The Bodleian Library*. Oxford: University of Oxford, 2000.

University of Cambridge. "The University and its Departments." http://www.cam.ac.uk/cambuniv/pubs/history.medieval.html. Accessed 14 November 2007.

University of Chicago Library. "Renaissance Humanism." http:www.lib.uchicago/edu/e/spcl/excat/berlin/renaissa.html. Accessed 5 July 2007.

"University of Paris: Courses in Theology [1271] and Medicine [1270–74]." http://history.hanover.edu/courses/excerpts/344ucur.html. Accessed 17 May 2007.

University of Vienna. "Renaissance-Humanism." http://www.univie.ac.at/archiv/tour/7.htm. Accessed 19 June 2007.

"Utopia Book Notes Summary by Thomas More: Plot Summary." http://www.bookrags.com/notes/uto/SUM.html. Accessed 2 August 2007.

Verger, Jacques. "L'étudiant maître de l'université," in *Historia*. Paris, No. 65, Mai-Juin 2000, pp. 36–41.

_____. "Naissance et premier essor des universités Européennes," in Pierre Riché and Jacques Verger. *Des nains sur des épaules de géants*. Paris: Tallandier, 2006, pp. 185–228.

_____. "Patterns," in Hilde de Ridder-Symoens, *A History of the University in Europe*. Cambridge: Cambridge University Press, 2003, pp. 35–67.

_____. *Les professeurs des universités françaises à la fin du Moyen Age*, in Jacques Verger. *Les universités françaises au Moyen Age*. Leiden : Brill, 1995, pp. 174–198.

_____. "Teachers," in Hilde de Ridder-Symoens, *A History of the University in Europe*. Cambridge: Cambridge University Press, 2003, pp. 144–168.

_____. "Université," in Jacques Le Goff and Jean-Claude Schmitt, *Dictionnaire raisonné de l'Occident médiéval*. Paris: Fayard, 1999, pp. 1166–1182.

_____. *Les universités françaises au Moyen Age*. Leiden: Brill, 1995.

Waddell, Helen. *The Wandering Scholars of the Middle Ages*. Mineola: Dover, 2000.

Wagner, David L, ed. *The Seven Liberal Arts in the Middle Ages*. Bloomington: Indiana University Press, 1983.

Wikipedia. "Hugh Primas." http://en.wikipedia.org/w/index.php?title=Hugh_Primas&printable=yes. Accessed 21 July 2007.

_____. "William Grocyn." http://en.wikipedia.org/w/index.php?title=William_Grocyn&printable=yes. Accessed 20 June 2007.

Williamson, Allen. "Joan of Arc, Brief Biography." http://archive.joan-of-arc.org/joanofarc_short_biography.html. Accessed 25 May 2007.

Winroth, Anders. "Domus Gratiani: Homepage for Gratian Studies." http://pantheon.yale.edu/~haw6/gratian.html. Accessed 2 August 2006.

_____. *The Making of Gratian's Decretum*. Cambridge: Cambridge University Press, 2000.

Yale University Press — London. "The Praise of Folly." http://www.yalebooks.co.uk/yale/display.asp?K=9780300097344&bic=HPCB3&sort=SO... Accessed 10 July 2007.

Zilsel, Edgar. "Methods of Humanism." http://www.compilerpress.atfreeweb.com/Anno%20Zilsel%20Humanism.htm. Accessed 24 July 2007.

Index

Abelard, Peter 9, 19, 20, 22, 23, 37, 46, 52, 53
Accursis 63, 68
amor sciendi (love of knowledge for its own sake) 27, 165
Angers (University of) 79, 127, 134, 135
Aquinas, Thomas 42, 87, 98, 99, 100, 101, 102, 103, 121, 154
Aristotle 19, 40, 43, 48, 50, 51, 52, 78, 83, 84, 102, 110, 117, 118, 148, 152, 156, 157, 173
artes liberales (the seven liberal arts) 42–43
Averroës 83, 84, 102

BA degree 45, 49, 50–52, 157, 170, 171
Bélibaste, Guillaume 8, 13, 14
Bernard of Chartres 27, 30
Bologna (city of) 18, 47, 52, 56, 58, 59, 61, 62, 64, 67, 69, 73, 138, 156
Bologna (University of) 19, 27, 54, 55, 56, 57, 59, 60, 61, 62, 63, 64, 67, 68, 75, 81, 98, 127, 128, 131, 132, 135, 141, 143, 147, 151
Bonaventure of Bagnoregio 97, 101, 102
Bulgarus 63, 67

Cambridge (University of) 10, 33, 35, 45, 73, 79, 108, 112, 127, 130, 131, 157, 158, 160, 170, 174
Chaucer 53
clericus ("clerk," the ecclesiastical title accorded to university students) 31

Deschamps, Eustache 15, 16

dialectical reasoning 20, 21, 30, 39, 42, 43, 45, 64, 65, 98, 145, 169
disputations (oral debates) 34, 41, 48, 49, 51, 52, 80, 97, 102, 113, 118, 169

feudalism 11, 124, 173
Fournier, Jacques 13, 14
Froisart, Jean 11, 88

Gasparino da Barzizza 62
Gerson, Jean 31, 87, 90, 91, 92, 173
Giovanni d'Andrea 63, 68
Glasgow (University of) 127, 138, 139
God (importance of this concept in medieval life) 12
goliard (free-spirited independent student; pl. *goliardi*) 33, 35, 37, 38
Gratian 59, 63, 64, 65, 66

hazing (of new students) 29, 30
Heloise 22, 23, 46
humanism 1, 19, 41, 62, 114, 140–145, 147, 148, 150–153, 155–157, 160, 163

Inerius 63, 64

Jacques de Vitry 77
Jean le Fourbeur 85–87
Joan of Arc 97, 103, 104, 105, 106, 172, 174
John of Garland 28, 47
John of Salisbury 9, 19, 27, 30, 42, 71

Latin (importance of in medieval universities) 1, 2, 4, 9, 13, 19, 21, 22, 28, 29, 35, 36, 38, 42, 43, 44, 46, 52, 62, 78, 89,

98, 101, 102, 111, 112, 114, 115, 116, 118, 131, 137, 142, 144, 146, 147, 148, 149, 150, 151, 154, 155, 157, 159, 160, 161, 163, 172
Lombard, Peter 52, 121

MA degree 52, 53, 157
magister (academic title equivalent to "professor") 1, 5, 49, 52, 67, 80, 98
meals (student meals) 34–35, 72
mendicant orders 81–82
Montpellier (University of) 42, 85, 127, 128, 129, 147

Naples (University of) 42, 85, 88, 98, 127, 132, 143

Odofredus de Denariis 61
Oldradus da Porte 63, 68
Orléans (city of) 9, 15, 135
Orléans (University of) 27, 28, 79, 85, 103, 127, 134, 136, 137, 155
Oxford (city of) 107, 111
Oxford (University of) 5, 10, 18, 19, 27, 33, 34, 35, 45, 49, 50, 51, 53, 63, 79, 107, 108, 109, 110, 111, 112, 113, 114, 115, 116, 117, 119, 121, 123, 124, 125, 126, 127, 130, 132, 142, 153, 154, 156, 157, 158, 160, 167, 168, 170, 171, 174

Padua (University of) 131, 141, 143, 149, 150, 151, 153, 156
Paris (city of) 8, 13, 14, 18, 19, 21, 23, 27, 28, 30, 33, 34, 35, 37, 45, 48, 52, 59, 63, 71, 72, 73, 74, 75, 76, 77, 78, 79, 84, 85, 87, 92, 93, 94, 98, 102, 104, 105, 107, 108, 117, 119, 133, 134, 138, 153, 159, 160
Paris, Matthew 8, 9, 13, 18, 78, 79, 131
Paris (University of) 2, 3, 13, 15, 21, 28, 31, 33, 35, 42, 48, 49, 56, 61, 71, 72, 73, 75, 76, 77, 78, 79, 80, 81, 82, 83, 84, 85, 86, 87, 88, 89, 91, 92, 93, 94, 95, 97, 98, 101, 102, 103, 104, 105, 108, 114, 117, 119, 127, 128, 130, 132, 133, 135, 138, 151, 152, 155., 160, 172, 173, 174
Pepo 63
plague 9
Prague (University of) 127, 137
Prince of Wales 8, 11

quadrivium (advanced courses) 45, 49, 78

Rashdall, Hastings 5, 7, 8, 17, 22, 34, 50, 56, 72, 78, 95, 107, 114, 115, 117, 126, 127, 130, 131, 132, 135, 170
Reformation 1, 2, 91, 123, 126, 160, 166, 173, 174, 175
Renaissance (in general) 1, 2, 28, 114, 140, 142, 145, 146, 147, 151, 160, 166, 173, 174, 175
Renaissance of the twelfth century 9, 19, 168

Schism (in Western Christianity) 88, 89, 91, 138, 172
scholasticism 1, 21, 39, 40, 41, 90, 130, 140, 141, 142, 143, 144, 145, 146, 150, 151, 160, 162, 163
Siger of Brabant 97, 102, 103
strike (right of university to go out on strike) 2, 61, 62, 74
student life 9, 15, 16, 17, 28, 29, 30, 32, 33, 35, 36, 38, 40, 42, 45, 46, 48, 49, 50, 51, 52, 53, 54, 56, 57, 58, 61, 62, 69, 72, 73, 74, 75, 77, 78, 81, 85, 86, 90, 92, 98, 108, 110, 116, 129, 131, 135, 137, 138, 139, 144, 163, 167, 168, 170

Tancred 63, 67, 68
theology (importance of in medieval universities) 27, 31, 33, 39, 40, 42, 52, 53, 65, 72, 73, 75, 78, 81, 89, 90, 91, 98, 99, 101, 102, 112, 113, 116, 117, 118, 119, 120, 121, 130, 131, 133, 135, 141, 143, 151, 158, 154, 156, 157, 160, 162, 165, 167, 168, 170, 171
Toulouse (city of) 133, 134, 135
Toulouse (University of) 28, 133
town-gown disturbances 62, 73, 78–79, 108, 111, 131, 133
trivium (beginners' courses) 30, 43, 49, 53

Vienna (University of) 35, 127, 138
Villani, Matteo 9, 18
Villon, François 92–94

Walsingham, Thomas 9, 18